IRREPLACEABLE

IRREPLACEABLE

The Fight to Save our Wild Places

Julian Hoffman

HAMISH HAMILTON
an imprint of
PENGUIN BOOKS

HAMISH HAMILTON

UK | USA | Canada | Ireland | Australia
India | New Zealand | South Africa

Hamish Hamilton is part of the Penguin Random House group of companies
whose addresses can be found at global.penguinrandomhouse.com.

First published 2019
001

Copyright © Julian Hoffman, 2019

The moral right of the author has been asserted

Set in 12.5/16 pt Fournier MT Std
Typeset by Jouve (UK), Milton Keynes
Printed and bound in Great Britain by Clays Ltd, Elcograf S.p.A.

A CIP catalogue record for this book is available from the British Library

ISBN: 978–0–241–29388–1

www.greenpenguin.co.uk

For Gill Moore and Owen Sweeney
And all those who fight for nature and places

How can you love something, how can you fight to protect it, if all it means is loss?
~ Helen Macdonald, *H is for Hawk*

Maybe the answer is to fight always for what you particularly love, not for abstraction and not against *anything.*
~ Wendell Berry, *Distant Neighbors*

CONTENTS

NOTE ON THE TEXT

I recorded a great many voices and stories while researching this book, nearly all of them informally, the conversations largely carried out while walking and exploring some place of personal, ecological or cultural significance to the person I was with. While many of these people were native English speakers, a number spoke the tongue as a second language. And for those who didn't speak English at all, their voices were translated for me by someone else in our company that day. While I've made no alterations of essence or meaning to anyone's narrative, I have made small changes to the structure of sentences for the purpose of clarity and continuity, primarily where tenses have disagreed, or non-native speakers have understandably confused plurals or mistaken words of a similar sound. I have retained throughout, however, regional particularities, such as the Yorkshire *t'* instead of *the*, and various Scots dialect terms, as these inflections are born of the very places where they are spoken. Sources for quotations can be found in the Bibliography.

Introduction

A testament of minor voices can clear away any ignorance of a place, can inform us of its special qualities.
~ Barry Lopez, 'The American Geographies'

Although the young man playing crazy golf wore shorts, the day was sharp and shivery on the pier. Glassy March light slid off the waves and broke into bright shards. Further out to sea, panels of dark grey rain had been hoisted against the horizon, blotting it from view. The arms of the Ferris wheel spun slowly on the promenade and the air plumed with the unmistakeable tang of the British seaside, a fusion of salt water, fish and chips, and candy floss. I walked Brighton's Palace Pier with the late-winter crowds, day-trippers and city residents mingling together to ride the rollercoaster and dodgems, dropping coins into the slot machines in the giddily lit amusement arcade, or to walk the length of the pier and back and feel the crisp, bracing wind against skin. Food shacks did brisk business, steady queues forming at Doughlicious Doughnuts, Hot Dog Hut and Moo-Moos, whose staff coned a dazzling rainbow of scooped ice creams, still popular in the biting cold. Loudspeakers garlanded the entire length of the pier; a middle-aged couple, already hand-in-hand and laughing at some-thing one of them had just said, rocked back on their heels and tapped out a two-step when Van Morrison's 'Brown-eyed Girl' rang out across the sea.

It was a few minutes to five when I chose a spot on the sunset side of the amusement arcade, staring across the water at the sad remains of the fire-destroyed West Pier and the skeletal crown of its sinking pavilion. A few other people had gathered alongside me, including a man setting up a camera and tripod. 'Photography is just my hobby,' he said, screwing in a long lens. 'I'm a financial investigator by day.' Another man wheeled his invalid father to the railings, the older man wrapped in a beige overcoat and brown woollen scarf, their wives jointly tucking a navy-blue blanket down the sides of the wheelchair. And then, at precisely 5.03 p.m., as hands were being rubbed together along the pier to kindle a little warmth, the performance commenced.

Eight starlings hustled overhead like a fan of thrown darts, roving the glimmering grey sea between piers. A minute later and another twelve had joined them, followed by countless small additions and accretions over the next quarter of an hour, so numerous that I could no longer keep track of their source. It was as if they were simply materializing from within the growing assembly in an endless process of self-replication, or being sieved unseen from the sea. As if in response to the swirling birds, several hundred of them now fusing into a mass of rippling black felt, dark clouds billowed westwards, pressing the last of the winter light into a thin shining seam between horizon and sky. And from that sliver of crushed sun, the rays flared outwards and over the sea, unwinding like a trawler's net and raining light on the wheeling birds.

Murmuration is the word given to these grand assemblies of starlings, descended from the Latin *murmur*, meaning *to surge*, though a friend of mine offered a lexical variation. 'It sounds like a compendium of murmur and admiration,' he'd once written. Which seemed about right to me – and I suspect to the many others gathered that evening on the pier. Not merely the ones who'd arrived especially for this regular winter event, but for those unknowing visitors pulled in by the sheer unexpected magic of it all. For the murmuration was difficult to ignore: it trembled off the coast as if the dancing images of a cinema reel were being projected onto the air itself.

Over a thousand birds had now coalesced into a single aerial mass, each flickering and feinting of a life form mimicked by its neighbour, the process repeated over and over throughout the gathering. Whenever I tried to follow the trajectory of a single starling, to glimpse individuality amidst union, my eyes lost focus within seconds, tugged inside the dense, darkly incandescent pulse of the cauldron. Together they shape-shifted into mystifying forms as evening fell around us – the black coil of a sinuous snake at sea, a bowl set spinning through salt air, a wine glass brimming with the last of the drained light. No sooner had a shape been perceived than it had already morphed into something radically unrelated, as if a sequence of ethereal phantoms, fugitive and fantastic in their unfolding. The starlings spiralled, ribboned and wavered, a vast tremulous cloud of intelligence, each curvature and warp in the air a response to their dynamic but precise volatility. And few movements seemed beyond their reach. Often congregating in such bewildering numbers to better survive the incisive attack of a predator, starlings have perfected the artful synchronicity of grace under pressure. A battle shield of weaving wings against the piercing talons of a peregrine.

The murmuration had a profound effect along the length of the pier. Two girls abandoned the selfies they were taking in front of the games arcade, standing side by side instead and re-angling their phones so that the camera lens faced out to sea. A woman, middle-aged and wrapped warm in a burgundy scarf, simply said *Wow* in the midst of it all, entirely transported by the spectacle. And the man in the wheelchair smiled weakly as he stared at the display. At one point the flock fractured into two distinct entities, each scrolling to the edge of the sea-stage before turning, floating inwards out of a desire to re-form. When they met in the middle, jointly arching upwards like tree boughs shaken free of snow, each flock dissolved into the other. They passed through as if ghosts instead of matter, without hint of contact or collision, their passage as perfectly executed as choreographed dancers crisscrossing through one another's lines. A group of couples in their late teens, done up for a Friday night at the pub once the pier closed, had got caught up in the sway of the starlings, excitedly flipping phones from their pockets, turning them sideways to film the unexpected dance in the air around them.

Starling murmurations are scientifically known as *scale-free correlations*, formations that most closely resemble *criticality* in their characteristics, this being the exact point at which systems stand on the brink of a radical transformation, such as water becoming ice or snow turning to avalanche. Each and every starling in the shifting body of birds is constantly moving in relation to its closest companions, regardless of the flock's size. According to an Italian study, orientation and velocity are precisely calibrated to a starling's seven nearest neighbours, so that the orchestral swing of a murmuration is governed by tiny deviations almost instantaneously transmitted by way of a ripple effect through the entire assembly. How starlings are capable of such synchronous correlations remains unknown, but there on the pier it was uncomplicated wonder that encompassed the experience, calling so many of us to the railings to dwell for a few minutes within its embrace, taking leave of other things in order to nourish the human need for mystery, beauty and wild creatures.

'Mum, look at this side!' cried a young boy, trampolining with joy on the wooden boards. 'They're over here as well!' And so we all followed him to the other side, as though the pier were in fact a tilting ship in a storm, its passengers sliding back and forth across the deck with the swell. The starlings were incoming now, their sky-vessel moored for the night. The murmuration began to unravel and fray as evening gradually darkened, each buoyant weave falling towards the sea before being drawn down in long ribbons into the structure of the pier itself, as if sucked inside by a vacuum cleaner. Within seconds the dreamscape of birds had vanished from the air.

I began to walk back off the pier, fizzingly aware of the momentous, transforming effect the starlings had had on us all. From beneath my feet I could hear a chittering chorus, the 'testament of minor voices' released from their murmuration until tomorrow. Roosting on the iron struts of the pier, beneath the weight of slot machines, doughnut vendors and fairground rides closing up for the night, hundreds and hundreds of starlings were huddled together and separated from me by only the worn wooden planking, the magic of their kind so close and living alongside us. I knelt down and peered through the gaps between the boards. There I glimpsed a blurry rustling and skittering of bodies, as those small informing voices rose through the darkling air.

*

A measure of loss is inevitable in these lives of ours. It is part of what makes us human – to share in an unavoidable absence, spanning the fading of our youthful energies to the eventual passing of friends and family. It is one of the few certainties that bind us together in this realm. But I struggle to think of many who would suggest that loss should be actively and continuously courted simply because it's a constituent element of existence – to enable it to dominate and painfully wear away at our days more than it already does. And yet that is precisely what we're doing when it comes to the natural world. That wondrous starling murmuration was at one time a common spectacle throughout the UK, its swirling winter magic and densely packed mysteries bestowed at dusk on every major city from London to Glasgow and Hull to Belfast. But the starling, once an everyday bird of our acquaintance, a creature known to some degree by nearly all in the nation, is suffering catastrophic decline. Its population is in such staggering freefall that their numbers in many urban areas are no longer sufficient to form a murmuration, the avian corollary of rural schools having to close because too few pupils are in the catchment area. And as starlings exit the stage, their incandescent sky-dance is peeled away from the common landscape a little further, revealing a poorer, leaner, thinner layer beneath. The spectrum of human encounters with the wild world – beautifully reflected in the wonder, joy, exhilaration and awe I witnessed on the pier that evening – is inevitably reduced by their leaving, tightened and compressed another notch as possibility itself becomes a rarer and more fugitive thing with each incremental loss. And so those two girls, absolutely thrilled when they'd turned to see the sky darkened by an inexplicable union of birds, are never torn away from taking selfies in front of the arcade games that night; the young couples abandon the pier without those attendant moments of connection with the starlings, huddling close as they head straight for the pub; and the middle-aged woman never whispers *Wow* to the stinging sea air, making her way home without knowledge of the wonder once there.

Between 1980 and 2012, it's believed that 40 million starlings vanished from the landscapes of the European Union, a loss of roughly 140 birds per hour. For over three decades then, almost 3,400 starlings have fallen from the continent's skies with each passing day. We're generally not witness to nature's actual thinning, nor are many of us attuned to decreasing numerical inventories of its abundance. We simply notice far too late in the day that it's been ages since we last saw a starling, or a hedgehog, or a firefly, and so these statistics, shocking and unequivocal though they are, can at times seem unfathomable. Like so many others, I was aware of large-scale loss in the natural world, but, beyond my own localized experience of it, it was primarily a cerebral understanding of depletion. I'd read about the vanishings and unfolding damage, discovering in articles and books the scientific figures that confirmed the devastating disappearance and unravelling of the world's biological richness, complexity and natural heritage, but I'd struggled to envision what this increasing leanness actually entailed, whether physically, experientially or spiritually, until a short journey turned abstraction into something vivid, relatable and real.

On a day of driven snow and skewering winds in April 2013, I travelled to the Hoo Peninsula in south-east England. I'd been invited there by a small group who were campaigning to protect and preserve their home ground and its many wild denizens from a proposal to turn much of the peninsula into Europe's largest airport, despite the landscape and its adjacent estuary being swaddled in a multitude of protective designations meant to secure its natural and cultural integrity for future generations. As my train pulled out of St Pancras Station into bristling snow that wintry spring morning, I had no way of knowing how greatly my life would be changed in the coming hours. I would be met on the peninsula by three people whose passion staved off the worst of the cold, and whose commitment to that place of theirs was both resolute and stirring; I would encounter the tangible realities of loss and the fragility of precious landscapes; I would witness the beauty of connection, the deeply felt but imperilled relationships forged between people and place; and I would experience persistence in the face of desolation. The Hoo Peninsula left such a profound mark on me that day that it has come to feel like a second home, its rich seams of wildlife and wonder woven indelibly through my days, as though it was a place I'd been looking for all my life.

*

Place can be powerfully transformative. It helps shape who we are, impressing itself upon us with all the force of a sea-storm, or as subtly as the unfurling of oak leaves by luminous degrees in spring, recalibrating our lives in conjunction with new and ever-deepening relationships. The Hoo Peninsula stunned me into silence when I first saw its vast and evocative marshlands at the edge of the Thames. Thrilling skeins of geese and trembling marsh harriers pushed on through the billowing bands of weather. Saline pools held elegant avocets and little egrets, their pure white feathers swiftly becoming indistinguishable from snow. And swirls of shorebirds blurred what remained of the horizon. Much of what I saw that day, winged and prone to aircraft collisions or susceptible to the destruction of crucial expanses of protected habitat, was threatened by a development plan that would radically undo the cohesion and plenitude of the peninsula. Suddenly those losses in the larger landscape were made tangible for me. I could see in magnificent detail the lives that were endangered, belonging to the same communities of wild animals that had prompted the protective measures sheltering the area in the first place. And it was then, as snow riffled past me and the words of my companions were spun away on the wind, that I began to understand a parallel kind of loss in the landscape, one as significant, pronounced and detrimental as the drastic decline of starlings and other wildlife from the world. It was the incalculable loss of place.

Charles Rothschild grasped the importance of place in an ecological sense long before the idea of habitat preservation became a standard tool of conservation. As well as being a banker in his family's firm, Rothschild was a highly respected naturalist and entomologist, so adept at teasing out the taxonomy of fleas that, in 1901, he discovered the Oriental rat flea in Egypt, scientifically describing for the first time the primary vector of human bubonic plague. Born in 1877, Rothschild is considered by many to be the founder of nature conservation in the UK. His ideas about the need for preserving the natural world were startlingly radical for their time, articulated in an age when nature's bounty was largely perceived as inexhaustible. But Rothschild saw the environment otherwise; he'd witnessed an indifference to what he considered to be its fragility, foreseeing a time when its inherent values could easily be lost from a lack of care and concern.

In the opening decade of the twentieth century, Rothschild would synthesize his thoughts in relation to the protection of wildlife, recognizing that for certain species, habitats, geological formations and interwoven floral and faunal communities, the preservation of place was critical to their continued existence. In 1912 he founded the Society for the Promotion of Nature Reserves (SPNR) with the express purpose of locating and designating places of particular ecological or geological value in Britain and Ireland. He asked for submissions of valuable local spots from across the nation, relying on naturalist friends, natural history clubs and members of the public to comb their particular land-scapes and regions for promising places 'most worthy of protection', those to be preserved, as he saw it, 'in perpetuity'. Long before it became common wisdom, he understood that pro-tecting threatened species without safeguarding their habitat was pointless, seeing in a place the entire structure of supporting ecol-ogy necessary to any thriving population of organisms. By 1915 Rothschild had compiled a list of 284 potential nature reserves; included in that list, which would eventually be known as Roths-child's Reserves, were chalk downland, ancient woodland, shingle beach, raised bog, mountain, sand dune and salting. The list was far from exhaustive, and it was subjectively weighted in favour of the preferred habitats of rare insect species and wildflowers, ento-mology and botany being more popular pastimes than ornithology in those days, but reading through its contents today gives a remarkable flavour of the wild presence of place over a century ago, its recommendations spanning such expansive and now iconic landscapes as the New Forest and the Norfolk Broads, alongside far smaller and more isolated pockets of wild country.

Any hope Rothschild had for the implementation of the list,

however, was dashed by the First World War, when priorities shifted dramatically in favour of land appropriation for the production of food. And his vision of a network of protected places that sustained a diversity of species in the British Isles was cast further into disarray when he committed suicide in 1923 after contracting encephalitis. But Rothschild's dream was kept alive by others, even if it took several decades to bear fruit. The SPNR would, in time, become The Wildlife Trusts, now managing a nationwide network of 2,300 nature reserves; and of the original places that Rothschild felt should be preserved for the future, nearly all of them, save those that fell victim to massive agricultural change, urban development and the depredations of two world wars, are now theoretically safeguarded in some way. Over a century after the list was compiled, his legacy of place and wildlife preservation lives on.

But place carries an even greater weight than these endeavours articulate: it is far too inclusive, multifaceted and prodigious a concept to be defined as a single thing, built up over time into a constellation of cultural as well as natural meanings that make it as essential and irreplaceable to humans as it is to wildlife. For place is what grounds us, holding us close to the Earth. 'A sense of place,' writes Rebecca Solnit, 'is the sixth sense, an internal compass and map made by memory and spatial awareness together.' Our instinctive desire to forge attachments to landscapes that impart personal meaning, value and identity as they intertwine with our lives and communities is known as topophilia, or the love of place.

While there have been many attempts at defining place – to differentiate and distinguish it from space or other dimensional descriptions – the one that still seems to me to come closest to elucidating its fundamental essence belongs to the artist Alan Gussow: 'The catalyst that converts any physical location – any environment if you will – into a place, is the process of experiencing deeply. A place is a piece of a whole environment that has been claimed by feelings.' Intuitively we understand the emotive power of a place that's been experienced deeply in our lives. Consider the irresistible pull that certain woodlands, urban neighbourhoods, rocky bays, national parks, city streets or mountain valleys have over us and you'll know the inimitable sensation of having a kindred connection to place. Or recall the physical settings of cherished childhood encounters, where place was the shore upon which formative experiences made landfall. We're often able to pick out their subtle yet luminous details with such clarity that it seems only yesterday we inhabited those landscapes of past familiarity. For such sites are the focal points of wonder and wellbeing, the enlarging apertures of exploration and identity. Dara McAnulty, a fourteen-year-old Northern Irish naturalist and writer, encapsulated this attraction in a beautifully succinct tweet about a day spent in the winter landscapes of Fermanagh, when he said, 'My roots are shaped by place and the freedom to explore. My mind is expanded by the sparks and connections which follow.'

Such indelible ties between people and place were lent even greater credence in 2017 with the publication of a National Trust study called 'Places That Make Us'. Examining the neurophysiological, emotional and behavioural responses of humans to place through magnetic resonance imaging (MRI) of the brain, combined with qualitative and quantitative questioning of subjects, the study uncovered 'the neural underpinnings of our need for place', ascertaining for the first time on a scientific basis the strong correlation between meaningful places and the left amygdala, the region of the brain considered responsible for processing primarily positive emotion. It was further revealed that places which are held dear instil feelings of joy, calm, peace, rejuvenation, security and belonging in those who frequent them.

Most startling, however, was the discovery through MRI mapping that significant places spark greater emotional resonance in people than personally valued objects, a particularly surprising find in a largely material culture, within an economic system that upholds the acquisition of things as almost the primary purpose of being on this planet. Not unexpectedly, this degree of personal connection with meaningful sites led 92 per cent of respondents to say that they would be upset if a place of importance was lost, an emotional strain becoming increasingly common as we strip difference and diversity from the landscape, grubbing up its fine particulars and characteristic details until we are left with a topography, both urban and rural, of increasing uniformity. Unless we protect and honour places that are meaningful to both human and wild communities, this rich tonal range of emotional, physical and psychological experience will be diminished alongside the impoverishment of the natural world already well underway as a result of rampant development, industrial levels of resource extraction, deforestation, overfishing and climate change.

*

Seeing the colossal threat under which the Hoo Peninsula existed, risking both wildlife and place on a ruinous scale, sparked in me a desire to explore loss in a way that wasn't simply elegiac but defiant. At a time when writing about the natural world is, of necessity, becoming archival, a record of remembered things that bears witness to continued disappearances, I wanted to go in search of a glimmer that I'd glimpsed amidst snow on the peninsula, a flickering resistance that lingered and shone with me long after my train returned me to London. It was a light born of the stubborn and unbending refusal to give way when the irreplaceable was at stake, digging in when it came to wildlife, unique landscapes, connections with the natural world, and a sense of home and belonging forged through attachments to loved places. For we are sustained by such things – some of the incalculable qualities that colour our richest days.

While I've sought the expertise of scientists and ecologists the better to understand the complex functioning of ecosystems and conservation efforts, and to bring a clarity of vision to the life stories of wild animals, many of the narratives here belong to people without any particular investment in the environment beyond their deep love and concern for it. Otherwise they are publicans, soldiers, schoolteachers, precision tool-makers and tribal hunters; they are café owners, scuba divers, subsistence fishermen, taxi drivers, plumbers and schoolchildren. The places and wild creatures they are committed to and care for are simply their near neighbours in this world, part of a wider landscape of home that includes the more-than-human in its midst. I wanted to listen to their stories of attachment to understand what is at stake when meaning and connection are torn from the world. I wanted to hear and record their voices in the hope that together, like those starlings of the murmuration, they might become a testament, informing us, as Barry Lopez suggests in his plea for revelation, of the special qualities of a threatened place or endangered species. I wanted to learn what still lived on this side of loss.

The Hoo Peninsula was just the beginning of this journey, one that would eventually take me to an array of landscapes, where I witnessed disappearance, grief, defiance and hope, as well as to radically different parts of the world in search of the many meanings – ecological, cultural and personal – of place. And wherever I travelled, whether to ancient woodlands, urban meadows, coral reefs or relict prairies, I found people acutely aware of what loss looked like. For them it was neither abstract nor actuarial; it was real, visceral and imminent.

Nature and place needn't be mutually exclusive ideas, as both are critically necessary to the flourishing of human and wild communities. On this basis I've chosen to explore threatened areas – ones whose eventual fate I had no way of knowing when I first travelled to them – on the premise of overlapping significance. And I have tried to approach them all equally, mindful that a place's cultural visibility or physical dimensions have little bearing on the depth of feeling that people have for it, or its importance to the wildlife that dwells there. What matters, as always, is the quality of our connections, honouring wonder, relationships and community in the face of potentially immense loss, the sustaining ties forged between people, nature and place.

Time after time I would hear the same words as I travelled: *Once it's gone, it's gone. And we can never get it back again.* Invoked in support of a threatened fragment of the world or a wild animal on the brink of extinction, these thoughts summed up what needs to be confronted when it comes to the natural world we are indelibly part of. Given voice in different languages, accents and timbres, I would find in these words that glimmer of resistance again and again. I wrote this book in the hope that we can seize that determination, spirit and resolve to hold on to the irreplaceable.

I

The Marsh Country

Ours was the marsh country, down by the river, within, as the river wound, twenty miles of the sea.

~ Charles Dickens, *Great Expectations*

I heard them long before I saw them. Their sound was faint at first, just a few far notes skimming like stones over water. Then the songs strengthened and rose, spiralling clear above the wind as I walked, a summer lament riding in on the river. I followed the curve of the coast until I reached the barnacled shell of the *Hans Egede*, slumped in a slick sweep of mud on the foreshore of the Thames. Built in Denmark in 1922, all that remained of the once three-masted ship was its exposed and broken hull. It could have been a beached sea creature the way its wooden ribs lay splayed on the shore at low tide, bedraggled and tinted green by seaweed. When I heard the sharp sea-whistling of the oystercatchers again, close by and clear this time, I saw that a pair of them had seem-ingly divided the wreck in two. They balanced the boat as crisply as a reflection – one at the bow, the other at the stern – in the same way that the *Hans Egede* was weighted equally between land and sea, forever beached at a crossroads, on a peninsula where the river meets the sea.

The Hoo Peninsula is a rich weave of water and earth at the edge of the Thames Estuary, taking its name from a word meaning 'spur' in Old English, jutting, as it does, into the widening waters like the prow of that beached boat. It's bordered by two rivers, the Thames to the north and the Medway to the south, and has been preserved from the sweeping tides by a sea wall that protects its lowest and most vulnerable edges. The peninsula is a mosaic of landscapes and characteristic features, a mingle of intertidal mud-flats, grazing marsh, thirteenth-century flint churches, pockets of threatened woodland where rare nightingales still thrive, centuries-old villages, orchards and agricultural fields in one of Britain's warmest microclimates, as well as shingle beaches, dykes, lagoons, saltings that were dug by hand for their clay, and saline creeks known locally as fleets. It's a place where a set of complex habitats, both human and wild, are woven into one.

But wherever you go, water is at the heart of the Hoo. It lifts boats from the riverbed with the rising tide, seeps up creeks like slowly moving mists and fills deceptively deep hollows with quickening mud, the entire landscape still under the jurisdiction of the sea, just as it's always been. Overlooking the marshes from St Helen's in the village of Cliffe, the churchyard's poignant charnel house is a reminder of that long maritime history and the intrinsic relationship that lends this place its unique character. Built in the mid-nineteenth century, the charnel house is a rare Victorian mortuary, one of only a few still to be found in Kent. Set in the corner of the churchyard nearest the marshes, at first glance the small building appears to be a chapel adjacent to the main place of worship. But as you move closer, drawn by a combination of exquisite stonework, the arched, wood-battened doors and the view over the marshes that unfolds as you near, you'll notice that the 'lantern' atop the sharply pitched roof is inset with angled slats that act as vents, allowing odours from inside to escape. Restored in 2008, this Grade II listed building was still in use up to the beginning of the twentieth century to store bodies until they could be identified and buried. Victims of drowning were often caught in a particular net of currents in the Thames that beached them on the rim of the peninsula; once pulled from the river, their bodies were carried or carted across the marshes and temporarily laid to rest inside the charnel house on a raised slab called the dais, kept cool by that stone pediment to slow the process of decomposition until the arrival of the undertakers. This watery, peninsular world has long been defined by its wild and shifting edges.

It's these same wild edges that have made the Thames Estuary home to such a spectacular array of birds. Over 300,000 of them winter there, arriving in autumn from breeding grounds as far north as the Arctic to feed from the extensive mudflats and salt marshes that are restocked daily by the tides. The estuary entertains spectacular rafts of wildfowl and aerial shoals of grey plover, knot and dunlin that twist and turn over the water like spools of ribbon unravelling in the wind. In recognition of this avian richness, holding globally significant numbers of wintering water birds alongside a diverse collection of marshland plants and rare invertebrates, as well as carrying out such essential hydrological functions as flood-water storage and shoreline stabilization, the Thames and Medway estuaries and marshes have been designated as Wetlands of International Importance, in accordance with the Ramsar Convention for the conservation and sustainable use of wetland ecosystems. Slotted between the two estuaries, the Hoo Peninsula is compelling in its own right: it supports significant breeding populations of avocets, lapwings, shelducks and oystercatchers; it's sleeved by protected land in the form of ecologically valuable marshes on both the Thames and Medway sides of the spur; it hosts one of the RSPB's oldest nature reserves, founded in 1955 at Northward Hill; and is home to England's largest heronry, where around 150 pairs of grey herons have colonized a stand of mature oaks. As a result of its notable habitats and the presence of these significant species, much of the wider landscape, both onshore and offshore, is covered by one protective measure or another, whether Sites of Special Scientific Interest (SSSI) – the basic building blocks of site-based conservation in the UK – Special Protection Areas (SPA) under the EU's Birds and Habitats Directives, or nature reserves, alongside the Ramsar wetland listing.

Taken together, the Hoo Peninsula and its estuarine surroundings have been accorded the highest level of protection in the UK, shy of being designated a national park. Despite this, and the unique rural character of its historic countryside and communities, the place has been under tremendous threat. I stood amidst slanting snow, peering out through a mire of Easter weather while Joan Darwell, a local parish councillor from the village of Cliffe, did her best to speak above the whistling wind: 'If someone came along and said, *We're going to build an airport on the New Forest*, people would be absolutely outraged. But they can here, because this area is so little known for its importance.' Together we looked out over the marshes, faint in the mist, as a skein of geese smudged the sky. The unspoken question that hung heavy in the air was this: how meaningful are these protective measures any more? Proposals to develop such protected places as Lodge Hill in Kent, Rampisham Down in Dorset and the Gwent Levels of South Wales have made clear – just as Donald Trump unwittingly did in 2008 when he convinced the Scottish government to ignore the

SSSI designation of a rare strand of shifting sand dunes, the fifth-largest dune system in all of Britain, so that he could build a luxury golf course in an area recognized for its unique ecological and scenic importance – that protection means little without the intention to honour it, without the desire to value a place for what it already is.

Our economic system has repeatedly emboldened politicians to override protective measures in the name of supposed national interest, as though only fiscal growth was of significance to the citizenry. Valuable natural environments that support and nourish us in additional ways to economic wellbeing have frequently been deemed expendable, to the point that 'protected' has become almost meaningless as a term, a word that's no longer absolute in definition but entirely flexible, reshaped as needed to suit the political whims of the day. Language is clearly part of the problem. In an article in 2017, the author and environmental journalist George Monbiot considered the relationship between words and wonder, noting that language 'possesses a remarkable power to shape our perception'. Condemning such terms as 'Sites of Special Scientific Interest', 'no-catch zones', 'reference areas' and 'natural capital' for a lack of vision when describing the remarkable vitality and richness of the planet we inhabit, he went on to write, 'Had you set out to estrange people from the living world, you could scarcely have done better.' The terminology of protective designations does little to inspire the engagement and enthusiasm of the wider public in challenging such political decisions, lacking the vibrant potency and compelling qualities that those places themselves possess in admirable abundance. And the lack of a suitable language twines with a second issue of concern – that of invisibility. Certain landscapes, and here I'm thinking particularly of marshlands in light of the Hoo Peninsula, have long lacked the cultural affirmation of downs, dales and lochs in the national imagination. For many, marshes conjure an atmosphere of dank desolation, a stretch of inhospitable flatlands rife with malaria and malignancy. These are places that have largely been omitted from the map of aesthetic attention – anonymous, barren and seemingly disposable, even when the cultural stereotype bears no resemblance to the dynamic and impressive actuality of the landscape. Without knowledge of such places, and all the beauty, wonder, heritage and meaning they contain, it's difficult to care about them. And without care, they're nearly impossible to preserve.

At a travel specialist's in London, I went in search of a map of the Hoo Peninsula. The assistant stared blankly at me for a moment, before asking, 'So where's that then?' It turned out to be a prescient question. I might have had better success in the shop if I'd asked for something on a remote Himalayan trekking route, as, over the following months, I discovered that this remarkable English peninsula, only thirty miles as the egret flies from where we stood in the shop that afternoon, occupied an essentially empty place in the minds of many people. So few that I spoke to had ever heard of it, or if they had, they knew very little about its landscape. It was as new to them as it was to me. 'I pass by on the train to the Kent coast sometimes,' a friend had said to me. 'There's nothing there, it's just marshes.' Even before I'd reached it, it had begun to feel as if the peninsula implied absence rather than presence.

*

George Crozer met me at a nearby railway station. In his late fifties, George was tall and reed-like, with wavy white hair and a moustache, and he spoke with the warm drawl of the Kentish coast. His easy style of conversation and personal engagement were most probably honed by working as the manager of his son's wedding band, the white van we travelled in through the billow of Easter snow no doubt doubling up as transport for their equipment. And as soon as we'd set off, George got to the core of the matter.

'You've got this magical place that's the North Kent Marshes and nobody knows about it. Nobody's celebrating it. And we should be. We should be putting this in the hearts and minds of people.' I asked George if he'd always been interested in wildlife and nature. 'Not at all,' he replied. 'All the years I'd lived here and I never even went to the RSPB reserve down the road from me.' I then asked him if there was a particular experience that had changed him. 'It was the first year that two egrets came back,' he said, 'and I went to Cliffe pools and saw this mating dance of theirs. And for me it was like being in Africa on the Serengeti. Just this kind of seminal moment.' His words reminded me how quickly place, and our experiences within it, can alter our perceptions in much the same way as language can shape our understanding of wonder and the natural world. 'The pools back then were still surrounded by dumped cars and stuff like that, but you could see through it for something like those birds.'

We drove to the village of Cliffe to meet up with Gill Moore and Joan. All three of them were parish councillors for the Hoo Peninsula, and loyal to the place they called home. As founders of the Friends of the North Kent Marshes, this wasn't the first time they'd been trying to raise awareness about this unsung part of southern England. In 2001 a Department of Transport study identified Cliffe as the potential site for a new four-runway airport.

Without the context of a corresponding landscape it's difficult to get a sense of scale when trying to visualize such plans, but there's a helpful viewpoint at the RSPB reserve at Northward Hill that takes in the sweeping vista of a portion of the Hoo Peninsula's marshes. From there I'd watched a marsh harrier wheel over the wetlands through falling snow one afternoon, before looking down at the long interpretive panel beside the path. It was similar to those boards you see in any number of cities, a panoramic guide to the skyline, denoting the names of each church, museum and historic building as you scan the urban landscape ahead of you. Only this panel was a guide to the marshes, bordered by photographs of some of its charismatic residents, including the nightingale, little egret and hobby. The panorama covered a vast area, highlighting sites of particular interest within the open country, such as Egypt Bay, where prison hulks were anchored in Victorian times, a nineteenth-century shepherds' hut, a flourishing old cherry orchard and a former marshland pub with a reputation for harbouring smugglers in times past.

While reading the descriptions I noticed a distinct red line across the entire illustration. It was drawn at the edge of the Thames, far off in the distance when I lifted my eyes from the board and peered through the mist and snow. I returned to the panel, still unsure what that sharp red line denoted after finding nothing at all that I could connect it to in the landscape, eventually discovering the explanation in a small box of text:

All the land from here out to the red line, plus that stretching several miles further round to your right, would have disappeared under the tarmac of Cliffe Airport had the plan been given the go-ahead. Northward Hill would have been bulldozed flat and the earth built up on the marshes in a layer 50 feet thick. Aggressive bird deterrent measures would have been brought in all around the airport to scare off the thousands of protected birds that would have posed such a huge risk of airstrike. The magnificent 'No Airport at Cliffe' campaign, which united community and conservation in the fight against the airport, saw the option rejected, hopefully for good, in December 2003.

I paused near the end: *hopefully for good*. A decade on from the Cliffe Airport campaign and the Friends of the North Kent Marshes were engaged in another fight on behalf of their home ground. 'We set up Friends of the North Kent Marshes because we could see there would be other threats coming along, whether it was airports or whatever else,' said Gill, 'because to some people it looks like a big empty space with nothing in it, but for us, it's a really important place filled with wildlife and lovely, wonderful communities, and we wanted to protect them.' She'd appealed to the critical difference between 'space' and 'place' – one a malleable territory largely devoid of culturally recognized characteristics, and therefore perceived as ideal for developing, the other a landscape of attachment, or Alan Gussow's 'piece of a whole environment that has been claimed by feelings'. Although the Cliffe Airport plan was quashed in 2003 on largely economic grounds, the three parish councillors were absolutely right about other threats looming over their landscape. The idea of an estuary airport hadn't gone away. In 2008 the possibility of one was revived when Boris Johnson, London's mayor at the time, called for a feasibility study to be carried out for a floating airport near Shivering Sands, off the Isle of Sheppey. And by the time the Airports Commission, headed by financial-markets expert Sir

Howard Davies, had begun considering options for increased aviation capacity in the south-east of England in 2013, Johnson, along with promoting a proposal for a floating airfield in the estuary, which became known as 'Boris Island', was avidly backing architect Sir Norman Foster's plan to build Europe's largest airport on the Hoo Peninsula as his preferred choice.

Gill, Joan and George have been tireless in telling the stories of this place, occasionally to the detriment of other aspects of their lives. 'The campaign,' said Joan, 'and all the time we have given to it, has hurt us sometimes with our families and our jobs, but we couldn't just turn away.' Ever since the airport proposal became known, they've galvanized their energies to raise awareness about what it would mean for both human and natural communities, persistently canvassing local opinion and setting up stalls at gatherings where they could spread the word about the threat, from Rochester's Dickens Festival to local village fairs. They've regularly travelled alongside local politicians to governmental summits and public consultations, taking a piece of this historic place with them each time, arguing in its defence and attempting to show how misguided the plan is, given what's at stake, highlighting the environmental protections purportedly shielding the North Kent Marshes from rampant development. Ultimately they've tried to reveal the extraordinary presence of this place rather than allow it to be defined by others, unveiling the remarkable blend of culture, nature and community that's been knitted together there over centuries. They've made clear what will disappear from the world.

'People don't realize the size and scale of it,' said Joan, endeavouring to conjure the airport over the misted marshes. If built, it would be a four-runway international hub, costing the public purse up to £123 billion, with sufficient flight capacity for 110 million passengers per year upon completion, a figure that could rise to 150 million through later expansion. To put that into context, Heathrow's passenger numbers for 2017 were just under 78 million. An airport platform that could host 140 flight movements per hour, descending and departing primarily over the bird-teeming estuary, would be partially built into the Thames itself, and would be 3.25 miles long and 2.8 miles wide. It would be connected to London by a high-speed rail link, a Crossrail extension and a six-lane motorway carving open the rural landscape. Parking stands for 300 aircraft would be attached to the terminal. To the west of the airport platform another 2,500 acres of farmland and marshes would be annexed for cargo facilities, while a further 544 acres would be asphalted for parking. Alongside the additional space given over to aircraft and maintenance hangars, inevitable infrastructure would spring up nearby – an 'Airport City' as it's referred to in the plan – including housing, shops, offices and hotels. Three entire villages would be lost for ever as a result, as well as over 4,000 acres of bird habitat, an area roughly two and a half times the size of Gibraltar and supposedly protected as SPA, SSSI and Ramsar sites. In their submission to the Airports Commission, Foster + Partners themselves admitted the following:

> The large terminals and operational buildings, offices, roads and car parks will interrupt the broad open scale of the marsh landscape. The network of ditches and creeks will be destroyed under the footprint of the airport. The settings of historic buildings and structures adjacent to the airport will be dramatically changed, assuming that they are not removed. The low hills of the Hoo

Peninsula rising out of the surrounding marshland will be lost entirely. The existing open views out over the estuary will be lost and replaced by terminal buildings, aircraft hangars and extensive areas of paving.

In order for a new hub airport to be viable, Heathrow, already Europe's busiest airport in terms of passenger numbers, would be closed and redeveloped. According to the proposal, Heathrow would be turned into a mixed housing and commercial zone which, in Foster + Partners' own words, would 'rival London Docklands', making the communities already dependent on Heathrow redundant in the process. In essence, then, the plan would be to shut down an operational airport near London, responsible for more than 200,000 jobs, either directly, indirectly or induced, many of them in relatively deprived boroughs, in order to build another airport on one of the last large-scale protected landscapes anywhere near the city.

The Hoo Peninsula is far from pristine; it's an area, like everywhere else in modern Britain, with a long and complex history of human use. Power stations and gas terminals anchor the Isle of Grain at the eastern end of the spur. The ruins of a nineteenth-century fort and a Second World War munitions testing zone are still visible, as is a radio transmitter station operational during the war. And at low tide one afternoon, I ran my hands along two steel launch rails that slid as smoothly as seals into the waters from the Brennan torpedo post that was embedded into the banks of the Thames in 1890 as part of Cliffe Fort. Yet each of these aspects of industrial or military use exists within the scale and span of the peninsula, a living landscape that continues to evolve within its physical parameters, comprising a mosaic of diverse pieces that never diminishes the foundational essence of the place itself. Slowly and surely over the centuries, the marsh country has absorbed them into its whole, a feat simply beyond its capacity when the latest proposal for the peninsula is an airport that would alter the geography to such a startling degree that a range of hills could 'be lost entirely'. The place would be gone in all but name.

*

I walked out of Gravesend, sloping down a rain-slick street to find the Thames the colour of dusk when I reached it. The marshes of north Kent stretch unbroken from there all the way east to the village of Grain on the far side of the Hoo Peninsula. Long-maned horses grazed the slopes down to the river to a chorus of fizzing song: skylark, reed warbler and swift. The marsh grasses rippled with wind, fanning open like a spread deck of cards as I walked the open country. Ahead of me I could see how the land swung north with the river, the bend that lends the Kentish coast its spur. I felt something shift at that moment, a tingle across my skin. That simple curve of coast, marking the true beginning of the Hoo Peninsula, called out to me in the way that promontories often do. Unlike islands, separation and escape aren't part of a peninsula's allure; instead, they seem to stretch possibility itself, urging you on to their very end.

I bent into the wind, swifts scything low across the grasses. A shelduck skittered on its wings like they were hobbled legs, feigning injury to lure me away: at the marsh's edge, a bundle of her grey and nervous young. I reached the bend in the river where a pond held a drowned car, windowless and rusted. Behind it, on an islet of gravel and mud in the first of the large pools near the village of Cliffe, nested a colony of black-headed gulls. I watched a few of them lift from their birthing grounds to join the common terns that were tearing open the air, hawking high over the water. A dance of white wings unfolded above me, a graceful solidarity between species so near to the industrial trinity of Tilbury power station, the petrochemical plants of Canvey Island and the factories on the outskirts of Gravesend. I stopped to enjoy the spectacle, to watch the gulls and terns bleach the dark canopy of cloud. And perhaps I watched for just a little too long, for suddenly one of the gulls peeled away from the dance, turning sharply and sweeping down on me with a rattling screech, the avian equivalent of an air-raid siren. The gull arrowed close to my head, then curled upwards like a child being pushed higher on a playground swing before falling back again, glancing near on its second attempt.

The islet of nests and young hadn't seemed particularly close, but like so much about the living world, it's easy to misjudge distances and intentions, to see things solely on our own terms, failing to consider – both individually and collectively – the impact of our presence. As with the shelduck that had pretended to be injured when it saw me, I was simply too near to all that the black-headed gulls held dear, the colony of vulnerable young they were raising in a fragile corner of a compromised landscape. A tern joined the dive-bombing gull, sheering across the pool, tilting its long scimitar wings to dip low on its approach. I kept my head down and sprinted along the riverside track. Looking back from a safe distance, I saw the birds circling high above their citadel again.

At the western edge of the Hoo Peninsula, Cliffe Pools, which hold 10 per cent of the UK's entire assemblage of saline lagoon habitat, owe their existence to quarrying, to the clay-diggings and river-dredgings of a nineteenth-century cement industry that left behind large pits that eventually brimmed with rain. Gill had archive photographs of quarrymen watching swans and herons while the site was still active, the industry unintentionally providing a whole watery world for them. Acquired by the RSPB in 2001, the combination of saline lagoons, brackish pools, salt marsh and scrub is now ideal for a range of breeding and migratory species, and in 2014, thirty years after last successfully breeding in the UK, a pair of rare black-winged stilts raised young on the reserve. But that wasn't the bird I was seeking when the sun finally eclipsed the clouds, drenching the marshes in a spill of sudden light. I crept alongside a thicket of alders lining a lagoon, edging slowly around the corner, and there, sifting water through their distinctively upcurved bills, were a pair of gleaming avocets, their snow-white feathers inked with the black curves of an elegant calligraphy. There is no wader that I know of as exquisite as the avocet. I'm not sure whether my feelings for it are because of the startling, zebra-like shades, the refinement of its tapered black bill or the hypnotic head-shuffle it performs while feeding in water, a movement that Gill told me she thought of as 'belly dancing' whenever she saw it, but I'm certain that something of its resurrection story plays a role in my reckoning.

The avocet holds a special place in the bestiary of British species. Driven to national extinction in the nineteenth century through a combination of hunting, marsh drainage and the collecting of their eggs for food, the avocet was adopted to feature on the logo of the RSPB in 1955 as the emblem of the organization's cause, the need to protect and preserve the UK's wild and often imperilled birds. It was only after the marshy margins of eastern England experienced a period of relative quiet during the Second World War that the avocet returned, gradually building up its numbers and slowly expanding to occupy its former range, until the RSPB logo on which it still appears, seen on everything from books and binoculars to bird feeders and bumper stickers, began to represent more than just a single, once-vanished species but also the possibility of recovery, a symbol of hope amidst a dwindling register of wild animals. Some 1,500 pairs of avocets now breed in the UK, all beginning with the handful of birds that colonized the Suffolk coast in the spring of 1947.

I watched the pair on the Hoo Peninsula lift and land, then rise again over the lagoon, their almost translucent blue legs trailing like ropes in water. The pools at Cliffe now annually host around 150 pairs of breeding avocets, and it's an unrivalled roosting place in late summer, recording the highest single-site count of the species – 1,930 – anywhere in the UK. I watched the avocets drop from the sky, wondering what an airport would mean for these recent returnees, more than a quarter of the nation's entire population regularly utilizing the Thames Estuary in some way. Chalk-white with sunlight as they landed, the streaks of coal running through their feathers turned to dark commas on their collapsing wings.

*

A poignant suite of graves huddles in the cemetery of St James', a graceful country church raised from flint and ragstone near the village of Cooling. The bundle of small stones, thirteen in all, marks the final resting place of the children of two local families, all but one of them less than nine months of age at the time of

death. The markers have become known as Pip's Graves, fiction-
ally memorialized in the opening scene of Charles Dickens's *Great
Expectations* as the 'little stone lozenges, each about a foot and a
half long', where Pip's five brothers are buried, nestled together
beside those of his mother and father. It is thought that Dickens
lowered the number of stones for reasons of believability, the real
figure of dead infants they commemorated perhaps too difficult
for his readers to accept.

'We want to preserve the Dickens landscape as well,' said Gill as
we stepped away from the graves. 'Because of *Great Expectations*
we say ours *is* the marsh country. We don't have the right to come
along and destroy it.' The Hoo Peninsula is a landscape that the
author often walked, particularly after moving to nearby Gad's Hill
in Higham a decade before his death. His appetite for walking was
prodigious, whether through London at night or the Kent countryside by day, and he regularly strode the five miles to the cemetery
at St James' to picnic there beside the graves and an ancient yew.
And it is there in the churchyard, with the 'dark flat wilderness' of
the marsh country beyond it, 'intersected with dikes and mounds
and gates', that the orphan Pip encounters Magwitch, who has
escaped from one of the prison hulks that were anchored where the
marshes join the Thames at Egypt Bay, a meeting that radically
alters the destiny of one of the most celebrated characters in world
literature. Other literary landscapes in Britain, such as the Yorkshire
moorland near Haworth, where the Brontë sisters lived, wrote and
sought inspiration, or the Lake District hills of the Romantic poets,
are revered, but it seems that this one, like so many other wet and
level landscapes, has for the most part been forgotten.

Gill was in her mid-sixties and tiny, her silver-haired head rising barely to my chest, but her age and diminutive size had

absolutely no bearing on her spirit; if anything, they only seemed to amplify and enlarge it. She was a powerhouse of passion and empathic intelligence, and everyone I've introduced her to in the years since our first meeting has without exception come away feeling simultaneously inspired and energized by her presence, made to realize just how much determination a single individual can carry. Completely unknown to her, she had a way of passing her inner strength on to you, even if in private she sometimes betrayed an acute vulnerability that was premised on a singular sensitivity to the world about her. I've never met anyone who combines the qualities of compassion and consideration with such dogged persistence as her. She spent a significant portion of her time looking after her disabled adult son, and large parts of the rest immersing herself in the ecology of her beloved marshlands. Extremely knowledgeable about the wild creatures on her patch, she was absolutely committed to their survival. 'Wildlife can't speak for itself,' she once said as we walked the marshes, 'so when it comes to responding to governments, the people have to do the speaking for the wildlife and the landscape. The landscape can't say, *Excuse me. Here I am, I'm beautiful.* It can't do that.'

I looked out over the marshes from the churchyard. 'Some people say the area is bleak,' said George, 'but I think that bleak is beautiful.' There was a Turneresque quality to the landscape, that pale collapsing of horizons and sky, the billowing updraught of rapturous mists. 'It's a beauty all its own,' added Joan. Over the course of numerous visits, I learned just how varied the beauty of this landscape in the pull of the estuary could be. Some days were exquisitely bleak, a hazy and atmospheric expanse riven with the ghostly calls of invisible birds. But on others, the place would be burnished as though some promised land, a longed-for shore of glossy grasslands backed by a ridge of deep-green hills in their summer sheen. The landscape itself, and the quality of light I have experienced there, wouldn't have appeared so different to Charles Dickens on his walks, having been shaped by human hand since Roman times, veined with channels and riddled with dykes that sluice water away so that animals can safely graze the reclaimed pastures.

The reclamation of salt marsh behind sea walls on the peninsula, a process known as 'inning', can be traced back through historical records to at least the early twelfth century. And although I saw a different generation of vessels than Dickens would have while walking the marsh country – vast, metallic freighters with such names as *Vespertine*, *Grande Brasile* and *Maersk Laberinto* instead of wooden, tall-masted clippers and schooners – I witnessed the same optical illusion that he would have experienced, the sea wall hiding the river when you cross the flatlands, so that the ships, by some strange estuarine alchemy, appear to be gliding over the land like meadow-boats, afloat on a sea of rippled grass.

The river and its estuary provided sustenance, transport and opportunities to the peninsular communities that prayed in these marsh-country parishes. Inside the church of St James', as a pale mist of light seeped in through the windows, I opened a door in the south-facing wall to a small vestry. It took me some time to work out what I was looking at in the gloom, until my eyes slowly adjusted. Although the church itself dates from the late thirteenth century, the vestry is nineteenth century in origin, a tiny, easily overlooked nook with a solitary desk and pew. But what marks out the vestry as beautifully rare are the thousands of cockle shells that plaster the walls in their entirety, as if a simple mosaic, the harvest of the sea its sole motif.

The inscription made by the embedding of shells in a pattern above the door is difficult to decipher, but the date appears to read either 1833 or 1888. Either way, the choice of cockle shells to line the inside of the vestry was apt. Not only were they one of the primary food sources gathered from the estuary, but the scallop shape is also the emblem of St James the Great, the patron saint of the church. Medieval pilgrims on the Way of St James carried a scallop shell as they walked to the apostle's shrine at Santiago de Compostela, showing it at churches, abbeys and houses along the route, where it would be filled with a charitable scoop of food or drink to sustain them on their long and arduous journeys. I ran my hands over the shells, some rubbed as smooth as a sea-washed stone, others crisply ridged with a pattern of grey waves. Together they told a story of belonging, the visible braids of a lived and anchored life, land and sea and place made one.

Standing in the way of the proposed airport are beautiful churches in the villages of Allhallows and Grain, dating from the twelfth and thirteenth centuries respectively, and the Foster + Partners' proposal states that any listed buildings will be reinstated elsewhere, 'should their significance warrant translocation'. The physicality of a church, however, the particular blend of beams, stones, arches and stained glass that lend it its architectural elegance, is merely one aspect of its overall significance. What can never be relocated, nor even measured, is its accrued meaning: the centuries of song that have been sung inside its walls; the murmured prayers and whispers of worship. Neither can the unique moments that have unfolded there be moved, all the weddings, baptisms and goodbyes, experiences given depth by Solnit's 'internal compass and map made by memory and spatial awareness together'. For the meanings of our relationships with the built and natural environment – their resonance echoed in that dense embedding of cockle shells – are inseparable from the places they were forged in.

Walking away from St James', snow flickering past us as we left behind the children's graves, Gill said, 'What's particularly strong is the sense of community spirit in these villages, and we don't think anyone has the right to destroy it.' Along with the churches, villagers in the doomed settlements would be rehoused in other parts of Kent, severing their physical and emotional ties to this place. 'Where could you put people where they could have their extended families near them and where they would be surrounded by wildlife?' asked Gill. 'It would be impossible to recreate this community.'

*

It's exhilarating out on the marshes, within earshot of the rising river. The wild estuary light continually shifts, filtered through salt air and sea-funnelled clouds, so that the mood of any moment can twist and turn, as sinuous as the peninsula's creeks. The wind pours in from the north or rides up the Thames on the tide, like the centuries of ships that have followed its promised course. And when the sun burns like a hot coin in the saddle of the sky, the marshes dance with a hazy shimmer, rolling towards the river, a green prairie slanting to the sea.

These wide open spaces lend the peninsula its particular and distinctive appeal – the way the sky over the estuary seems uncommonly deep, the way the drawl of a river boat, or the call of curlews arching high overhead, is gathered up by the air and held there for longer than usual, so that the sound sifts down, as lightly as snow. Together these expanses encourage a corresponding openness within; they leave space for weather and light, all the tangible atmospheres of our living, breathing world. To be out there on the peninsula, at the edge of the spangled sea, can be as liberating as it gets in a landscape.

But what value do these qualities of place carry in this age? What credence is given to open skies, to the ability to experience a place that hasn't been turned entirely to our own convenience? In a statement to support the submission of Foster + Partners' proposal to the Airports Commission, Sir Norman Foster said that 'we have reached a point where we must act, in the tradition of those Victorian forebears and create afresh – to invest now and safeguard future generations. Why should we fall behind when we could secure a competitive edge?'

The airport proposal would have us believe that their plan is radical and brave. Yet little has changed since the Victorian age they evoke; our approach to economic growth has long been premised on extraction and building, to level and reshape on a vast scale in order to spur and stimulate fiscal activity. Whether it's skyscrapers, motorways or airports, large-scale building is the status quo, and Foster + Partners' plan merely follows that well-trodden route, breaking yet more new ground with old ideas. While they insist that their proposal is a way to 'safeguard future generations', the obvious question in reply is, What will be safeguarded for them?

'What kind of world are we going to leave to our children and grandchildren in the future?' asked Gill. 'We can't destroy absolutely everything.' Given how global firms increasingly feel they can get away with the development of unique and protected landscapes – and with governments steadily more content to grant them their wishes – what of the world will be left for those future generations to cherish other than a 'competitive edge'? Those Victorian forebears of ours that Sir Norman Foster extols were equally well known for their enthusiasm for empire, and perhaps that is a more accurate comparison: a misplaced sense of rightful dominion over local communities, landscapes and wildlife. Reading their proposal in the same year that the UN's Intergovernmental Panel on Climate Change released its most comprehensive findings to date, stating that 'unequivocal' global warming 'threatens our planet, our only home', a plan to build Europe's largest airport from scratch seems to have very little to do with safeguarding anyone's future.

*

Standing off the coast of the Isle of Grain, the London Stone at Yantlet Creek had intrigued me from the moment I first saw it. It was one of two evocative boundary markers on the Thames that once delineated the eastern jurisdiction of the City of London. The stone pillar rises where the river meets the sea on the rim of the peninsula, exposed on the shining mudflats when the Thames retreats. But having little experience of the tides that envelop the estuary, and even less knowledge about the strange alchemy of silt stirred with water, I had no plan to cross the riverbed to reach it.

The tide was out as I curved along the sea wall from the village of Allhallows, revealing a palette of worn browns and rinsed blues where the river had run. Sandy mud was ridged into the shape of the vanished waves. Seaweed slicked the shore, dark and glistening. The clouds in the wide estuary skies were in spate, streaming out to sea with a violent westerly. With each step the stone obelisk rose more clearly into view, far out and solitary on a midden of crusted rocks. I knew then, seeing it isolated by tides and exposed to the winds and rain that stampede across the estuary, that all my earlier intentions had been suspended. I suddenly wanted to be in its presence, near the barnacled base that has held it steady through nearly two centuries of swirling currents. I wanted to stand in the sway of the emptying river.

What is it that forges these connections, these strong allegiances that emerge between people and place? In response to such compelling resonances, the Czech author Václav Cílek has suggested that 'a place within a landscape corresponds to a place within the heart'. Having spent considerable time with Gill, Joan and George on the Hoo Peninsula, I could clearly understand the indelible ties and tetherings between their lives and this expansive terrain. They were linked to it in multiple ways, rooted by the human compulsion to seek meaning in the physical world, whether through the embrace of entire topographies or the cherishing of small and knowable local spots. For we each have our own resonances that chime inside us. As far back as I can remember I've been drawn to stones; whether set on a bleak, storm-weathered dale or in a green-leafed glade, they've spoken to me in the same way as stories. Like paths that have radiated and been remade across the land for millennia, they express meaning that is native to the places they are found in. Some of the commonest stones have been guides to a territory, set as navigational signs to preserve a sequence of safe steps across moorland or marsh, marking a way for the solitary traveller, or tributaries of trade. Unlike the formal monoliths raised to commemorate empire and victory, the stones discovered along the edges of rivers and fields speak a more vernacular tongue. They are ancestral and confiding, bequeathing to us patterns of past use.

The water in Yantlet Creek was trickling out to sea when I reached it, like sand in an hourglass. I knew that I needed to be quick, unsure how swiftly the tide might surge when it turned. The slippery sides of the hollow creek were shiny with mud and my first step nearly sent me spilling down the slope. Finally I found a litter of crushed bricks that led to a narrow waist of water, where a few rocks had been tipped into the stream as a makeshift bridge. When I hit the beach on the far side the clouds were suddenly flung open like curtains, revealing the sun in a window of sky. In the hot white light, Shelley's 'lone and level sands' stretched away, a mire of tidal flats that touched the distant, silvering sea.

Even in the knowledge that place is a physical space or environment that's been claimed by feelings, Gussow's definition provides merely the most basic of scaffolds upon which our relationships can be raised. For wherever in the world it is found, place is composite in the extreme. It's woven through a combination of weather, seasons, shared experiences and livelihoods. It's assembled from architectures and underlying geologies, the flush of spring wildflowers and the sounds of city streets. It's composed of traditions and temperatures, wind patterns and topographies. It's shaped by animal paths and the whirl of a bird's wings. And it's worn and deeply scored with communal histories, songs and stories that correspond to some region of the human heart.

I crunched over a reef of countless sea creatures, their shells as bright as cleaned bone. Large freighters slid into the distance, surrounded by a shimmering haze that made them appear to float through air. I walked fast along the beach and, finally, out onto the riverbed, stepping slowly across a watery glaze that was pitted with black rocks. Nearly at the stone, the sands started to give way, parting with each step so that my boots vanished into the sudden, deepening folds. I turned back to shore, eyeing the elusive stone column that stood sentinel off the coast. Working my way around the headland I eventually found a path, a causeway of small rocks and clinker laid down over the years, which led me across the sinking sands.

The London Stone marks a place first measured out by the charter of King Edward I in 1285. Standing 33.5 miles from London Bridge, the stone – linked by the invisible Yantlet Line to the Crowstone at Chalkwell, on the north side of the river – once marked the extent of fishing rights on the lower Thames, which had been the exclusive preserve of the Crown until 1197, when King Richard I sold them to the City of London in order to finance massive debts incurred by his involvement in the Third Crusade. Although the obelisk itself is Victorian in origin, it's probable that a marker of some kind has existed at this same site for the past seven centuries.

To stand beside the London Stone was to open the old river to view. I was able to envisage those countless other correspondences that have left their traces across the threatened peninsula. One of the beauties of place is that it has the ability to imprint itself upon us in an instant. Many will have known that immediate, electrifying symmetry upon arriving somewhere that seems to fit so perfectly with your life as to be predetermined, the place you were always meant to find. And that connection, embryonic and swollen with possibilities, can begin with something as simple as a stone. The markers of a landscape act as folk memories, reminders of the ways of life that governed the age of their making, from the histories of dockers and lightermen crisscrossing the Thames to the bootleggers and fugitives that hid in the marshes alongside it. This silted curve of coast has steered generations of men and women out to sea, or returned them at journey's end, and this column, caught up in the tangle of salt water and fresh, seemed to speak for them all.

I reached up and pressed my palms against the weathered stone, where other hands had held it to shape and raise it tall, before I headed for the shore. I followed the watery path that my feet had dimpled across the sands and safely recrossed the creek.

When I turned for a last look, the clouds had settled heavily over the estuary, lending an altogether different, more brooding aspect to the scene. For all the complexity of place – the compound aggregate of countless particularities that resonate and shimmer inside us – it can be radically altered by something as simple as a shift in the angle of light. At any moment it's remade.

*

'They can talk about community,' said Gill as a tin of cake and biscuits was being passed around the table, 'but the government thinks it can pick us up, bricks and mortar, and move us somewhere else. But community's not like that, because a place is inside you. A place is in here.' She tapped at her heart as she spoke.

We were still discussing the airport proposal – the serious risk of bird strikes in the estuary, the prevalence of dangerous fog – but had moved on to more personal things as well. George talked a little about managing his son's wedding band and his love of motorcycle touring. Gill spoke about her volunteer work at St Helen's church and organizing village fêtes and heritage events for the community. And Joan, who juggled a busy set of commitments between her obligations as a parish councillor and airport campaigner with her full-time work in the Rochester office of her family's custom car bodywork business, told me the story of turning up years ago for her first walk across the marshes wearing high heels and fancy trousers totally unsuitable for the wet and muddy terrain, laughing at how naïve and unprepared she was all that time ago. The three of them had been brought together by their love of this place, each of them, in their own personal and particular ways, coming to make connections within a wider landscape they were a part of. None of them were biologists, environmental scientists or legal experts. Instead their endeavours were, at their very heart, about protecting a sense of home in its widest and most inclusive of meanings, grasping how it radiates outwards like the spokes of a wheel from its central hub. The airport proposal focuses much of its energy on the importance of hubs, intoning the need for greater connectivity in a globalized age. And yet you could speak to any one of the Friends of the North Kent Marshes, or the many other residents I've met during my time there, and see how connectivity is already well established on the Hoo Peninsula.

'At sunset, in summer, the air turns pink with the glowing, and the white egrets actually turn pink as well, which is absolutely magical,' said Joan as we finished up our tea. 'One day I walked up to the viewpoint on my own and just looked at the landscape. It was stunning – it was so beautiful, all the wildlife, the birds. It actually brought a tear to me. And I just thought, *It cannot be destroyed. It just can't.*'

I had only ever planned on spending a single day on the peninsula, sufficient time to meet these campaigners and learn enough about their home potentially to write an article about its predicament, but sometimes a place finds its way unexpectedly inside you, holding fast to some ineffable interior, so that it leads you back again and again. On each of my subsequent visits I encountered richness wherever I went, each step bringing some new quality of the marsh country into focus. Yet with it came a simultaneous disquiet: the knowledge of its fragility. Avocets swept across the shingle like a sudden squall of snow in the place where aircraft would descend; water-light, that gleaming meld of sea and sky, spilled over the marshes where terminal buildings would loom; and a barrage of peeping redshanks fired from the marsh grasses where the impermeable surface of a car park would be

laid. Even the long-standing London Stone, after surviving centuries of storms and tides, would be swept away by the airport.

I climbed through soft rain one day to reach the spine of the peninsula. It was only four o'clock in the afternoon and mid-June, not
far off the longest day, but already it was darkening all around me.
It was soon about to pour. As I looked from the crest of the low
ridge, I suddenly had a clear sense of where I was; not because I was
nearing the end of my day's journey, but because from that humble
height I could see both rivers, silvering to either side of me. While
I'd spent hours poring over a map of the area when I was first getting
to know it, trying to divine some sense of the place from a flat rep-
resentation that I'd kept folded in my rucksack, I could now see
clearly before me how the spur of the peninsula rode into the estuary,
tapering into the tide like a creature of the sea. That ancient name
for the Hoo Peninsula was no longer abstract but experienced.

I peered through falling rain to see three egrets stitch a white
weave into the dark sky, and I began to wonder if that was how the
Hoo Peninsula was perceived by those who wished to level the hill
that I stood on – the way that it appears on a map, empty of all that
it holds, a flat and featureless quarter slotted between London and
the sea. Just a litter of marsh names that confirm, for some, its sour
insignificance: Whalebone Marshes, Cooling Marshes, St Mary's
Marshes, Allhallows Marshes. But what is a map, any map, however subtle its scale, to the song of the skylark? What is a map to
the arc of the avocet, that slow flight back from extinction to survival? What is a smooth sheet of paper to the centuries of evensong
sung in peninsular churches, to the thousands of cockle shells
embedded in their walls? What is a map to the murmur of the rising tide, to those three white egrets, aglow in the pewter sky?

All that I'd walked across that day would be gone, either

physically destroyed or irreversibly lessened to such a degree by the constant noise and industrial processes of a twenty-four-hour airport and its attendant infrastructure that it would amount to the same thing: the complete obliteration of a place and its communities. And while standing on that hill that would be razed I remembered Gill's words from the morning I first met her: 'We're just custodians of the world, that's all.' Peering across villages that had endured in the marsh country for centuries, I struggled to fathom the sheer scale of it all; not of the airport, but of the blindness, vanity and loss.

Although the Airports Commission eventually rejected the Thames Estuary proposal from Foster + Partners in September 2014, having conducted a feasibility study that raised serious concerns about its enormous cost, viability and impacts, relief was tempered by experience on the Hoo Peninsula. 'We're pleased that Howard Davies saw this idea for what it is, a huge environmental, economic and social mistake, but we've been here before,' said Joan, remembering how an airport at Cliffe was ruled out in 2003. This most recent decision was non-binding, and Boris Johnson immediately went on to dismiss the commission as 'irrelevant' and its ruling against his pet project as 'myopic'. He was so committed to the idea that, while still mayor, he refused to amend his London Infrastructure Plan 2050, in which the airport features heavily, even after the decision by the commission was announced. And so the threat, while pushed back out to sea for the time being, awaits only a favourable wind to come ashore again. And if it does, there'll be a formidable resistance to greet it. 'I have no money, but I'll give all my time and energy to protect our places,' said Gill as we sat at a table in St Helen's one morning. 'Don't destroy everything we love and care about and expect us to live with it.'

2

Woods of Old Knowing

Landscape may have no plot, but it has much by way of revelation.
~ Anne Enright, 'A Return to the Western Shore'

'I was first in these woods in 1947, as a Scout, and it were paradise.' Five of us wandered Smithy Wood at a gentle pace as Geoff
Driver spoke, brought together on a hot summer's day when light
leached through the leaves in shimmering waves, as if it were
being fanned downwards from above. It reminded me of J. A.
Baker's notion in *The Hill of Summer* that a wood is 'essentially a
field of light overgrown by trees. It is not the trees themselves that
make a wood,' he wrote, 'but the shape and disposition of the
remaining light, of the sky that descends between the trees.' Few
landscapes besides mountain and woodland let you soar without
leaving the ground.

Despite the colossal changes he has seen it undergo in his lifetime, Geoff had lost none of his childhood fervour for this ancient
woodland north of Sheffield. In the sixty-eight years between his
first visit and our walk in the woods in 2015, he'd seen it ravaged
by a coking plant whose spoil was bucketed away through the
trees on an automated aerial flyway, where it was dumped on
adjacent Hesley Wood; he'd watched as the M1 snaked ever

northwards and cleaved the wood in two in the 1960s, destroying much of its original footprint, and he'd been witness to the recent vandalism caused by countless quad bikes churning the woodland floor and its wildflowers into a stricken, muddy mess.

'As an elderly fellow, all I can do now is stroll about and walk dogs, and look for nuts and seeds and fungi, and watch birds. But I've known it all my life. And I suppose it's like a favourite pair of slippers. I mean they may be worn out, but I'm still reluctant to throw them away. I don't want to part with what I've got.'

His frequent use of these local woods has inculcated in Geoff a sense of responsibility for their care. Now seventy-five years old, Geoff has done what he could to help them in this changeable landscape. On the spoil heap of coke in neighbouring Hesley Wood he would drop acorns from his pocket and sink oak saplings into its ravaged black waste to help regenerate it after the collieries closed. And now, after seeing that wood spring back from the ashes only to be cut down by a company called Recy-Coal while still seeking planning permission to create an open-cast mine to salvage usable coal from the waste heap, he was desperate to raise awareness of what could be lost in Smithy Wood as well. These woods – still immensely beautiful after all they've endured, graced with tall ashes, oaks and sycamores, a glossy green canopy that breathed and rustled in the hot coiling air, parted in places by spears of light that pierced the last of the year's bluebells – are an essential part of who he is, having helped fashion his way of being in the world. Walking the earthen paths that morning, he'd pointed a walking stick that he'd sculpted from the compressed wood of a discarded pallet towards hazels, beeches and luminous dells of wildflowers he'd known his entire life. Each was a glimmering of the here and now, a vivacious tracery of woodland life so close to the thrumming traffic of the M1. But it was also a refracted light for him, bounced back from all the springs and summers he'd ever known there.

'I can remember coming in t'wood,' said Geoff, 'and going off t'path and just sitting and thinking like I often used to do, and I saw two snakes, two grass snakes, entwined together. And they were in a shaft of sunlight. And they were entwined in courtship, and for quite a while I just sat and watched them. Then two women came by, talking about last night's episode of *Coronation Street*, and they didn't know I were there and they didn't know the snakes were there. And that's what I appreciate about this wood.'

Experiences of this kind couldn't easily be found in the town's parks, let alone its urban centre. To borrow from Walt Whitman, the wood contained multitudes, being a space of democratic and inclusive usage, there for solitary contemplation, dog-walking, talking, birdwatching and snake-coupling. Like the finest of the world's places, it was a reflection of local diversity.

I'd been in the warm company of Yorkshire kindness and dry humour from the moment I stepped off my bus, met by four members of the Cowley Residents Action Group, named after the estate where they all lived. It could have been a Ramblers outing to the Pennines I was setting out on, good-natured, courteous and keen, all of us paced by Buddy, an excitable ginger Labrador. The difference, though, was that everyone but me was simply walking next door from their homes, Smithy Wood being a neighbour to them all. Jean was the group's spokeswoman, a sixty-six-year-old former deputy head teacher at a primary school in Rotherham, now giving part-time home tuition to a local boy battling cancer; Mick Harrison was seventy, a retired motor mechanic who loved

photographing orchids and woodpecker nests in the wood; a control engineer by profession, Paul Brackenbury was sixty and now
director of a training company after teaching engineering for
many years; and Geoff, the elder statesman of the woodland fra-
ternity, was a retired tool-maker, who'd spent his working life
making precision equipment for Rolls-Royce and British
Aerospace.

The Cowley Road Estate was nestled in a shallow valley at the
southern end of Chapeltown, a working-class town of some
10,000 people ringed by Rotherham, Barnsley, Sheffield and the
Peak District. Like so many of those South Yorkshire communities, coal mining had been one of the primary engines of its
economy, the stout stonework of buildings still darkened by the
legacy of old soot from the coking plants and pits. Both Mick's
and Geoff's fathers, as well as all their uncles, had worked in the
collieries, one of which was sunk under the southern edge of
Smithy Wood in the early twentieth century.

The group joked easily about their ties to place. 'I'm a new-
comer to this area,' said Paul, a grin on his face. 'I only moved up
here in 1973.'

'And I'm an incomer from Ecclesfield,' added Mick in a warm
Yorkshire burr, a town a whole two miles south of where we
stood.

Despite the joshing about these distinctions, these were people
who believed deeply in the value of connections, that underlying
sense, hard won through the slow practice of paying attention, of
being grounded in a specific locality. They spoke of the living
wood with the fluency of the familiar.

'You could sit quietly and listen t'wildlife,' said Mick. 'And you
could see wildlife. You could see woodpeckers in t'wood, you

could see treecreepers, you could see nuthatches, you could see all this if you just sat quietly.' Smithy Wood was bound together with their experiences and wellbeing, not merely as a place to escape to, though they all saw it as a quiet refuge in their working lives, but as a place that informed their characters, personalities and community. They were witness to its transformations, having undergone their own along the way. 'Just about where t'middle of motorway is now, there were what we used to call t'Jumbo Tree. A massive beech, probably that far across,' said Geoff, both arms spread outwards as if celebrating a goal from the stands, 'and it had a branch that came out like that, down t'ground, like an elephant's trunk. And we used to bounce up and down on this Jumbo Tree. And of course t'motorway came along and wiped that out.'

*

Woodlands were once the living heart of Britain, the pulsing rhythm of its culture, economy and communities. Since around 11,000 BC, when the last ice sheets and glaciers of the most recent ice age peeled away from the encased landscape, allowing the frozen ground to thaw and resprout with such boreal, cold-adapted colonizers as willow, aspen and birch, treed landscapes have been inseparable attributes of these islands. In time, as the climate gradually warmed, the woodland over the British Isles diversified and thickened with pine and hazel, followed later by oak and alder. Even later still came lime, elm, maple, hornbeam, holly and ash, all adding to the land's native arboreal record; names that would eventually be sown into the vocabulary of its human residents, remembered easily on the tongue because they were essential to survival. Since the days of this primeval wild-wood, woodland has ebbed and flowed in terms of its character and cover. Climatic changes have meant contractions or expansions of certain species of trees; non-native diseases have resulted in the near loss of others. But by far the biggest influence on the shape of British woodlands has been the human hand.

Ever since the days of Neolithic settlers hollowing out clearances some 6,000 years ago for agricultural land, the relationship between people and woods has been one of considerable complexity. An odd duality existed around woodland that greatly affected the human response to it in the landscape. While necessary for firewood and myriad forest products, it was also a physical impediment to farming and the expansion of settlements. Because of this, woodlands faced a two-pronged set of pressures as the population gradually increased during the Bronze and Iron Ages and into the early medieval period, gutted for agricultural clearance while also being locally degraded through untenable harvesting practices. By the time of the Norman conquest in the eleventh century, when only 15 per cent of England is believed to have still been wooded, treed landscapes were primarily composed of wood pasture, a savannah-like landscape of grasslands studded with large trees that provided both grazing and timber for local communities. The type of dense arboreal landscapes that we recognize as woodland today were increasingly relegated to the edges and remote corners of parish boundaries, often consigned to sloped and stony settings that were lowly choices for villages and tilling. But in response to this pressure on vital resources, a cultural transformation in attitudes towards woodland occurred near the end of the twelfth century, one that has had enduring effects on the landscape.

From a shallow depression on the floor of Smithy Wood a solitary yellow archangel rose in a spire, its hooded lemon petals
sheltering beneath umbrellas of dark leaves along the stem. Some
forty wildflower species in the British countryside show considerable
attachment to ancient woodland; plants that require a stable
woodland setting over a long period of time and which typically
colonize new sites vegetatively rather than by seed, making their
expansion beyond the perimeter of trees a slow and arduous process. Of these indicator species, yellow archangel is one of the
most persuasive pieces of evidence when compiling the family
tree of a wood's ancestry. Found in conjunction with others, particularly in the company of such strong indicators as wood sorrel,
yellow pimpernel, sweet woodruff, barren strawberry, lily-of-the-
valley, bush vetch, wood anemone and nettle-leaved bellflower,
there's a good chance of the woodland being ancient in origin.

In Britain, an ancient wood is any area of woodland that,
through documentary, archaeological or botanical evidence, can
be shown to have been in existence in the year 1600. This date
represents a pivotal point in British history, a time before the
widespread planting of trees became popular in the mid-1600s.
Prior to the pervasiveness of planting, trees prospered solely
through natural regeneration and the process of succession,
meaning that woodland in existence at that date testified to its
native antiquity. This doesn't mean, however, that today's ancient
woods are necessarily of the wildwood, that original arboreal
canopy that flourished in the wake of ice. Fragments of them may
be its descendants, but far too many social, economic and land-use
changes have occurred since the withdrawal of the glaciers to be
precise about the provenance of any particular wood. To suggest
a connection to the wildwood would also muddy the meaning of

ancient woodland, for its continuing presence in the contemporary landscape is a direct result of innumerable human interactions with the land, the way woods were worked, managed and preserved for a multitude of medieval needs, the age in which the majority of them originated. Instead, according to woodland specialist Professor Ian Rotherham, ancient woods are best understood as semi-natural, eco-cultural landscapes, enduring fusions of the natural world and human activity that have enabled a remarkable diversity of wildlife to flourish within them over an extraordinarily long period of time. They are the venerable offspring of joint parenting.

The yellow archangel rose from one of the hollows that dotted the topography of the wood. Roughly circular depressions, these dips were significant indicators in themselves, another strand of the interwoven narrative wrapped like a shawl around ancient woodland. 'They dug a shaft down to a depth of about thirty foot with a ladder,' said Paul, describing the process of ancient ironstone mining in Smithy Wood. 'Once they're in, they excavate, and the reason they're called bell pits is because they excavated in that kind of a shape.'

Rudimentary in design, each mine shaft was unsupported, and consequently at risk of collapse if extended beyond the small circumference of the bell shape hewn by the miners. Once the iron ore had been removed, the cavern was backfilled with spoil as the next pit was dug, so that the land eventually settled into a series of pond-like hollows. While many of Smithy Wood's primitive bell pits date from the early sixteenth to nineteenth centuries, some are believed to hark back to the place's beginnings, when the cultural relationship to woods was first altered after centuries of vanishing trees.

Less than a hundred years after the Domesday Book of

William the Conqueror, that remarkable inventory of 1086 which itemized the spoils of his new kingdom, the idea of woods took on a wholly new dimension in the British landscape. They began to be named and noted on maps, enclosed behind boundary walls, ditches and stock-proof fences, and also managed, through a meticulous set of systems governing all aspects of their use, in order to provide a continuous and dependable supply of renewable resources. Documentary evidence suggests that Smithy Wood was managed in this way as far back as 1161, when the monks of Kirkstead Abbey in Lincolnshire were granted a monastic 'grange', a landholding held by the monastery, on nearby Thorpe Common. There the monks established two furnaces and a forge in which iron was smelted from the ironstone seam found within Smithy Wood, a process fuelled by charcoal produced by woodcolliers from the woodland's trees.

When the monks of Kirkstead Abbey eventually departed in the second half of the thirteenth century, Smithy Wood was managed as both wood pasture and a coppice wood, appearing again in the documentary records in the early 1600s as just a coppice wood, or 'spring wood', so named because multiple shoots sprang from the tree's base, also called a stool, when cut for renewable cropping. Coppicing, common to many of Britain's woodlands at the time, not only provided regular wood for a variety of needs, but also prolonged the life of the trees, making them less susceptible to weakening and disease, or being felled by lightning and storms. While the shoots are repeatedly renewed, the stool from which they spring could well be centuries old, radically altering our perspective of what an ancient tree might look like. This cutting was carried out in cycles that varied according to the species of tree and reasons for felling, ranging from every few years to as many as thirty. And each tree species had a particular place in the pantheon of woodland crafts that once flourished in the countryside, such as elder for clogs or rowan for tool handles.

While the days of large-scale woodmanship in Britain are now over, pushed aside by the availability of coal, oil, plastic, chemicals and synthetics, woodlands were once essential to society. Coppice was systematically cut for basketry, fencing, fodder, pegs, pails, bowls, heating and charcoal, which was itself the primary fuel for the iron forges and smithies of the land. Timber trees were felled for hogshead barrels, houses, barns, pit-props, railway ties and ships. Bark was stripped to be ground and turned into a liquor for tanning leather; bundled twigs tied to a coppice pole to make brooms. Nearly every last part of a tree was used in some imaginative and inventive way. You can still get a sense of the former signifi-cance of woodland by totting up all the surnames that are in some way connected to trees, woods or historic woodland occupations, including, amongst many others, Hirst, Greenwood, Shaw, For-ester, Greaves, Oakes, Ash, Underwood, Maples, Wainwright, Tanner, Woodman, Barker and Warren. By the end of the nineteenth century, the coppicing tradition was in serious decline, and many woods were converted to high-canopy forests for timber production through the addition of non-native trees, creating the type of wood-land we are most familiar with today. And while the livelihoods of those woodlanders are now primarily echoes of the past, many of the ancient woods that sustained them are still with us, described by the Woodland Trust as 'irreplaceable'. They are the living mu-seums of a landscape that has witnessed radical changes in the course of its history, their distinctive flora and fauna still largely intact and dependent upon the long-standing stability of relatively undis-turbed soils. Preserving an intricate archaeological inheritance, ancient woods are an archive of accumulated use, each one an inimitable repository, uniquely alive and a treed embodiment of both past and present.

*

'You look at these trees,' said Jean in Smithy Wood, 'and you think, *How on earth can anybody even contemplate chopping them all down and building a concrete service station?*'

Motorway services: that's what was being proposed for this ancient woodland. To convert an irreplaceable cultural and natural treasure with potentially 850 years of continuous wooded history to a service station off the M1 at Junction 35. The plan, submitted to Sheffield City Council by Extra Motorway Services (Extra), envisions a petrol station with eight islands and sixteen filling stations on the main forecourt, and a further four filling stations on the HGV forecourt; an eighty-bed hotel; 3,000 square metres of retail and food court space, presumably anchored by a Little Chef, Burger King, McDonald's or the like; and parking for 600 vehicles, including thirteen coaches and fifteen caravans. Access and circulation roads would enter the site at both ends, and 'natural landscaping' would adorn a picnic place and dog-walking area. Over half of Smithy Wood's remaining twenty hectares would be immediately destroyed by the development, grubbed up together with its singular historical legacy in order to tarmac its ancient earth.

'It's like that song,' said Paul, 'about paving paradise to put up a parking lot. That's actually where we're heading.'

Department of Transport guidelines recommend that motorway services should be approximately twenty-eight miles apart – roughly thirty minutes' driving distance in normal traffic. Woolley Edge Services are exactly 13½ miles north of Smithy Wood, while 14 miles to the south sit Woodall Services, making the distance between existing services 27½ miles.

'And then there's Meadowhall down the road,' said Jean, referring to the enormous shopping centre off the M1 north of Sheffield. 'If anybody needs to stop off, Meadowhall is there. There are two service stations, there are about five hotels, there's a truck stop. There's lots of parking, free toilets. Why would you need a service station just down the road?'

The answer to that is in the detail: in 2013, the British government removed the minimum distance between services that had previously been stipulated by law, reframing motorways as linear economic opportunities and handing local councils the overall decision on placement without regard to density or limits.

With Sheffield City Council considering the application, the Cowley Residents Action Group endeavoured to pre-empt the decision by applying to have Smithy Wood protected as a 'village green'. While the archetypal image of the British green, formed from period dramas and historical novels, is of a gentle lawn set squarely in the middle of a town or village, its grass kept as short as nibbled nails and peopled by white-clad cricketers on summer Sundays, the reality is far more varied in texture than this rural idyll might suggest. For greens are common land, and under British law that can denote any place where a significant number of local residents have indulged in lawful sports or recreational pastimes for a period of twenty or more years. Which means that even private property, such as Smithy Wood, can be considered a village green. Owned by St Pauls Developments, a company that has made a name for itself through the regeneration of former collieries, the wood has never been fenced off in its entirety nor signposted as private. No one has ever been asked to leave it, and it's been utilized as community woodland for as long as anyone here can remember. Since at least as far back as Geoff's initial visit with the Scouts in the 1940s, Smithy Wood has been used 'as of right', meaning openly and without forced entry, despite the lack of formal permission, in a way that entails repeated communal usage, potentially conferring the traditional rights of a village green, or common, upon it.

The group's village green submissions contained written evidence detailed by each member of the housing estate willing to speak at the inquiry set up under the guidance of an independent inspector. Reading through this large collection of material made me realize that, while the traditions of woodmanship have been eclipsed, the varied relationships forged between people and woodlands over many centuries continue to thrive. The form of the engagement has simply altered with time, as seen in the experiences of the estate's many residents, briefly selected from below:

> I would collect berries in the autumn time and would often go out in the early morning, especially if the weather had been stormy, to look for any damage which may have been done to the wood or its animal inhabitants.

> We went for nature walks armed with nets to catch butterflies, jam jars in which to put insects. They would be inspected then released. [My children] collected and learned how to identify leaves in autumn and learned the names of the trees to which they belonged.

> I picked beech leaves to preserve in glycerine as decoration for my neighbour's wedding.

We often took sticks to 'look for lions', and [my son], who is in the RAF now, has recently informed me that he was more afraid looking for lions than he was serving in Iraq or Afghanistan!

We would often hear owls if we went there in the evening time.

Many speak about the peace and tranquillity that they find there. One lady went there after a bereavement exactly for that reason.

[My children] collected seed casings etc. for spraying gold or silver for Christmas decorations, followed the animal tracks in the snow in winter and tried to identify them. In autumn we would all collect blackberries for pie.

I fear this loss for myself, for future generations, for local people – but most of all for the ancient woodland. It cannot, after all, speak up for itself.

Although their application for village green status was rejected (the inspector, a London barrister, described the residents' use of the wood as 'trivial' and 'sporadic' in his report), the process focused the group's thoughts about the significance of Smithy Wood, while raising further questions about the way in which ancient woodlands are treated.

'I think the problem now is people want everything to create an income,' said Paul.

'Yeah, that's the thing,' agreed Mick.

'Everything has got to have an economic value attached to it and a worth. Greenery and woodland have now got to be something that returns an income.'

'It's like art,' said Mick. 'People like to just go and watch and look at art, *Fantastic, look at that painting there.* And this is the same. It's alive and moving.'

Perspectives on places can shift easily when damage is visible. While responses in the area to the development were overwhelmingly negative, some support for the motorway services did exist, particularly amongst those who described the wood as a focal point for anti-social behaviour. While the overall impression of Smithy Wood was one of complex and historic richness, an unmistakeable ugliness was present as well. The quad bikes had broken the understorey, leaving it rutted, oil-stained and spoiled; trees had been set alight and beer bottles smashed in a circle around their blackened trunks; rubbish had been fly-tipped in great heaps. 'I find it curious that a building can be "Listed" and subject to restrictions and protections,' stated one of the citizen submissions, 'yet these same restrictions and protections do not seem to extend even to the valuable and irreplaceable ancient woodland that is Smithy Wood.' As with so many others, this woodland faced multiple threats.

Professor Melvyn Jones has done more than anyone for ancient woodland in South Yorkshire, identifying nearly all of its remaining sites in the Sheffield area through detailed fieldwork and a meticulous survey of documentary archives. I met Melvyn at his home just east of Smithy Wood; avuncular and bearded, he had the calm and stoic stature that I would have imagined of a man whose working life was pitched somewhere between woodlands and libraries. On the wall behind him hung an oil painting of charcoal-makers in a shadowy wood by John William Buxton Knight. Melvyn was thoroughly steeped in the world of trees. Careful and considerate with his words when I asked him questions about the history and economies of ancient woods, there were also moments of undeniable anger. And it exploded in his voice mostly when considering what might happen to Smithy Wood.

'A big plank of their argument is that it's not a very interesting wood. And it's not a very interesting wood because it's been abused *mercilessly* for a century and a half. First for industry and then by off-road bikers and God knows what. But if it were managed sympathetically, the seed bank would just burst. There's a holistic value to it – the human history and the archaeology, as well as the wildlife.'

His view on this damage and its potential reversal was corroborated by Nicky Rivers, an ecologist with the Sheffield and Rotherham Wildlife Trust. 'To be fair, it's not supporting the amount of biodiversity that an ancient woodland in good condition would be,' she said after joining us on the morning walk through the wood, 'but it hasn't been managed. It's been completely neglected for a long time.' She was quick to put the place into perspective, something so easily forgotten when seeing it solely in its current incarnation. 'It could recover. It's been here since the 1100s. You've got to think of the long term, not just what's happening today with it in this short window of time.' She was dismissive of Extra's claim that this was *necessary* infrastructure. 'The public are not crying out for motorway services. They're not writing to their MPs and newspapers saying, *We really need a new motorway services.*'

Smithy Wood is far from an anomaly. Over 700 ancient woods are currently under threat in the UK according to the Woodland Trust. HS2, the high-speed rail line being routed from London to Birmingham, and then onwards to Manchester and Leeds in future phases, threatens ninety-eight ancient woods alone. And even where ancient woods are not in jeopardy, all too often they are neglected. Melvyn believed that a 'golden age' in woodland care had now passed in Sheffield. He dug out a folder from another room and slid out a single sheet of paper. 'This draft is

called "To Maintain Woodland in Perpetuity in a Healthy State",'
he said, 'and was adopted in 1987 by Sheffield City Council as
their woodland policy.' He cleared his throat before beginning:

Most of the city's broadleaf woodlands are ancient and have
existed for centuries if not thousands of years. It is because our
predecessors protected and conserved these woodlands that we
are able to enjoy their many benefits today. We have a similar
obligation to future generations, and the development of healthy
woodlands and their perpetuation is therefore of primary importance and must take precedence over all other considerations. It
would be both tragic and irresponsible for us to allow our woodland heritage to be lost. It is beyond human ability to create
ancient woodland. Once it is destroyed, it is destroyed for ever.

We sat in silence when he'd finished. It was easily the most
progressive governmental policy on the environment I'd ever
encountered, though clearly one that no longer carried much
weight, as the city council, rather than immediately reject the
Smithy Wood application, has instead returned to the developer
numerous times for additional facts or reworkings of its proposal.
'You'd think if you read that out at any inquiry,' said Melvyn,
dropping the document on the coffee table, 'they'd just chuck the
Smithy Wood proposal straight out.'

*

I'd spent an evening in Smithy Wood on my own, the woodland
floor ribbed with sunlight and dark shadows. With my back to an
old oak, bluebells nodding in the murmur of a breeze, I'd tried

imagining what life would have been like there over the centuries. It was a challenging task: ancient working woodland would have smelled, looked and sounded very different from the woods we know today. While I could approximate a basic scene of charcoal-burners before me, or possibly a panorama of the working wood at a given moment in its history – its various spaces tended to by wood-cutters, bark-strippers and broom-makers – to do justice to Smithy Wood, and to understand why its significance outlasts any single occupation or particular time, I would have needed to conjure all the gathered layers of generational heritage and history, together with the complex evolution of its floral and faunal systems. Not just a single day; not merely a season; not even a whole year of systematic and unwavering use of the wood, but century after century of stewardship. The essence of ancient woodland is continuity, its accrued value gathering like the slow accumulation of soil from decaying leaves. At best I could summon a snapshot of the wood in an earlier age – though even that was approximate, since the charcoal-making process was often a closely guarded secret, passed down like an heirloom from one generation to the next.

'You've got to think about what it's like to live here. Not just to visit it, as it's now this leisurely landscape,' said Ian Rother-ham, Sheffield's former city ecologist and now Professor of Environmental Geography at Sheffield Hallam University. 'You can't nip down to Sainsbury's, you can't go round to Homebase, and you can't go to B&Q. You've got to actually live off this land. You are attached to it, generation to generation. You don't move, or you're not allowed to move. This is the place that you would know intimately and that you relied on.'

We were submerged in Ecclesall Woods, another of the city's ancient woodlands, meandering between sunken trackways, charcoal hearths, towering oaks and beeches, and fragments of stone walls. Around us rang a grand summer symphony, the tell-tale notes of robins, blue tits, blackbirds and wrens woven as one. We stopped to examine a coppiced holly that soared into the upper reaches of the canopy, its enduring stool, Ian reckoned, perhaps a thousand years old and the recipient of countless cuttings.

Ian was leading us towards a memorial that was shaped like a gravestone, inscribed to a charcoal-maker who'd died on that precise spot in the woods. It read: *George Yardley, woodcollier, was burnt to death in his cabin on this place Oct 11 1786.* Yardley's char-coal hearth can still be seen nearby. Beneath the inscription are the names of those friends who paid for the memorial: William Brooke, salesman; David Glossop, gamekeeper; Thomas Smith, besom-maker; and Sampson Brookshaw, innkeeper. Brookshaw was the publican of the Rising Sun, a pub still serving ale today just opposite an entrance to Ecclesall Woods. The memorial sud-denly made clear to me how few histories and names we are left with of the men and women who worked these landscapes. Most of today's ancient woodlands were once places of labour, tradition and toil, but the only names we know are those of the manor. The ones that come coupled with hereditary titles, power, authority and respect; the ones belonging to dukes, earls, lords and knights, the double-barrelled owners of the land.

The real enduring richness of our ancient woodland heritage, though, belongs to commoners: the bark-strippers, carefully incis-ing and levering off great coils of bark to be ground for the tanners; the coopers, meticulously shaping and stretching lengths of cop-piced wood for hogshead barrels; the coppice-cutters, working their way laboriously through stands of oak or willow in winter, felling, shaving and stacking its poles for the basket-makers, clog-makers and charcoal-makers as snow fell about them; and the carpenters, who, in the knowledge that they would never see the exquisitely finished work, searched for specific shapes in young trees, imagining how their future physical forms and profiles would fill out, selecting in adolescence the ones that should be preserved for up to a hundred years, until in adulthood they would be felled by someone else for their seamless fit with a ship's keel, or to be the beautiful exposed beam of a manor house. The ancient woods of Britain are essentially working-class landscapes, the places of the George Yardleys of their time, each one layered through a continuum of raw rural industry, and I wonder if that is one of the reasons they remain persistently under threat, because of a cultural indifference to their origins.

*

A great deal of our contemporary knowledge about ancient woodlands, and the historic countryside associated with them, originated with the unrivalled work of the late Oliver Rackham, the environmental scholar and field ecologist who sought out the gnarled and unsung old hawthorns riding the ridges of upland Britain as much as the majestic lowland oaks and beeches of enormous public affection. A lifetime of looking closely at woodland within the larger landscape meant witnessing the loss of significant features, wildlife and habitats across its historic range. In his book *The History of the Countryside*, Rackham isolates different kinds of loss in the landscape:

> There is the loss of beauty, especially that exquisite beauty of the small and complex and unexpected, of frog-orchids or sundews

66

or dragonflies. There is the loss of freedom, of highways and open spaces . . . There is the loss of historic vegetation and wild-life, most of which once lost is gone for ever.

All are recognizably visible losses, palpable and traceable. He also identified, however, a fourth kind of loss, one that is primar-ily intellectual and emotional in extent, a human extrapolation from the landscape that is no less important in character but which is critically reliant on cohesiveness for it to be fully felt. He called this 'the loss of meaning', the gradual stripping away of all that has made us and our societies what they are today. 'The landscape is a record of our roots and the growth of civilization,' he writes. 'Each individual historic wood, heath etc. is uniquely different from every other, and each has something to tell us.'

Rackham had a visionary understanding of the landscape, able to leaf backwards through a historical book of changes, each page a record of some particular aspect of place, whether a woven hedge, a coppice wood or an ancient vale. But while we have come to honour henges, barrows, castles and towers for the significant residue of history that clings to them, all part of a trad-itionally recognized, accepted and solemnized countryside of heritage value, for Rackham other landscape features were equally charged with momentous importance, and he categorized ancient woodland as the pinnacle of the nation's irreplaceable sites. Believing their destruction to be a form of cultural vandalism, the digging up of the very roots of shared history, he concludes his paragraph on loss with this simple fact: 'to recreate an ancient wood is beyond human knowledge'.

The loss of meaning is the most difficult to articulate within an economic and political system that largely shuns such uncountable and fiscally unverifiable values within the framework of the free market. Both cultural and ecological meaning, stemming from a reflected expression of our natural heritage, a sense of rootedness or connection with landscape or community, or a broad and complex spectrum of biodiversity within a place, are regularly trumped by a political belief that the value of any single thing is transactable, exchangeable, negotiable. That everything, ultimately, has its price.

In their proposal to Sheffield City Council, Extra offered a compensatory package that included the planting of two new woods and the management of three privately owned ancient woodlands as community amenities. The offer is intended to persuade decision-makers to grant planning permission to the proposal, and on the surface it sounds appealing. In exchange for the 10.76 hectares of Smithy Wood that would be directly lost to the footprint of the motorway services, the developers would plant nearly sixteen hectares of new woodland and manage a further seventy hectares of nearby woods. But this offer, generous as it might seem, is set against national planning policy, which categorically states that 'planning permission should be refused for development resulting in the loss or deterioration of irreplaceable habitats, including ancient woodland . . . unless the need for, and benefits of, the development in that location clearly outweigh the loss', which raises its own questions about the method of measure. Smithy Wood is also safeguarded under national Green Belt policy and Sheffield's Local Nature Site provisions, unless 'very special circumstances' dictate the loosening of those strictures. According to Extra's proposal, those special circumstances include the benefits of road safety (even though the distance between the two nearest current motorway services falls within recommended government guidelines), social and economic benefits through the creation of 250–300 jobs (albeit in a ward with 3.3 per cent unemployment according to the 2011 census, well below the English average of 4.4 per cent), and an overall 'enhanced environment'.

'Enhanced environment' is currently a key phrase in development papers, along with such increasingly hollow terms as 'sustainable development', intended to gloss the proposal obliquely with a positive natural veneer. Within the Environmental Impact Assessment for their Smithy Wood plans, Extra make their intentions clear:

> Although planning permission is not required . . . for the new woodland planting, the proposed afforestation forms part and parcel of the 'development' . . . The courts have made clear on several occasions that where works are properly to be regarded as an integral part of an inevitably more substantial development, it is the more substantial development which must be assessed as a whole for its environmental effects, and not only that part of the development for which planning permission is being sought.

While the proposal doesn't explicitly mention 'biodiversity offsetting', that is in effect the essence of the offer – the replacement of a habitat or ecosystem to be destroyed by the creation or augmentation of another one. Of the two new woodlands that Extra propose to establish, the first would be located to the north-east of Smithy Wood, on the opposite side of the M1, and be 'planted with nursery grown sapling trees of local provenance and of similar composition to the adjacent woodlands'. The second, using similar techniques alongside the relocation of sapling trees from the original woodland, would be created to the south of Smithy Wood.

These proposals sum up, for me, the primary failure of biodiversity offsetting: they transform biodiversity – 'the variety of life on Earth, in all its forms and its interactions', according to environmental journalist Damian Carrington – into an equation, a system of exchange organized around a false sense of equivalency.

Age-old places and habitats aren't tradable forms. They are the accumulated result of long periods of complex interplay between species and soils, climate and geologies, people and landscape. Species can't be selected, collected and inserted elsewhere in the countryside without an accompanying loss of structural meaning. Ancient woodlands, as we have seen, are threaded into the landscape by way of unrepeatable conditions and the relationships between people's livelihoods and the natural world, stitched together over exceedingly long spans of time. Their ecosystems, each one unique from the next, have been forged through formidable challenges, then adapted, consolidated, strengthened and vivified by that compound interlacing of culture and nature. George Monbiot has captured the essence of this issue: 'Accept the principle of biodiversity offsetting and you accept the idea that place means nothing. That nowhere is to be valued in its own right any more, that everything is exchangeable for everything else.' No matter how many hectares of new plantings are offered up into the bargain there can be no comparison between a wood potentially traceable back to the forges of Kirkstead Abbey's monks, its biodiversity evolving over seven centuries of human interaction, and a stand of newly established saplings. In time those new woods may well become reservoirs of considerable biodiversity and cultural history themselves, but they can never replace what has been lost. And deep down we all know this, because to take this concept to its logical conclusion, that a place

of enormous historical value can be replaced without any altera-
tion to its fundamental meaning, is to suggest that the duplicate
of King Tutankhamun's tomb – recreated using period materials
and historically accurate techniques and tools – which was show-
cased for about fifteen years in the Luxor Las Vegas Hotel and
Casino before moving on to the Las Vegas Natural History
Museum somehow has the same aura and value as the original.

*

Several years ago I stayed with a friend who lives in the foothills
of the Santa Cruz Mountains in California. On a languid blue
afternoon in late March, Jenny introduced me to a grove of
ancient redwoods. Never before had I been in the presence of
something quite so moving and enlarging of heart. Well over a
thousand years old, those trees exceeded in both magic and mystery anything I could have ever imagined of them. Stands of
coastal redwoods, forever dependent on the dense fogs that roll
in from the ocean and guard them against drought, are sometimes
referred to as cathedrals. They claim a silence from you irrespective of your beliefs: that wondrous and respectful hush that is a
descendant of awe.

My first impressions were tactile rather than visual. It was
noticeably warmer inside the grove than out. A damp, sensual and
lemony humidity percolated about the trees that I could feel on
my skin, as if a plume of hot-spring air had suddenly risen from
invisible fissures in the earth. Redwood rainforests gather heat and
moist vapour inside them, acting as vast organic reservoirs that
release a lavish coniferous scent into the antique atmosphere.
When my eyes finally scaled their heights, ascending a colossal

column of cinnamon-red bark that was vertically ribbed with shaggy, flaking fibres, they just seemed to keep going and going, traversing the initial, horizontal spars of broad burly boughs and eruptions of buttressed wood, rising ever higher past secondary masts seeded midway up the trunk, iterations of the tree itself that rose beside it like a hand-holding child, carrying on beyond the tangled riot of burgeoning dark greenery and the tensile living bridges of branches fused to adjacent trees, until, finally, small detonations of sunlight conferred sudden lustre on the highest crowns. And even then, it felt as though there was no end to how far my eyes might ascend, the tree growing ever more prodigious by the day, its needled spire steepling into sky and the fine far sprays of luminous new leaves paling to gold in the sweeping light of the sea.

Old-growth redwood groves are irreplaceable for reasons very different from those applying to Britain's ancient woodlands. While the latter are primarily cultural landscapes – living places that have been cut, worked and preserved – the former are the largely undisturbed epitome of the virgin natural world. And while the age of old-growth coastal redwoods reacquaints us with the humbling smallness of human life (the cross-section of one cut in northern California in 1934 is labelled with growth-ring markers denoting such iconic events that the tree had lived through as the birth of Christ and the founding of the Mayan city of Chichen Itza), it was the height of the trees that most profoundly affected me. Coastal redwoods are the tallest organisms on the planet. The loftiest of them currently alive is named Hyperion. Discovered only in 2006 in Redwood National Park, it soars into the sky for a scarcely believable 380 feet 4 inches, and at such a height something remarkable and equally unbelievable begins to occur around the spires of these trees: they nurture an ecosystem near their summits entirely different from that lower down. It wasn't until tree-climbing scientists Steve Sillett and Marie Antoine began their complex and exceptionally dangerous ascents of redwoods in the 1990s that the accepted scientific assumption that the redwood canopy must resemble some kind of high-altitude desert, a cold and bitter zone that supported precious little wildlife at such exposed and rarefied heights, was disproved, a discovery that managed the difficult task of making old-growth redwoods even more fantastical and astonishing than they already were.

High amongst the tree pinnacles, where vapour regularly congeals into cloud and branches tangle and twine with the profusion of a tropical rainforest, Sillett and Antoine discovered a magical, mysterious realm, a place described by Richard Preston in his book *The Wild Trees* as a living 'lost world'. Up there in the mists, the first people to ascend to the dizzying summits of old redwoods, the pair found ornate gardens of ferns adorning the spires, hanging tapestries and mats of epiphytes which absorb such enormous quantities of rainwater that they are the densest mass of plants growing on other plants in any forest canopy in the world. Accumulated soil, wind-blown and settled over centuries in the nooks and crooks of branches, plays host to an aerial forest of entirely different tree species, enabling a strange gallery of bonsai-like miniatures of Douglas firs, hemlocks, Sitka spruces and California bay laurels to lay down roots hundreds of feet from the ground. Huckleberry, currants, salmonberry and elderberry grow in profusion up there, producing a succulent harvest for foraging birds. Stranger still, colleagues of Sillett and Antoine discovered a previously unknown species of earthworm inhabiting the canopy soil, as well as a sky-borne population of wandering salamanders that, unlike their ground-hugging kin, appear to carry out their entire life cycle high in the redwood towers. Other scientists have since discovered copepods living in the water-retentive fern mats near the tips of the trees, a species of aquatic crustacean generally found in the gravel beds of forest streams and the open ocean. No one knows quite how they ended up inhabiting the canopy, or much at all about the complex strands that make up this unexpected world, a dream-space kingdom out of reach of the earthbound human eye.

Scientific knowledge is inseparable from the aims of nature conservation. Such deliberate inquiry shown by tree-climbing biologists makes the dense intricacies of the natural world more readable for the rest of us, together with revealing additional reasons for the vigilant protection of these virgin trees and their accompanying habitats. The committed diligence of skilled scientists enlightens the general public on the complex workings of functioning ecosystems, the threats of climate change and ocean acidification to the living fabric of our planet, and the minutiae of life cycles and wild organism behaviour, informing critical policy at local, national and global levels. Alongside the science, though, it is equally important that everyday intellectual, emotional, spiritual and psychological responses to the natural world don't go unheard in the larger environmental discussion. Old-growth redwoods resonate with us in multiple ways, calling forth fascination, inquiry, curiosity, awe, attachment, wonder and love. For us to have any hope of salvaging what remains of the world's biological plenitude – and while clearly fragmented and diminished, it still remains astonishingly vibrant, beautiful, resilient and needed – it's imperative that those two voices complete and bolster one another when their trajectories overlap or align. Harnessing the essential energies of varied communities and elevating the abiding and indelible need that humans have for the more-than-human world will require both science and stories.

We mustn't refrain from naming our feelings about the natural world. Especially at a time when to do so is criticized by some as sentimental and out of touch with 'the real world', as though there is another world lurking invisibly beside this one – dependably wealth-creating, largely male and strikingly self-contained – that has nothing to do with the limiting physicality and life-dependent processes of our planet. *This* is the only world we have, the one whose water and air we need, and from whose substance we shape our lives. If there is any sentimentality or out-of-touchness to be found in any of this, surely it belongs to the quixotic notion that we can exist outside the planet's natural systems and verifiable parameters. In light of how rarely the environment, biodiversity loss and climate change receive even cursory lip-service in election campaigns and debates, speaking up about our attachments to landscape and place, talking in whatever forums are available about our connections and love for the natural world, takes on an urgent political hue.

So many of the names associated with the saving of old-growth redwoods around Santa Cruz are largely forgotten outside of the study of environmental history – Carrie Stevens Walter, Andrew Putnam Hill, Josephine McCrackin, Charles W. Reed, Kate Moody Kennedy – and yet these people had a profound effect on their local environments, both then and as it exists today. From the turn of the twentieth century onwards, these were individuals who either founded or helped energize such organizations as the Sempervirens Club and Save the Redwood League, gaining sufficient political traction for their cause that legislation was eventually enacted to safeguard these old-growth trees. Less than 5 per cent of the world's virgin redwoods are still in existence, found in fragments of bewildering beauty, but if it hadn't been for the concerted voices of local citizens and scientists alike we would have none of their celestial splendour left at all.

*

We descended from trees, which might, perhaps, be part of the reason they continue to have such a hold over us. As the renowned naturalist and conservationist John Muir once wrote, 'Going to the woods is going home.' The seat of our canopy-dwelling predecessors, the leafy arboreal heights of the jungle played an essential and defining role in our ancestral development. Even after we had climbed down from them to walk out into a wider world, trees still studded the savannahs of our landscape origins, a form of countryside that echoes with remarkable similitude the ancient wood pastures of Britain's early medieval past. It is in the core of our being that trees are embedded; they are simply a part of who we are.

But what if your wellbeing depended on a wood? It might seem fanciful, but there exists considerable scientific evidence illuminating the healing potential and health benefits of spending time amongst trees. The Japanese have even incorporated the practice of 'forest bathing' – essentially the act of immersing yourself in woodland, or going for a walk in the woods to put it another way – into their national health programme. It was coined *shinrin-yoku* by the government in 1982, though premised on older Shinto and Buddhist practices of being in contact with nature, and a detailed series of studies carried out by health officials and university medical departments between 2004 and 2012 determined that 'bathing' amidst trees boosted the immune system, reduced stress and lowered heart rate and blood pressure. Forest bathing also turned out to be therapeutic psychologically as well as physiologically, study subjects showing increased liveliness and reduced depression and hostility scores after being in the company of trees. But what if your life *truly* depended on a wood?

Hopwas Wood slopes steadily up a hillside from the flat fields of Staffordshire, a wide cone of trees and summer leafings between the market town of Tamworth and the cathedral city of Lichfield. Sinuously riddled with public bridleways, walking paths and self-made mountain-bike runs, the wood is immensely popular. First noted in the Domesday Book of 1086, and previously known as Hopwas Hayes Wood, this glorious ancient woodland was one of the 284 places selected by Charles Rothschild to be preserved in 1915, one of the few woods to make it onto his schedule of significant natural sites. It was an enclosed hunting preserve in the Middle Ages before being managed, like Smithy Wood, for coppicing. In 1903 the War Office bought a portion of it, and the wood is now part-owned by the Ministry of Defence (MoD) and the building-materials company Tarmac. There was widespread condemnation from residents across the region when news broke in the autumn of 2014 that Tarmac had submitted a proposal to include Hopwas Wood in the county council's local mineral strategy, seeking the extraction of 9 million tonnes of sand and gravel from beneath its trees for a period of thirteen years, at a rate of 700,000 tonnes per year. The intended quarry would be fifty hectares in size, or just slightly smaller than Scotland's Loch Ness.

One of those most profoundly shaken by the news was a young

man who I'll call Charlie for reasons of privacy. In his mid-twenties and working in the music industry, Charlie and his friends regularly met up in the wood. It was a small piece of freedom for them, he told me, where they could ride their mountain bikes over its scored undulations and gather round in its quiet spaces to put the stresses of their lives to one side for a while. Being the largest wild green place near his home, the woodland had a gravitational pull on him, and its possible loss prompted him to start a Facebook page called Save Hopwas Wood. The response to it was startling; within a single day it had well over 5,000 followers, many of whom shared personal thoughts, memories and reflections about the woods. Much to his own surprise, Charlie had galvanized a latent feeling for the woods in these people, a powerful sense of responsibility and belonging that was vividly described in their own words. He connected with them easily, painting himself to the page's followers as an 'average joe – much like yourselves', linking to a *Tamworth Herald* piece about the threat and adding, 'This article put the fire in my belly, from sadness to anger to disbelief.' Over the following days, Charlie made a passionate case for solidarity and community resistance on behalf of the woods, framing the place through intimacy: 'Hopwas is a place of peace, tranquillity and incredible beauty that must be protected,' he said. 'I don't want to go anywhere else to clear my head or to hang with my friends.' I sent Charlie an online message asking if he'd be willing to talk to me about his connections to this place and why he felt so strongly that it should be preserved. 'It's quite simple actually,' he said in reply, going on to briefly sketch me his story.

Hopwas Wood was a place of healing for Charlie. Diagnosed with manic depression when he was young, he'd already tried killing himself several times in his short life. But his world had undergone a radical shift in balance when he was taken to Hopwas Wood on a therapeutic retreat. There, amidst the silence and light and serenity of trees, the place had moved something inside him, creating a space in the pain for solace and realignment, a restorative understanding that his days had meaning despite the formidable weight of depression. Hopwas Wood had saved him from trying to kill himself again. 'It was these woods that gave me back my life,' he wrote at the end of the message, 'so I'll do anything to protect them.'

Charlie wasn't the only young person to start a campaign to save Hopwas Wood that week. Only a few miles away, Georgia Locock was fifteen when she set up a petition on change.org to try and save the ancient woodland. Her words tumbled ahead of her as we walked those same summer spaces several months later, joined by her mother, Jen, on a damp afternoon. Jen occasionally reeled her daughter back to the river of our conversation when she excitedly took one of the tangential tributaries of thought that kept appearing to her. Being with her was like watching sparks fly from a fire: all the rich firings in the forge of her young mind, leaping and fusing in the air. It was hard to accept that Georgia had only just turned sixteen when we met, particularly as her passion for the natural world was not only fiercely felt but also profoundly grounded in practical knowledge. She spoke with a wisdom well beyond her years.

'I remember when I first heard about it, and I was like, *What the hell is going on?* It really shocked me; it's an ancient woodland,' said Georgia, the wood's expansive stands of birch, oak and beech rising in deep vistas. 'I thought there was some sort of law behind it, because of the wildlife and all the species which are here. Reading into it more and more, it really got me interested in how the natural world and politics are quite closely linked.'

The earthen scent of old woods rose like mist off a lake around us, the intricate aromatic labour of countless networked bacteria in the soil breaking down centuries of fallen leaves to a fine litter of humus. Places like Hopwas Wood highlight the importance of ancient woodland for wildlife as much as human lives. Dead and rotting wood support whole ecosystems: the infinitesimally small nests of fungal spores awaiting replenishing rains; the mined cross-hatching of tunnels made by insects and larva tenanted within. Such charismatic creatures as the stag beetle and the rhinoceros beetle are completely reliant on dead wood for their life cycles, the logs and limbs of the forest continuing to live on in a transfigured yet sustaining way. In total, 650 beetle species in Britain are found almost entirely in ancient woodland or on old trees, a commensal relationship of long-standing and essential monogamy that helps lend Hopwas Wood its richness.

Georgia had aimed her petition at Staffordshire County Council, hoping, with a self-confessed outsider's chance, that she might get one hundred people to sign it. But the numbers rose as soon as she'd set it up, its momentum rapidly snowballing. And just like over at Charlie's Facebook page, many of the signatures were accompanied by comments reflecting on long and memorable associations with the woodland. But Georgia didn't cleave solely to a digital realm to champion change; she saw social media and its associated technologies merely as tools, there to be used in effectively shaping, sculpting and amplifying a cause. It was the world outside, she believed, that raised awareness of itself better than anything else. 'Even though doing something like a petition over the internet and social media is very good and helpful, it's also very important to get hands-on with it. I don't mean like big violent protests, but just making people more aware and showing them why it needs to stay. Not just saying, *Sign a petition, that's it*; sort of showing them why we shouldn't be letting this go. The atmosphere and feeling you get from just being surrounded by all this fantastic woodland. Why do we need to get rid of a place like this?'

Within days of submitting their quarry proposal for Hopwas Wood, and in response to the loud local outcry, Tarmac withdrew their plans, stating that they prided themselves on 'working in harmony with local communities'. There is nothing necessarily permanent about this truce, of course. As long as valuable resources are privately owned within a much-loved ancient wood there remains every chance of future extraction and opposition.

On the day I met Georgia I'd asked directions from a woman at her garden gate. I explained what I was doing there, which immediately resulted in an invitation to return after my walk to look at a map of the wood from the late eighteenth century. That afternoon I would sit with Liz and John Smith over beers as they graciously welcomed a stranger into their home while their Sunday dinner roasted in the oven, sharing stories with me about their love of the wood and John's career in the army. 'There cannot be a person in Tamworth that hasn't been taken as a child to walk in that wood. It was wild here at the time,' said Liz at one point, referring to the local mood after the proposal had become public. 'And thank goodness for girls like Georgia, who managed to harness it. Because it was there, and she was able to tap into a massive feeling for the place.'

*

Sixty years separate Georgia and Geoff. Both are similarly open and confiding in conversation, blessed with a frank and personable sincerity that makes communication with them easy and enjoyable. And yet each inhabits a radically different world from the other. Enormous technological changes have left their respective eras appearing in some ways unconnected. I first met Georgia through Twitter, and have kept in touch with her through email, blog posts and podcasts. If Geoff has an email address then I don't know what it is, let alone any social media handles. While Georgia was know-ledgeable about environmental issues that spread far beyond the circumference of home, including spring hunting in Malta and the lack of scientific evidence for a badger cull to eradicate bovine tuber-culosis, controversies and concerns that she kept herself digitally updated about, Geoff was a practitioner of the particular, a man whose life had revolved around the specifically rich details of his home ground. On the surface there was little resemblance between their lives, and yet, despite the span of time, experience and topog-raphy that divided them, they both sought the same thing, to preserve an ancient wood of great personal, cultural and ecological importance. They understood not only its value, but also the reach of its possible loss.

At the end of our Smithy Wood walk, Geoff had invited me to the pub instead of exchanging electronic details. The only thing better than a walk in the woods, he said, was a chat over pie, peas and a pint. 'You could walk through there, quietly, on your own like,' he said as we found a table, raising our glasses in a toast to the wood I'd just experienced. 'And I relish that. I want to be able to seek a bit of solace.' After spending time with Georgia and Geoff and the rest of the campaigners, I came to understand how uneasily the term 'protestor' sits on the shoulders of these people. It's a word that carries considerable baggage in our culture, its connotations often perceived as negative, typically summarized as opposition rather than advocacy. 'Protestor' just doesn't have the same responsive resonance as 'dissident', or even 'activist', lacking the sense of social justice and righteous honour caught up in those words. Few peaceful protests ever seem to reach the airwaves, and it's become a term that's been co-opted by politicians, economists and developers to frame the debate in favour of those in power. You can hear the derision in Boris Johnson's words when he once said that 'it's tragic we have these protest groups talking about *this ancient woodland*' – simultaneously ridiculing the value of old woods by claiming 'there's no tree in this country that's more than 200 years old' and conveniently dismissing those campaigning to preserve them by calling them 'protest groups'.

In a society tied to the road of infinite growth, the term 'protestor' is used as shorthand for those who are seen to be *against* what is considered the natural order of things. They are cast as being against development, advancement and wealth creation. Essentially against progress itself. But Geoff and Georgia's protest, their *againstment*, is merely the by-product of something that runs far deeper in their veins, a purposeful seam of meaning that elicits protest solely as a secondary reflex and response. First and foremost they are *for* their woodlands, not *against* progress. They are guardians, ordinary citizens compelled to speak out on behalf of the nation's natural and cultural heritage in the absence of the political will to do so. The ongoing case around Smithy Wood has been framed as an issue of small-scale local obstruction to much-needed development, and yet the fundamental principle of the campaigners has been to honour a place of inimitable importance, to rightfully question the location of those planned works, articulating the sensitivity of place in the process. No one I've spoken to has suggested that an additional service station shouldn't be built if there is a demonstrable need; rather, they argue that an irreplaceable ancient woodland is not the place where it should happen. In this they are the voices of common sense as much as advocates for the natural world, following in the steps of John Muir, for whom true conservation was 'not blind opposition to progress, but opposition to blind progress'.

For each ancient wood that is bulldozed and developed, we eradicate yet another opportunity from the wider landscape to encounter Rackham's 'exquisite beauty of the small and complex and unexpected'. We remove one more prospect for freedom, to explore an open place on our own terms. We eliminate historic flora and fauna from the celebrated tapestry of a place that's been in use for several centuries, nullifying its vast array of natural and cultural meanings embedded into the timeline of a region. And for people like Geoff, Jean, Mick, Paul, Charlie and Georgia, and countless others yet to come, we lessen their world.

'You felt like you were doing something wrong by speaking up about your memories of this place,' said Geoff over our afternoon beer, considering his feelings about the village green inquiry. 'It made me feel grubby.' Centuries on from its beginnings, that wood of old knowing was still there, the place Geoff had cleaved to as a sanctuary throughout his life, but whether a new generation will ever know it remains unclear.

3
The Land of the Lynx

The rarer they get, the fewer meanings animals can have. Eventually rarity is all they are made of.

~ Helen Macdonald, *H is for Hawk*

They were days that had been cast like a spell, stretched taut and shining and seamless between seasons. There was a ripe fullness to the autumn air, like pressure building up in the inner ear. Even the immense blue sky seemed too small to hold it all. I had no memory of when those unseasonable days had begun; it was as though they had been with us all along, a radiance that had been summoned to stay.

At the end of a stony dirt track that had corkscrewed us from a valley into the hills, Ljupcho Melovski and I stepped from his car into a stunning extent of grasses. They swayed and swept upwards into sky, sun-cured, tawny and magnificent. Setting out that morning to traverse the dense mountain forests of Mavrovo National Park, winding through dark tangled stands of beech, oak and fir in the north-western corner of North Macedonia (known until February 2019 as the former Yugoslav Republic of Macedonia), I would never have imagined that by late afternoon we'd emerge into a surprisingly prairie-like world, but I knew that Ljupcho would have good reason to bring us here. He understood landscapes and their ecologies with the finesse of a conductor, perceptive to the tiny but essential nuances that combine at the heart of a composition. A Professor of Biology at SS Cyril and Methodius University in Skopje, and former president of the Macedonian Ecological Society (MES), Ljupcho was someone I'd known for several years because of his cross-border work in the Prespa lakes basin where I live in Greece. I'd once joined him and his colleagues on a mountain trek to a refuge secluded high in the peaks beside a glacial lake still reefed by snow in mid-June. I came to appreciate the hardy and passionate stamina so typical of his people that day. Undeterred by torrential rains, they had hiked and smoked their way to the summit, stopping to identify and admire wildflowers and insects with a keen appreciation and knowledge of the land, all the while hauling sacks of cheese, bread, sausages and booze like Sherpas, supplies that later sustained us late into the night while they sang traditional folk songs with raucous Balkan ardour.

I had an especial fondness for Ljupcho. In his late fifties, his fierce intelligence could make him seem distant to newcomers, but over time I began to realize that what I'd at first misinterpreted as remoteness was in fact a generous contemplativeness, the product of a philosophical and attentive outlook on the world that dovetailed with an irrepressible love for its nature. He could be spare with his words, not feeling the continual need to impress himself or his considerable knowledge on an experience; instead his quietness enabled a space to develop where the surprising could arise. And he was modest about his highly regarded professional stature. 'I'm more of a nature lover than a biologist,' he once told me. 'I just want to know everything around me.'

Ljupcho's attachment to his ancestral uplands hadn't been

lessened by living in the capital city for fifty years, and while he travelled extensively throughout the country, deftly knowledge-able about many of its unique places, traditions and landscapes, I had the sense that all paths led back to Mavrovo for him. We passed our evenings there in a haze of smoke in the kitchen of his family's stone house in Galičnik; a fault with the flue on the open fireplace meant we had to throw open a window occasionally to vent the room or risk suffocating. Over a rich country stew we talked of this place of his, drinking wine and rakija, scoring chest-nuts with a carving knife to roast on the stove. Whenever I stepped outside for the outhouse the skies were utterly silent and still, strung with starlight and a gibbous moon. We were perched 1,400 metres up the forested slopes of Mount Bistra in the second-highest village in the country. Though this was Ljupcho's place of birth, the village was nothing like it had been when he was born. Once a wealthy settlement of sheep-farmers and skilled labourers, whose men regularly travelled elsewhere to work as stonemasons, carpenters and painters for months or even years on end, by the 1970s the village had withered as its residents, includ-ing Ljupcho's family, migrated to cities. One evening he walked me to a rocky crest that nudged forward like the prow of a boat over a deep sea of trees, oak and hornbeam falling steeply away, their leaves spangled by senescence to crimson, ochre and gold. 'This place is called Ukalen,' he said, 'which comes from the verb to shout. It's where the women of the village yelled goodbye to their men when they were leaving for work, walking the paths down into the valley.' No one now lived in Galičnik all year round to wave goodbye to anyone else; its elegant stone houses were opened and aired solely for summer once snow had finally melted from the road.

Unlike Galičnik, many of the other forty settlements that sit within the boundaries of the park are still permanently inhabited. Ljupcho broke them down into three distinct geographical and social groupings as we stood on a crenellated pillar of stone that rose from a river valley. He'd unfolded a map to point out their locations: Gorna Reka, or Upper River, was a collection of villages primarily Albanian in ethnicity, but Orthodox Christian in religious practice; Dolna Reka, or Lower River, is where the Torbesh people lived, Slavic Muslims who primarily inhabited the slopes of Deshet Mountain; and, finally, there was the region of Mala Reka, or Small River, which included Galičnik and other Slavic Orthodox Christian settlements within its circumference. These were all part of the complex and fascinating cross-stitching of ethnicity and religious belief still found throughout the Balkan peninsula, lands composed of compound communities and ancestral intricacies. Where villages had been abandoned you could discern the clearings of their fields and pastures now reseeding with trees, the patterns of altered lives being rewritten in wood.

Unlike the ancient woods of Britain, the forests of the Balkans still sustain some of the top predators on our planet. Roaming these precipitous slopes were brown bear, wolf and lynx. For Ljupcho, born in this environment and understanding its landscapes better than anyone I know, these totemic creatures were the whole point of maintaining large protected areas. 'A national park is a home for large carnivores,' he said as we stopped to examine fresh bear scat on the track. 'We need them to preserve what is valuable, what is vulnerable. And hopefully to spare them.'

Ranging in habitat type from dense forest and alpine meadows to limestone bluffs and river valleys, Mavrovo supports plenty else alongside its apex predators, its extensive terrain encompassing the dwelling grounds of corncrake, lesser horseshoe bat, Balkan snow vole, wildcat, hazel hen, Orsini's viper, lesser mole rat, eagle owl and chamois. Over 1,400 species of plant are denizens there as well, erupting into a kaleidoscope of colour in the alpine spring and summer. The deeper we sank into the park's forests, where occasional hamlets unexpectedly appeared, consisting of little more than a few simple houses and a church, the more enthralling its landscapes and autumn shades became, the dancing candled lights of poplars set against the evergreen firs and russet leaves of beech. A griffon vulture sailed so near to us that the wind against its wings became a haunting hymn.

When we walked out into that unexpected prairie world, pushed forward on a warm wind, the grassy swells bevelled and broke as they rolled to the horizon. I was entranced by the sweep and stillness of it all. In a fold of the hills snaked a narrow blue river. If we were to have crossed it, stepping from stone to stone above its dipper-skimmed ripples, then risen up the next shimmering slope, we would have entered Kosovo on foot, the invisible border lancing through the light of the land. Instead we stood above that blue crease in the hills, the thin rivulet that Ljupcho had wanted me to see. He'd brought me to the source of his worries.

*

There are few animals that conjure as much mystery for me as the lynx. Like many creatures that stake claim to our fascination, it's one I've yet to encounter in the wild. Rather, the lynx exists for me as an unseen but prodigious presence. Walking certain forests in the Balkans, I know that this singular emblem of the wild could potentially be nearby, infusing the landscape with its electrifying spirit regardless of whether it is seen. It has the ability to pad silently over a litter of dry leaves, as though its corporeal presence has somehow been shorn of weight. It has the aptitude to dissolve mercurially into the landscape, lying up during the hours of daylight almost invisibly on a rock face, moulding itself so faithfully to the underlying foundation that you would mistake it for stone. Its gilded billow of lustrous brown fur and spectral underbelly lend tonal comparison with the barn owl, another ghostly tenant of the shadows. And it shares the alchemical essence that clings to all of the large cat species, whether lions, snow leopards or tigers – a marriage of pliability and coiled strength, the smooth tense vitality of predatory felines. Part shape-shifter, part flow of distilled energy, the lynx is an animal that reminds me of the unrestrained movements of light, wind and water; it passes through dense forests with equal ease. For all its compelling resonances, though, the lynx's magic has a limit. It's built from the same basic materials as other wild mammals of these lands, an exquisite but composite creature of blood, flesh, nerves and bone, making it vulnerable to the same common ravages they all face in their lives: poaching, disturbance, climate change, persecution and habitat destruction – threats particularly egregious when a small number of individuals make up the entirety of a species.

The Balkan lynx is a distinct subspecies of the Eurasian lynx. Found only in North Macedonia, Albania, Kosovo and possibly Montenegro, the Balkan lynx has lived through tumultuous times in south-east Europe, sharing its wild, precipitous spaces with complex human communities and their legacies of conflict and strife. Studies carried out between 1935 and 1940 estimated that 15–20 Balkan lynx were present in the whole of the peninsula, the known nadir of the species. After the Second World War, when the attendant environmental pressures of the hostilities began to slowly ease, the lynx population rebounded, particularly in the Yugoslav areas of Kosovo and Macedonia, so that by 1974 there were thought to be some 280 of them in the region. But this population spiralled in the wake of the savage disintegration of Yugoslavia, dropping to 80–105 individuals by the year 2000. And by 2012 their numbers had declined yet further, reduced to a mere 40–60, the shrinkage most likely triggered by the pervasiveness of guns and poaching after the collapse of the Albanian state and the subsequent looting of its military depots. Of those few dozen Balkan lynx alive today, the vast majority are found in Mavrovo National Park.

Mavrovo is the reservoir of the Balkan lynx. The species pools there in the vast forests that Ljupcho had guided me through, the animals naturally moving along feeder streams that wend their way through connective woodland and grassland corridors to replenish small populations in Albania and Kosovo. For years there was no proof that reproduction of the Balkan lynx even occurred outside of Mavrovo, until a camera-trapping team from the NGO Protection and Preservation of Natural Environment in Albania (PPNEA) captured images of a mother and a cub on two separate occasions in the Albanian highlands.

'Mavrovo is by far the most important place for the Balkan lynx,' said Dime Melovski as he stirred a stew in the stone oven outside Ljupcho's family house. 'If it wasn't for Mavrovo, the lynx would be extinct in five years.' As well as being a Balkan lynx expert, Dime was Ljupcho's son. He'd inherited his father's thoughtfulness and blended it with an acute pragmatism and analytic precision. These skills made Dime key to the Balkan Lynx

Recovery Programme; begun in 2006, it brought together MES, PPNEA, the European Heritage Fund (EuroNatur) and the large carnivore specialists KORA in a cross-border project funded by the Swiss MAVA Foundation. The recovery programme's aims – to secure the long-term survival of the rare lynx species and spread awareness of its presence and fragility through educational projects in schools and local communities – required a baseline understanding of the animal and its ecological needs. Such data isn't easily retrieved: the Balkan lynx successfully clings to its last territories primarily because of their isolated and rugged character, landscape qualities that fit neatly with its monkish nature. 'Lynx don't want to be seen – never,' said Gjorge Ivanov, another of MES's lynx ecologists. 'It doesn't want conflict or contact; it is elusive.'

The field work carried out by the recovery team is arduous. In order to assess population numbers and use of territory, the biologists run camera traps in some of the most intimidating and difficult-to-access parts of the Balkan massif. The cameras' placement requires challenging traverses of the snow-clad hinterlands in winter, the period in which the animals' activity is most prevalent and noticeable. Furthermore, the ecologists of MES have been live-capturing lynx in box-traps in order to fit them with transmitter collars; their signals can be followed through radio telemetry to determine distribution routes and range, information that is vital to formulating a long-term strategy that could incorporate newly protected corridors to encourage the expansion of territories. Large box-traps are baited with catnip, beaver-oil extract or straw soaked in urine from a zoo lynx, and are set only in the late winter months to increase the chances of capturing pregnant females. Often placed in remote mountain forests with little or no accessibility by vehicle when snow is heavy on the ground, the trap has a GSM module and SIM card attached, instantly sending a signal to the recovery team's mobiles when triggered by an entering lynx.

'We are 24/7 prepared for a potential capture,' said Gjorge as we walked limestone ridges along the border, examining traps and remote camera footage. As the largely nocturnal lynx is most likely to enter the trap at night, the team is primed to ascend these snowy slopes on foot in complete darkness to tranquillize the animal before taking measurements and DNA samples and fitting a radio collar. The whole operation lasts forty-five minutes, after which the lynx is released back into the welcome embrace of the night.

Fortunately for the prospects of the Balkan lynx, Mavrovo National Park provided a strong base for the hopeful recovery of the species. It was one of Europe's oldest protected spaces and large enough to sustain both the necessary prey species and sufficient undisturbed habitat critical to the animal's wellbeing. Or so it was believed. In 2011, North Macedonia's government made it clear that it saw other opportunities in that wild alpine world. Wishing to exploit the many rivers coursing through the park to bolster energy production, they sought to implement twenty-two hydropower projects within its confines. The two largest of the dams, called Boskov Most and Lukovo Pole, were to be funded by the European Bank for Reconstruction and Development and the World Bank, respectively.

Ljupcho had taken me to the most northern point of the park, where Mavrovo meets Kosovo in a seamless spread of grasses, to show me the location of the Lukovo Pole dam. That crinkle of blue water in the valley was the key to his concerns. 'It will be seventy metres high,' he said, pointing to the place where the walls of the dam would be raised, 'and water will cover all of this land.' That luminous world we had been encircled by would drown, the footprint of the dam directly affecting 3,546 hectares of supposedly safeguarded national park. Beneath the water would perish specimens of seventeen endangered plant species, including the gorgeous, purple-flowered Macedonian fritillary; the project would also severely impact on thirteen European priority habitat types, including pine heath and Balkano-Pontic fir forest. As with Boskov Most, however, the dam at the southern end of the park, the direct damage would be only one aspect of the project's overall impact. The infrastructure and industrial processes required to make these hydropower plants viable – numerous kilometres of virgin, widened or asphalted roads; supply pipes and transmission lines erected across the wooded hills; and the siphoning-off of tributaries above the dams – would initiate snowballing ramifications of their own, the drying up of rivers and streams through lack of recharge and increasing accessibility for tourists, poachers, loggers and other encroaching development plans.

'The lynx can swim the Danube, so the lakes that would be created are nothing for them,' said Dime, 'but the disturbance during construction and afterwards, including tourist settlements around the water, could seriously affect the prey population.' The Balkan lynx primarily hunts roe deer, a species present but not prolific inside Mavrovo. 'If the roe deer move from a lynx's large territory because of disturbance it could affect both kill rate and breeding success. We're talking about roughly twenty lynx here, so if you affect one pregnant female this is already 5 per cent of the whole population.'

The land of the lynx could be unravelled beyond recompense, threatening the fragile existence of the species in its primary homeland. Resistance to the plans was immediate throughout the country and elsewhere, aligning scientists, ecologists, nature-lovers and NGOs in the condemnation of the invasive development of the park. Eventually taking the case to the Directorate-General for Environment in Brussels through a large coalition of NGOs, MES helped seek an injunction on the plans in light of the frail status of the Balkan lynx – listed as critically endangered on the International Union for Conservation of Nature (IUCN) Red List of Threatened Species – and the lack of a comprehensive environmental assessment for the projects. Their approach to the EU went down poorly with the North Macedonian government, which immediately banned MES from carrying out any further scientific work on the Balkan lynx within the boundaries of Mavrovo National Park. The place of Ljupcho's birth was no longer his nor his son's to conduct studies in, and the sanctuary of that sublime and secretive creature looked distinctly imperilled, bringing the Balkan lynx ever closer to the edge of extinction.

*

We pass our days amidst incremental changes, constant and largely unalterable processes, some as intimate as the ageing of our bodies, others as vast and cyclical as the seasons. Natural change is what continually animates the world, allowing present to become future. We sift meaning from such gradual transform-ations. But change can also signify a monumental rupture, a snapping of those threads that make up the living weave of the world. We need only think of tsunamis and earthquakes to see the devasta-tion made possible by violent, planetary processes. Or the five mass-extinction events that have irrevocably altered Earth through the geological ages; the last of these most likely the result of an asteroid smashing into the planet near the Yucatán peninsula at the end of the Cretaceous period some 65 million years ago. In conjunction with massive volcanic eruptions that had already weakened and destabilized whole ecosystems elsewhere on the globe, the impact of that asteroid, which left a colossal, 180-kilometre-wide crater as the signature of its visit, freed such volumes of soil, pulverized rock and debris from the earth, flung high and wide into the atmosphere, that the world turned utterly dark, as if night had fallen for ever, triggering a killing period of cold and preventing the sunlight necessary for photosynthesis and the functioning of the food chain from reaching the planet's surface. The best-known victims of this ruinous collision were the dinosaurs, but the Fifth Extinction also took with it countless other organisms into the darkness. All life that we know today has descended from the survivors of those dim, obliterating years.

'Background extinction' is always with us; the term is used to refer to the natural rate of evolutionary disappearances, a measure generally gauged over epochs rather than anything as small as a century or millennium. Background extinction differs from mass extinction in its slow trajectory and relative rarity, the result of natural climatic alterations, localized overpopulation and disease. Unlike mass extinctions, which are rapid and widespread events that condemn a multitude of life forms to oblivion in a startlingly short span of geological time, background extinctions are gradual affairs, spun out over the ages. The expected background extinction rate of modern mammals, for example, pieced together after meticulous study of the fossil record, could be, according to author Elizabeth Kolbert, roughly equal to one species disappearing every seven hundred years. What we are witnessing today, however, the large-scale contraction of multiple species in both range and numbers, a shrinkage spread across floral and faunal families and already resulting in extirpations that might be, according to American and Mexican scientists in 2015, up to one hundred times faster than background disappearances, has been interpreted by a considerable number of scientists to be human-induced, the result of industrial civilization, overpopulation, resource extraction, climate change and the twin pressures of consumerism and consumption. We have initiated, it seems, the Sixth Extinction.

We live in an age of diminution, thinning, disappearances. We live alongside shadows – ghosts of our own making. There is no easy way to convey the magnitude of loss currently underway in the natural world. It is, for the vast majority of us, simply beyond our comprehension, dealing in figures that we struggle to interpret or personalize. They are abstract to the point of absurdity. But these numbers are absolutely necessary; they act as mathematical shorthand for individual lives and the existence of entire species, unique expressions of life on this planet, that we must find ways of continually keeping in mind, clearing away space in our busy lives for all those intricate and evolutionarily complex organisms and fellow beings, many of which pre-dated our arrival on this planet by some considerable margin. They are no less the inheritors of this Earth than we are.

In 2013, following the co-ordinated efforts of twenty-five environmental organizations to evaluate Britain's wildlife, the State of Nature Report formalized the harrowing news, long suspected in anecdotal terms but never before proclaimed in such a wide-ranging and comprehensive manner. It was explicit to the point of shame. Since the 1960s, the nation had lost some 44 million breeding birds. In the decade prior to the study, 72 per cent of butterfly species had decreased, including some that were once ubiquitous. Since the beginning of the twenty-first century, sixteen different counties had been losing a plant species every other year to extinction. Of the 3,148 species of wild organisms that quantitative assessments of population trends existed for, 60 per cent of them had declined in the past half century and 31 per cent had strongly declined. Two-thirds of 337 moth species surveyed between 1968 and 2007 were waning in numbers, with as many as 37 per cent of them by over half. And so the report went on.

In the following years, corroboration of these figures came from multiple sources. Research in 2014 revealed that Europe as a whole had lost approximately 421 million individual birds in the previous thirty years, a loss most momentous for such perennially seen species as the house sparrow, skylark, grey partridge and starling; around 90 per cent of the losses were accounted for by just thirty-six formerly common bird species. Monarch butterfly populations in Mexico fell from a high of 682 million in 1997 to just 42 million in 2015. And a 2017 study in Germany, painstakingly assembled by the volunteer-run Entomological Society Krefeld, revealed the catastrophic loss of flying insects in nature reserves across the country, a decline of 76 per cent in just twenty-seven years in a group of invertebrates critical to the pollination of crops. I could go on, but Elizabeth Kolbert soberly sums up the situation in her vitally important book *The Sixth Extinction*, noting that, according to estimates:

> one-third of all reef-building corals, a third of all fresh-water molluscs, a third of sharks and rays, a quarter of all mammals, a fifth of all reptiles, and a sixth of all birds are headed toward oblivion. The losses are occurring all over: in the South Pacific

and in the North Atlantic, in the Arctic and the Sahel, in lakes and on islands, on mountaintops and in valleys. If you know how to look, you can probably find signs of the current extinction event in your own backyard.

The natural world familiar to Georgia from the Hopwas Wood of today is very different from the one that Geoff once knew as a boy around Smithy Wood. Born in Chapeltown in 1939, Geoff came of age just prior to a period of enormous change in the British countryside, when industrial agricultural practices, fuelled by a readily available brew of toxic chemicals, productivity-maximizing machinery and the corrosive nature of Common Agricultural Policy payments, began to drastically alter the textures of old farmland, removing the grace notes from its score of companion species. His encounters with wildlife in the 1950s and 60s would have occurred in countryside demonstrably different in biological plenitude from the one that Georgia began exploring in the 2010s: the science makes that distinction clear. And yet our connections to the natural world, as with our relationships to fellow humans, tend to pivot on the personal; they are interactions of the intimate, the tactile, the seen and the heard. In the presence of wildlife, whether a jay in Smithy Wood or a nuthatch abseiling down a beech in Hopwas Wood, we generally accord the immediacy of the moment its due. And the past becomes that other country we scarcely know.

In his poem 'Binsey Poplars', written in 1879 after the felling of a row of beloved trees by the banks of the Thames near Oxford, Gerard Manley Hopkins wrote:

After-comers cannot guess the beauty been.

What Manley Hopkins evoked nearly 140 years ago was essentially the shifting baseline syndrome, the generational acceptance and normalization of a degraded planet and diminished biodiversity due to the empirical perspectives that largely shape our engagement with nature. An idea first developed by fisheries expert Daniel Pauly in response to fishery management and the inability of scientists to determine a pre-human baseline of species abundance and fish sizes, the idea has gone on to be relevant to a far wider set of relationships with the natural world. Defined by the writer Julia Whitty as the 'phenomenon of forgetfulness', the syndrome relates to our necessarily limited perception of change, a result of relatively short lives and our circumscribed personal knowledge of historical time. Young people discovering three or four butterflies on a summer's walk would have little way of truly comprehending that the verb 'teem' could once have been applied to Britain's butterflies in the country's wildflower-rich meadows, 97 per cent of which have been lost to urban development and modern farming techniques since the Second World War. Drivers pulling into Smithy Wood Motorway Services off the M1 to grab a coffee and a sandwich would have an inadequate ability to 'guess the beauty been' of the lost ancient woodland if that project were to proceed. And so in the process we become inured to loss, understanding our current age, particularly in relationship to our childhood, as the baseline of biodiversity. Excited by an elegant quartet of birdsong in a summer's wood, you might possibly recall that it was a chorus when you were young, but you'd have little way of knowing, in an experiential sense, that it was once, long ago and before your time, orchestral. As the present becomes our measure of abundance, we end up unwittingly celebrating paucity.

But while Geoff was born into a world considerably richer in wildlife than the one Georgia then inherited, his era would have been noticeably poorer than the one his parents and grandparents were familiar with. The 1960s have been identified as a watershed period in terms of biodiversity loss for a number of important reasons: it was a time of turning for agricultural practices that profoundly thinned the countryside; it was the age in which quantitative data about wildlife numbers and population trends began to be collected in a more rigorous manner; and it was the period in which our rising population numbers and industrial consumer societies most dramatically colluded to affect the planet's web of life. But while that decade was indisputably a critical milestone, it's important to bear in mind that none of us can guess the beauty been. We're all susceptible to the shifting baseline, for we're all after-comers, all arriving in times less lush.

In the nineteenth century, American settlers reduced the un-imaginably complex beauty of the tallgrass prairie vista to almost nothing, ploughing under within a few decades all the old dwellings of prairie chicken, bison, meadowlark, compass plant and big bluestem. And a 1905 account by the writer Herbert Job of a London auction lot of heron and egret feathers for the millinery trade revealed that some 193,000 birds had been killed on their nests for that single sale, filling 1,608 packages with beautiful plumes to be worn in women's hats. 'Is it, then,' he asked over a century ago, 'any wonder that these species are on the verge of extinction?'

Our tendency towards nostalgia, and the accompanying assumption that things have worsened since our personal prime, can make the shifting baseline syndrome crippling, yet for a very long time humans have been inheriting less of the beauty, intensity and charge of the living world. I've sometimes heard the argument, from otherwise articulate and passionate advocates for nature, that there's no point in trying to preserve what remains of Britain's wildlife because there is so little of it left. But even three or four butterflies met on a summer's walk can be as magical and transformative as those teeming meadows of old. The wonder of the wild world, whether poorer or not, is no less meaningful on an individual level for the changeable status of its base material. For Georgia, for others of her age, and for what remains of the astonishing and resilient tapestry of life on this planet, there is still *everything* left.

*

Wreathed in egret-white waves, the rippled hills of the Californian coast glittered in hot light. The sky was a flawless turquoise, a near match for the glazed and glistening sea. I walked with a friend through a warm bevel of sand, sinking into the smooth sweep of dunes that were perpetually on the move, each solitary grain slowly cartwheeling south with the wind and waves on one of that coast's few active dune fields. We'd come to Año Nuevo State Park, a windswept spur of mudstone about ninety kilometres south of San Francisco, to see a single species, one that came into focus as we rose above the dunes.

Although it was the end of the breeding season, a number of northern elephant seals were still sprawled across the shore. Breeding was first recorded at Año Nuevo in 1961, and no year has since passed without them returning to this place of theirs. Dozens of pups lay like plump sausages on the sand, occasionally humping forward with the flap of small, wing-like flippers to bask at a new angle. Each year a mother elephant seal will raise a single pup, fattening it with milk so rich that her young will gain 150 kilograms in less than a month. When they finally push off from land, these youngsters will run a gauntlet of great white sharks in the strait, the primary reason why only 50–60 per cent of them will survive their first year. But until then, the pups are content to settle in sunlight beside the few adult males and females still lingering at the end of the season.

If it weren't for the Mexican government, the seals wouldn't be there. After nearly two solid centuries of mass killings, not a single northern elephant seal was sighted between 1884 and 1891, despite having once numbered in the millions. In the following year, 1892, a Smithsonian expedition located eight seals on Guadalupe Island, nearly 250 kilometres off the coast of Mexico, promptly killing seven of them to take back east as museum specimens. According to Charles H. Townsend of the New York Aquarium, however, only three of them eventually made the journey, the other four unforgivably left to rot on the shore where they were killed. Townsend embarked on a further expedition in 1911, counting 125 elephant seals on the same island. They were the sole survivors of countless massacres carried out by sealers from San Francisco, Santa Barbara, San Diego, Hawaii, the American East Coast and Mexico; entire sedentary colonies slaughtered for the oil stored in the animal's blubber – oil which helped fuel the Gold Rush and the rapid expansion of settlement across the American West. Sealing sporadically resumed when word spread that there were still a few animals lingering around the coasts, but in 1922 the Mexican government unilaterally declared the northern elephant seal a protected species in its territorial waters, where Guadalupe Island was found. Their move was followed a few years later by the United States. If it hadn't been for that initial, shielding decision, to announce that a living creature mattered beyond its industrial usage and commodification, it is highly unlikely that the species would be with us today. Instead, because of that singular choice and, more critically, its continued enforcement, northern elephant seal colonies and numbers continue to grow. There are between 200,000 and 250,000 present in the oceans of the world today, all tracing their lineage to that small island in the Pacific.

A male rode in, like a king coming ashore. We'd seen him in the distance, breaching with a twist of white water until he caught a necessary swell. Even the enormous energy of this ocean couldn't carry him far. A male weighs between 1,800 and 2,300 kilograms when he beaches at the beginning of the breeding season, losing around 500 kilograms by its end. This one seemed stranded between worlds: the buoyant blue gloss of sea and the inflexible gravity of shore. The seal reared up in sudden, lumbering movement, a muscled torque of motion that held it steady on its torso. It was sphinx-like at the edge of the sea, gleaming in spray. The long pendulous nose of its name was now visible as it heaved forward, a blubbery shuffle that brought it another metre onto shore.

Seen there, hauled out and dozing on the sands, the elephant seals gave little inkling of their majestic oceanic lives and migrations. For it is to the sea that they truly belong. Leaving Año Nuevo after breeding, the females chart a coastal course northwards to Vancouver Island in Canada, before veering into the Pacific, feeding on rays, squid, eels, fish and small sharks. Once far out in the ocean, capable of diving to a depth of 1,550 metres and holding their breath for a hundred minutes or more underwater, they'll loop southward, boomeranging back to Año Nuevo. The males travel even further, journeying as far north as Alaska, where their westward curve follows the sprinkled volcanic trail of the Aleutian Islands. They are far closer to Asia than their natal shore when they eventually turn for home, spearing across the deep sea for the Californian coast. As remarkable as these migrations are in their own right – long pelagic peregrinations that return them to the precise place of their birthing and breeding – these northern elephant seals in fact make the journey twice each year, returning not only to reproduce but also to moult in the summer months, before setting off seaward again, following that Pacific sea-path encoded deep in their blood and bones.

The sea-light glittered, caught up in the sway and swell of waves. A black oystercatcher whistled from the ridge of breakers. At the edge of the water, the elephant seals basked and rolled. A dead pup was pecked at by ravens and gulls. There was a strange and indescribable beauty to being in the presence of such animals; once imperilled by human action to such a degree that only a single population on a lone island stood between their continued existence and an entry in the history book of extinction, they'd been returned to the world by a decision to alter course, a realignment of moral direction, confirming that, however depleted the planet might appear, what remains always matters.

*

The shattering sound of gunshots, two in swift succession, cracked the ceiling of low clouds and was returned to us, echoing sharply off the winter valley walls. Only silence followed their fading. Nove Angelkoski had pulled a Walther P99 pistol from his rucksack soon after we'd discovered the mule. It was tethered between oaks not far from the border village of Drenok, where Nove lived in North Macedonia. With only two other families inhabiting this

once thriving settlement, he knew that the mule belonged to neither. It had been brought across the Albanian border by illegal
loggers, he said. And so Nove had fired his pistol as a warning for
the men to leave.

The entire border region was tinted with a mixture of ambigu-
ity, wariness and intrigue. Earlier that morning, from a kerbed rib
of limestone, we'd looked across a valley at the village of
Kodźadźik, where the paternal grandparents of modern Turkey's
founder, Mustafa Kemal Atatürk, had lived. In a sign of the
region's myriad Ottoman legacies, it's a village that to this day
remains predominantly Turkish-speaking. In the era of Albania's
paranoid and vengeful dictator, Enver Hoxha, that line on the
map crossed by the loggers would have been deadly for anyone
who dared risk it. And for Nove, a gentle man who wore a neat
grey moustache, round glasses and camouflage gear, the area held
emotional resonances beyond the simple fact of it being his birth-
place; his grandfather had been killed along the border by
Albanian anarchists during the Second World War.

Having worked in the chemical industry in Skopje before retiring to his ancestral village, Nove now fussed over a menagerie of
various animals at his home. Mandarin and wood ducks mingled
in a netted enclosure together with bullfinches and buntings, while
flamboyantly coiffed pedigree chickens strutted through the yard.
His home held a gallery of furs and the stuffed skins of creatures
he'd hunted. Now sixty-seven years old, Nove had fed from this
land, both physically and emotionally, all his life, even when he
lived in the city. He instinctively knew, however, that something
was missing from it. 'The lynx belongs to this landscape,' he simply said as I walked in his footsteps, rising across whale-backed
ridges in thin, silver light. 'It is a part of it.'

His breath smoked in the cold when we stopped. 'When the lynx team came I knew they needed someone who understood the area and where they should put their traps and cameras. And I wanted to help the wildlife, to help any species that is threatened.' Still barred from Mavrovo by government decree, the recovery team was having to study less promising areas in the hope of finding lynx to track, and so had migrated to the mountains south of the park's boundaries. 'The plan,' said Gjorge, 'was to concentrate on the core of Mavrovo and then work on the outskirts, but we have to do it the other way round.' And so local knowledge and the commitment of hunters working with the team became irreplaceable to this phase of the project; they were the eyes, ears and experience of the land. 'We couldn't do this work without the hunters,' said Dime. 'They've been responsible for some of our most important findings.'

Nove had last crossed paths with the reclusive Balkan lynx almost twenty years earlier. And it had been six years since he'd discovered a set of their prints in the hills. 'Ever since I was a young boy I've loved and admired wildlife,' he said as we returned to his house, his pistol packed away again and dozens of illegal snares he'd found in a glade now coiled around a strap on his rucksack to dispose of. 'My father was a passionate hunter as well,' he added, 'but not for the type of hunting that just killed animals, but for the type that involved loving wildlife.'

The Balkan lynx recovery project insists and depends on alliances, the convergence of people that might otherwise steer separate courses through life. It bridges different worlds through shared interests. Travelling northwards through the park with Dime, having made sure we weren't carrying any incriminating equipment in the car, the Radika River was slung to one side, rippling downhill in lucent teal torrents; it was one of the sources of this river that Ljupcho had taken me to on the border with Kosovo. If the Balkan lynx programme had brought together people from different spheres of life in the name of protecting a rare species, the threat of dams had encouraged communities with different stakes in the landscape to take action in the national park's defence as well. The region's rivers were the cornerstones of local communities, their waters used for drinking, fishing and recreation, as well as being immortalized in traditional songs and customs. Residents of Mavrovo rallied on a walk to the location of the Boskov Most dam, taking part in a 'picnic with a message' and filming short videos about their relationships and attachments to the watercourses. Others hauled stones from the banks of the Radika and placed them together beside the river in the shape of fish, creating symbolic deaths out of water.

While the Balkan lynx was the primary focus for MES's scientists, there was the concurrent worry of rivers disappearing as well, a confluence of concerns that harmonized science and story yet again. Extinctions that would steal the heart of the land for the people of Mavrovo, as well as threatening such endemic species as the Macedonian stream crayfish and the Radika trout. As the hydropower proposals entailed the construction of flush dams, water would steadily build up behind the wall before being released in a single surge each day, a technique that involves the catastrophic destruction of downstream wildlife, sweeping away creatures of all kinds in rapid floods. With Ljupcho I'd seen how water levels within the park had dropped due to a number of small-scale hydropower projects already in place. The beneficiary of many tributaries, the Radika relied on a widespread circulatory system of water. Some of these feeder streams were now largely dry, tapped for electricity, their courses siphoned and shipped through pipes. Anything once alive in their waters had already been banished from their beds.

The Balkans are veined with some of the last free-flowing rivers in Europe. They rise across the mountainous hinterland in rocky crevices and pine-studded gorges, spilling off undulating plateaus and bending through broad valleys of beech, juniper and oak, before fanning across the plains to the sea. In recent years many of these cold cascading streams, sage green or glacial blue and home to sixty-nine endemic fish species found nowhere else in the world, as well as 40 per cent of Europe's endangered snails and freshwater mussels, have been stoppered like half-drunk wine bottles, plugged with cement corks and rerouted through plastic tubes. As of 2017, there were 2,800 hydropower projects under consideration in the Balkans, 37 per cent of which were set to be located in protected areas, either national parks, like Mavrovo, or EU Natura 2000 sites. This boom in hydropower, called a 'dam tsunami' by Ulrich Eichelmann, director of the NGO River-Watch, translates into a 300 per cent increase in proposed dams in just a two-year period. On the surface river energy makes persuasive sense for the region; without nuclear power and having little in the way of natural gas, Balkan nations lean heavily on coal for their electricity production. While around a third of the EU's electricity is derived from coal, that figure rises to well over two-thirds in the case of south-east Europe. Power plants are often old, dilapidated and fuelled by lignite, also known as brown coal, the lowest-quality and dirtiest form of coal in existence, pollution being a major health hazard in areas where it is open-cast mined and burned. But so-called green energy doesn't necessarily mean without cost. In Valbona National Park in Albania, local inhabitants have been left without drinking water after three dams were constructed in the area, while people in other parts of the Balkans confront radically reduced water supplies for crop irrigation and dried-up riverbeds where they'd once watered their animal herds, let alone the environmental destruction to protected places.

Energy issues are a litmus test for our valuation of land, as the United States' decision in 2017 to begin drilling for oil in the protected Arctic National Wildlife Refuge affirms, stating their intent to open previously untouched and legally preserved grounds reserved solely for wild species and indigenous peoples. While inhabiting an economic environment built upon continual growth, there are no easy answers to the complex issues that converge around the provision of energy and the preservation of a country's natural and cultural heritage. In such a climate, without a real commitment to protected lands and ecosystems, new energy supplies will always be sought, and not necessarily as an alternative or replacement for more damaging forms, but rather as additional sources in order to meet the rising demands that are inherently sewn into a neoliberal economic system. Unless we find a way to wean ourselves from perpetually increasing energy 'needs', along with harnessing less damaging forms of renewable sources, these conflicts will continually arise. Some Balkan waterways, particularly in Albania, Serbia and North Macedonia, could be clogged with so many dams that you would need to find a word other than 'river' to describe them.

Save the Blue Heart of Europe, a group advocating for the protection of the Balkans' pristine rivers, argue that the environmental and cultural value of the waterways means that a spatial plan should be initiated across the entire region in order for energy production to take place that benefits human communities while simultaneously safeguarding the most unspoiled and significant of the rivers, making space for the more-than-human within our shared world. We cannot continually drive towards a horizon where the utilization of all land and water is geared towards human purposes without looking in the rear-view mirror and seeing countless wild creatures and species fading from view behind us.

In an article about the scale of invertebrate extinction, the journalist Jacob Mikanowski wrote that 'much will vanish before we even knew it was there, before we had even begun to understand it'. Three aquatic insect species entirely new to science were discovered on a Mavrovo stream in 2015, but these caddis flies and stone flies were already at risk of disappearing into the same bleak darkness that followed the Cretaceous asteroid, the biological void we call extinction. 'To know that all this will disappear,' continued Mikanowski, referring to the millennia of interactions between vanishing species and their environment, alongside behaviours developed over countless generations, 'is like watching a library burn without being able to pick up a single book. Our role in this destruction is a kind of vandalism, against their history, and ours as well.' The rivers of the Balkans are far more than just conduits of potential electricity; they flow with their own immutable energy, nourishing innumerable wild creatures and communities as they trace winding routes across the borders of some of the most bitterly disputed territories in history, bridging, braiding and sustaining whole worlds on their way to the sea. Amongst the last relics of an older continent, a land less worn, depleted and shaped for human ease, their continuity amidst considerable change enables an incalculable richness to persevere, pulsing and rushing with the rhythm of wild and living things.

*

In the 1920s, the writer Henry Beston spent a year living on the outer shores of Cape Cod, tethered to the furthest scarp of land on the eastern seaboard of the United States. There he built himself a small cabin in the dunes, the vantage point that gave name to his beautifully luminous book *The Outermost House*. Other than the time ceded to hauling supplies in his rucksack over the shifting hills of sand, Beston spent his hours intimately observing the passage of the wild world as it prevailed on that remote rim of land shelving into sea. He watched fierce storms ransack the beach before him, exhausted deer crack pools of ice in their winter desperation, vast shawls of seabirds ripple darkly southwards on migration, and skates and dogfish surge through the tempered sea in pursuit of prey, only to be stranded on the shore by violent, banishing breakers.

Beston became well acquainted with the endurance asked of seaboard creatures, including humans. He was witness to their daily travails for an entire year. The only people we glimpse in the book, other than the author, are surfmen; assiduous and dogged wardens who patrolled the shorelines of the cape every night, whether snow-riven, still or bitter with pillaging winds, swinging lanterns as they kept solitary watch for signs of wrecked vessels, or the distress lights of troubled ships at sea. At any given moment the sea could be devastating for all, and Beston saw how everything that journeyed his way, whether sailors, shorebirds, surfmen or skates, struggled with equal, vibratory persistence, spending their inheritance of skills and evolutionary adaptations to overcome the odds with every ounce of energy they possessed. In the aftermath of strandings, or other perilous happenings, Beston understood that to view wild animals as somehow lesser than us was a failure of the imagination, an inability to empathize with other creatures and see with clarity their own inimitable brilliance. His passage on our relationship to the more-than-human world is no less important or resonant today than when it was written in 1928:

We need another and a wiser and perhaps a more mystical concept of animals . . . We patronize them for their incompleteness,
for their tragic fate of having taken form so far below ourselves.
And therein we err, and greatly err. For the animal shall not be
measured by man. In a world older and more complete than ours
they move finished and complete, gifted with extensions of the
senses we have lost or never attained, living by voices we shall
never hear. They are not brethren, they are not underlings; they
are other nations, caught with ourselves in the net of life and
time, fellow prisoners of the splendour and travail of the earth.

The ingenuity and capacities of humans can rightfully astonish
us (though they may equally dismay, depending on how they are
put to use), but despite all their splendid diversity they account for
only a fragment of the impressive animal behaviour displayed
across the living world. While we're shuttling astronauts into
space, African dung beetles, creatures that are smaller than the nub
of my thumb, are navigating by the glow of the Milky Way, utilizing that celestial band of starlight as a vast cosmic compass. While
we've raised temples and cathedrals and the Taj Mahal, certain
ant species, notably the Florida harvester ant, have been doing
similarly elegant work underground for considerably longer,
burrowing down through the sandy soil of pine groves and removing each and every particle in the way with their mandibles, passing
it up ant by ant to the surface, and fashioning elaborate, spiralling
networks of living space, composed of vertical shafts and horizontal chambers. The entirety of the nest resembles an inverted
chandelier that might hang to a depth of four metres. And never
do the shafts veer at an angle, but drop directly down as though
following a carpenter's plumb line. In order to achieve this, the

ants must have some sense of the relationship between depth and surface; beyond that, according to ant specialist Professor Walter Tschinkel, the construction of these intricate and magnificent nests largely remains a mystery: 'They do this without a blueprint, without a leader and in total darkness.'

Even consciousness, the attribute alongside language and the transmission of culture that we've long held sacred as the exemplary and distinguishing feature of our kind, the self-awareness that sets us apart from the rest of the living world, may not be ours alone. African elephants express an extraordinary fascination for the bones of their kin, returning to a carcass to examine it in great detail, sometimes covering the remains with leaves, or raising a foot over the body in an unusual display, something which never occurs around the skeletons of other animals. Some scientists and anthropologists have argued that elephants are mourning the deceased in some way that's unknowable to us. If so, it might suggest that their grieving, if that's what it is, contains a cognizance of mortality, a self-awareness about the parameters of existence that is only possible through consciousness. While there is no definitive proof that consciousness exists in these majestic mammals, neither can we negate the possibility of its presence, or that 'self-awareness' to an elephant doesn't register in ways entirely different from human-defined expressions of self-knowledge. What transpires deep in the mind of the elephant, a creature with the greatest brain mass of any land animal and already acknowledged to be extraordinarily intelligent, empathic and remembering, is simply beyond the reach of us.

There are countless reasons why we should celebrate, preserve and repair the natural world wherever possible, from its beauty to our wellbeing and all points in-between. But perhaps the most compelling for me is its innate right to exist, to be able to express itself uncoupled from human needs. To persist and flourish on its intrinsic, evolutionary course; part of the multitudinous, patterned, compound and mystifying world we've mutually inherited. We are not solitary on this planet; we never have been and never will be. And yet so often we seem to live as though we're alone, shorn of ties or tethers to other creatures, inalienable and exclusive in our demands despite our late arrival on this planet and the interwoven relationships we were immediately and necessarily a part of. We simply wouldn't be here without the intricate living web we're enmeshed in. To substantiate the intelligence we so fervently claim for ourselves requires the wise recalibration of our commonality while simultaneously acknowledging our differences; to see in those other nations not 'underlings' but fellow species with an inherent right to wild existence within the 'net of life and time' that we share. To transform *them* to a radically different kind of *us*.

*

In his article on extinction, Jacob Mikanowski noted that, 'We live in an invertebrate world.' He went on to say that, of 'all known animal species, less than 5 per cent have backbones. About 70 per cent are insects. Fewer than one in every 200 are mammals.' If we are to take Henry Beston's notion of encouraging a wiser concept of animals to heart, our embrace of the natural world needs to extend beyond the reach of the iconic animals that so intensely captivate the human imagination. To give greater consideration and credence to those dung beetles and harvester ants along with elephants and the lynx. We have tended towards the totemic in our cultural appreciation of animals, seeing in whales, tigers and polar bears the visceral magnificence of the wild world, reminders, perhaps, of the planet we once knew with inescapable intimacy in all its primal magnitude, violence and awe. We have leaned towards the readily accessible grace of birds, their physical beauty combined with an enviable ability to move through air with ease, as if gravity held no sway over them. Invertebrates, though, with such notable exceptions as butterflies, have generally lacked the cultural impress of mammals and birds in our connective aspirations, receiving relatively little attention despite comprising the bulk of the animate world. Whole empires of invertebrate life are passing us by all the time – some of them potentially for ever.

The horrid ground weaver spider is known from just three places in the entire world. You could easily visit them all in half an hour, its distribution confined to a few disused limestone quarries on the rim of Plymouth in Devon. A whole species, an entire evolutionary link unique to the planet, entrusted, as far as we know, to such small dominions that they'd avoided detection until 1989. And of the three sites supporting the spider, one has now vanished beneath an industrial estate and a second was proposed for housing, making the continued presence of the species on this planet even more tenuous and fragile than ever.

The horrid ground weaver is a tiny money spider that takes its name from the Latin *horridus*, meaning 'bristly', describing the hairy legs and abdomen of the amber-tinted arthropod. It was first described in 1995, proving to be a new genus as well as species to science. And when I visited Radford Quarry in 2015, the proposed site of the fifty-seven houses Wainhomes was hoping to erect, only nine specimens of the spider had ever been found in total. Radford Quarry is a deep and unexpectedly beautiful bowl of scoured limestone, its worked walls the colour of old snow and studded with lone shrubs along vertical fissures. Its floor is self-seeded and greening with willows and grasses, but rocks of all shapes and sizes litter the hemisphere of hewn takings. And somewhere in that spill of stone was a spider whose existence proved little more than a mystery. Not even a photograph of the living creature existed; and so little of its ecology was known that its relationship with these mined sites was guesswork at its most nebulous.

'We don't know where it lives,' said Andrew Whitehouse, refreshingly candid about uncertainty in his field. Andrew was an ecologist at Buglife, an environmental charity that works on behalf of insects and related species in the UK. 'We don't know whether it lives in the cracks in the quarries. We don't know whether it's subterranean, a species that only comes to the surface when you quarry. We don't know anything about its life cycle. We don't know if these are remnant populations of something that was spread out across the countryside. All we do know is that it's been found by turning rocks over on the floor of quarries.'

I began turning stones, prospecting for money spiders. Not in the real hope of finding a horrid ground weaver, but out of a desire to participate in its remarkable story – the fact that a whole life form could exist within such limited habitat so close to mass human habitation. There was an obvious irony to it all: human housing so visibly erasing the dwelling places of other species. But as Henry Beston had hoped, at times the human imagination has found its footing, making space to envisage animals in a realm outside of self-referential needs: to grasp what extinction means, not in an experiential sense, but an ethical one. When Plymouth Council rejected the housing proposal, Wainhomes took the decision to a public inquiry that eventually found against the developers as well, largely due to the threat of extinction.

'Over 10,000 people signed the petition, which is incredible,' said Andrew as we carefully lifted rocks, referring to the crowd-funded conservation plan that enabled Buglife to give evidence at the inquiry on behalf of the horrid ground weaver. 'We got 10,000 people to sign a petition for a spider that they'd never seen, that they're never likely to see, and that has absolutely no relevance to their lives!'

As studies have shown, it's often not facts, figures or information that prompts us to act with regard to the natural world, but rather a potent combination of feelings and morals. Our enlightened care for nature may well best be measured by our attitudes towards the things we'll never experience – where self-interest doesn't commandeer the equation. Most of us will never encounter the polar bears that increasingly suffer starvation as sheet ice breaks apart or thaws too soon for them to hunt seals at the Arctic floe edge because of a warming world. Most of us will never have the opportunity to glimpse a Balkan lynx as it flickers through a forest like firelight. And most of us will never upturn the precise rock that shelters a rare spider in a quarry.

'It's the principle of knowingly causing the extinction of a species, whether it's large or small, that is wrong. Morally wrong,' continued Andrew. 'And I think that's what people were signing up to. They weren't signing up to save this money spider, they were signing up to save a species. And to say, quite strongly, that this is wrong. It's not worth causing the extinction of the horrid ground weaver for fifty-seven houses.'

Of course the safeguarding of singular places isn't a magic remedy for biological loss; the causes of the Sixth Extinction are too systemic, wide-ranging and indelibly woven through the consumptive, economic, industrial and agricultural systems we inhabit. To deal with them adequately requires wholesale change on a political scale that is global as much as regional, transformative rather than reactive. But neither is the protection of place merely a salve, a tonic for our troubles when it comes to the plundered abundance of the natural world. As envisioned at the turn of the twentieth century by Charles Rothschild, who understood that some wild organisms cling to specific sites with a degree of fidelity not dissimilar to humans, protecting places for their ecological integrity has a critical role to play in the process of preservation. Such seemingly small and isolated acts as helping safeguard a species confined to just three places in the world should never be underestimated. These struggles are the small stones of conservation, dropped into waters with no possible knowledge of how far their swells might roll.

Despite their overwhelming differences as landscapes, Radford Quarry and Mavrovo National Park are indelibly bound by a shared quality. They both shelter a species that exists in few places outside their perimeters. Nearly unique in their holdings, they are of unquestionable value if, as Helen Macdonald points out, rarity isn't to be all these animals are made of. The World Bank and the European Bank for Reconstruction and Development finally withdrew their promises of funding for Mavrovo's large-scale dams after recommendations from the European Commission, the IUCN and the Bern Convention on the Conservation of European Wildlife and Natural Habitats that the government halt their hydropower projects, a decision taken largely on the grounds of the risk to the fragile and threatened Balkan lynx population. A national election in 2017 also brought a change of government for the first time in eleven years, the new administration immediately reinstating permission for MES to continue their critical work with the endangered mammal inside the park.

In a span of just two weeks in the autumn of 2017, Balkan lynxes were recorded on camera traps in both Albania and North Macedonia. For an animal whose population amounts to only fifty or so in the entire world, this twin sighting was nearly as rare as their presence on the planet. For the Albanians, their still image opened up the hopeful prospect of an entirely new region being colonized by lynx. For MES, their set of photographs, captured by a group of hunters working alongside the ecologists, confirmed that reproduction was taking place outside of Mavrovo, in a mountainous region close to that border with Albania of so much historical enmity. It showed that stones cast ripples across land as well as water.

I peered closely at one of the photos on my computer screen; none of its monochrome, infrared graininess could dim the beauty of the scene. At an earthen pool in a dell of winter-bare beech trees, a mother lynx and her cub flatten themselves against the ground to drink. Their pointed ears are distinctive in the gloom, like pinched candle wicks. The cub's white, reflecting eyes are fastened onto its mother, watching closely for guidance and signs in this tremulous new world that it's emerged into. It's a tender snapshot of secretive forest lives lived largely out of range of human eyes. Despite all that they faced, this mother and cub were still precisely where they should be, rightful parts of this world we all share.

4

Nocturnes

. . . there are things not human yet of great honour and power in this world.

~ Edward Thomas, *The South Country*

It was nearly midnight when I stepped into the garden. An almost full moon hung above the mountains, frosting the willow leaves in cool, spectral light. Nestled in the neat crease of a mountain fold, ours is the last house at this end of the Greek village that my wife and I have lived in since the year 2000. The valley rises through the old, mostly forgotten, fields, orchards and meadows of the region's past, redolent reminders of a time before the country's civil war emptied this village of most of its souls. While neighbours have salvaged plots to sow summer gardens of tomatoes, peppers, potatoes and beans, and a few shepherds steer goats and sheep between dense palisades of hazel and cornelian cherry, much of the valley has been left to its own graceful ageing.

I was ready for bed when a song cracked the stillness of the night. The source of the spellbinding sound wasn't far, some five or six plots along the track that wends like a river from our house, but I hesitated for a while before finally grabbing a torch from inside. I almost never walk the valley at night. Alongside unpredictable sheepdogs keeping watch over their flocks, this patchwork of fields and thickets veined with cold mountain streams is the haunt of brown bears. During the day I'll often find the remains of their nightly meals, great mounds of fresh scat peppered with identifiable seeds, stones and pips. And at times I'll discover upturned granite boulders; huge, awkward and heavy, they'll have been levered from the earth by long, raking nails, and then lifted as easily as pebbles picked by children on a beach. Lining the empty socket after a bear has eaten its fill are the visibly breached tunnels of an ant's nest, threaded through the soil like a map of a nation's rivers.

But that night moonlight emboldened me. I climbed the grassy track as the nightingale reeled me in, its song sparkling in the dark. I could just make out the silhouette of a walnut tree in a meadow as I neared, and cradled somewhere in the great candelabra of its boughs was the bird I'd come to hear. Across its southern European range, the nightingale is common in the right places – which can mean any patch of scrub or dense thicket of lowland trees. Even a humble roadside bush, filmed with exhaust fumes and dust, can suddenly burst into bright music when you drive by with the windows rolled low. And on spring days the upper reaches of our valley shimmer with their songs. Arriving with the wild plum blossom of April – stunning constellations of unfurling white stars – nightingales sing right through the snowfall of their flowers and the luminous opening of leaves. Their music stays the course through much of June, into those first hazy days of summer, when the valley begins to brim with humidity. And for that annual span of time, the resplendent notes of male nightingales conjure the image of lead violinists, their intense and fluid phrasing slicing through the underlying orchestral score of oriole, blackcap, cuckoo and cirl bunting. So interlaced do these songs become that it feels as though the music is reflecting off the thickets, echoing and reverberating until it becomes dreamlike in its presence, lush, liquid and enclosing.

For all the brilliance of those diurnal concerts, though, there is a reason for the nightingale's name – one that reaches back, according to Mark Cocker in his remarkable compendium *Birds Britannica,* 'at least 1,400 years and recognizable in its Anglo Saxon form, *nihtingale*'. Meaning 'night songstress', its name originated from a belief that it was actually the female that was doing the serenading. The bird's glorious night arias are made particularly mesmeric because they're isolated from most other natural sounds, cushioned and amplified by the enfolding dark until there is little else to distract from their presence.

I sat on a stone beneath the walnut tree. Somewhere above, concealed by darkness and leaves, was a bird whose song has for centuries inspired literature, philosophy, music, folklore and poetry as a symbol of romance, love and enchantment. It's not solely the overwhelming volume that such a small creature is capable of producing that makes its song so wondrous, but the seemingly endless tonal variety and diversity of styles it has to draw on. In a study referred to by Cocker, a 'single male was shown to possess as many as 250 different phrases compiled from a repertoire of 600 basic sound units'. And those phrases are being continually reworked in the midst of the bird's performance with improvisatory gusto. What makes the nightingale's song so spellbinding for me is exceedingly simple: no matter how many times I've heard one sing, I have no idea what to expect next. Inside each passage of music is the gift of surprise.

*

On 19 May 1924, the BBC made history with its first live broadcast of a wild animal, setting its microphones and sound equipment in the leafy Surrey garden of cellist Beatrice Harrison as she performed a duet with a nightingale. Against all the expectations of BBC founder Lord Reith, who'd reluctantly agreed to the idea despite believing the nightingale would be an unco-operative prima donna, the broadcast proved profoundly entrancing, commanding an estimated audience of a million listeners and making Harrison internationally renowned. She was the recipient of 50,000 pieces of fan mail in response to the serenade, some of them addressed simply to 'The Nightingale Lady'. The duet captured the imagination of a nation, fusing together the experimental artistic energy of the post-war period with the comforting appeal of revered British fauna.

The broadcast was also an occasion for bringing the natural world into the living rooms of people who'd never heard a nightingale, but who would have been familiar with the bird from the compendium of poems, folk songs, symphonies and stories that it appears in. In *Broadcast over Britain*, published shortly after the duet streamed across the airwaves, Lord Reith wrote that the BBC had 'broadcast a voice which few have opportunity of hearing for themselves. The song of the nightingale has been heard all over the country, on highland moors and in the tenements of great towns.' Appealing and inclusive as this project was, the inescapable and awful irony wrapped up in Lord Reith's words, written nearly a century ago, is that it was nevertheless considerably *easier* back then to hear nightingales in Britain than it is today. Its song has become more myth than reality, taking up far greater space in digital libraries and sound archives than in the living landscape.

Although Britain's nightingale population, demarcating the

north-west limit of its range in Europe, was never as dense as in its southern heartlands around the Mediterranean, it was once, not so very long ago, substantially greater and more widespread than today. Nightingales had been plentiful enough in Victorian England that they were regularly sold as caged birds in London markets. And they could at one time be heard as far north as South Yorkshire and westwards into Wales after arriving each spring from Africa, hitting the coast and fanning out in search of mates. But those days of plenitude are long gone. The nightingale's span of song has contracted sharply since the 1960s, leaving it confined largely to southern England. It is difficult to contemplate the mathematics of the nightingale's plight without imagining a numerical error. But sadly, and accusingly, they're true. The British Trust for Ornithology (BTO) estimates that since the late 1960s the range of the nightingale has shrunk by 43 per cent, while its population numbers over that same period, gauged by spring surveys of singing males, has plunged by 90 per cent. Which means that in only half a century – roughly my lifetime – nine out of every ten nightingales in Britain have vanished.

I spread my hands in front of me when I read the numbers again, then one by one fold down all the fingers until I'm left with a solitary thumb still standing. It is overwhelming losses like these that enable the shifting baseline syndrome to take hold, making it feel to those coming of age today that nightingales have always been the very epitome of rarity. A feeling only deepened by the BTO's prediction that the nightingale could be extinct in Britain within the next two to three decades.

*

'I said, *We know you're in there, you beggar, I wish you'd sing.*'
Owen Sweeney and I stood beside a thicket of wild roses woven
by summer growth into a tangle of impenetrable darkness as he
recounted a visit to this precise spot some years earlier. I'd known
Owen for only about thirty minutes, the length of time it took for
him to collect me at Strood railway station in Kent, drive to Lodge
Hill on the Hoo Peninsula and set off on our walk, but already I
felt a deep affection for him. Along with a wonderfully dry sense
of humour, there was an unmissable light in his hazy blue eyes
that reminded me of the estuary skies he spent so much of his time
watching.

'We dinnae hear it and so we went somewhere else and then
came back. Now, I don't know if you've done this, but if you do
the first few notes of the nightingale's song, well . . .' The startling sounds of a nightingale's opening refrain snapped the
morning stillness as suddenly as a car alarm. Owen laughed in the
wake of his perfect rendition, and I asked him whether it was at
all possible that there'd never been any nightingales in the area at
all, just a retired Scotsman lurking about the bushes at night. He
clapped his hands together and leaned back on his heels into even
deeper laughter, a sound that was to become as memorable for me
as the nightingale's that day.

There was an apt symmetry to exploring the outskirts of the
former military base of Lodge Hill with Owen, as he'd spent
thirty years working for the MoD, primarily as a personnel manager in charge of training and development. He'd moved south
from his native Perthshire in the 1960s, and had spent most of his
life in Kent since then, except for an unforgettable few years in
divided Cyprus with his wife Linda. After returning to England
in the late 1970s, Owen devoted his spare time to studying and

surveying birds in his local surroundings, assisting the Kent Wildlife Trust and the Kent Countryside Forum whenever he could, a
passion that stemmed solely from the uncomplicated joy of being
in the company of wild creatures. But it was the nightingale that
roosted nearest to his heart, and to which he'd given most of his
energies in recent years. And it was because of this great affection
that we were spending the day at Lodge Hill.

Along with a number of other military sites, Lodge Hill is currently mothballed and being disposed of as the MoD aligns itself
with new strategic realities and financial concerns, shedding some
of its extensive portfolio in the process. It's a large and varied
place spread along the ridge of the peninsula, partially nested
within a leafy vale bordered by the ancient wood of Chattenden
and a housing estate of the same name. Although we lacked permission to access the strictly guarded interior of the base, there
were enough public rights of way to get a feel for how this entire
military landscape has developed into a mosaic of rare and exceptional diversity. We walked woodland and scrub beneath sea-blue
skies, slowing for speckled wood butterflies and pyramidal
orchids, for kestrels, song thrushes and long-tailed tits. And
whenever the familiar song of a nightingale sparkled from the
dark green heart of a thicket, Owen knew the particular territory
it belonged to. All day it felt as though we were dropping in on
his neighbours to say hello.

Nearing his seventy-second birthday, Owen had arrived in
crisp black trousers and a smart purple shirt, looking more like he
was on his way to Sunday lunch at a country pub, except for the
binoculars slung around his neck. His default position seemed to
be happiness, or at least a constant and generous openness to its
presence, knowing that joyfulness was related essentially to

awareness, to what might arise in the smallest of given moments. He would peer for the thousandth time in his life at types of butterflies, birds and trees as though it were his first. Shortly after we'd set out I'd asked him if there was something specific about the nightingale that appealed to him. 'Because I'm Scottish,' he replied, 'and we haven't got any up there!' Another of his fulsome laughs rose buoyantly into the air. 'I just took to them,' he finally admitted, 'because there's not a singer like them. You just gasp, don't you?'

Ours wasn't a random outing in search of nightingales, however. I wanted to understand a place at the heart of a long-running conflict, whose avian inhabitants had unexpectedly taken centre-stage in the drama. While the nightingale continues to dwindle throughout Britain, Lodge Hill acts as an unexpected haven for the species. When the BTO conducted a national nightingale census in 2012, Owen was one of the surveyors who discovered this remarkably concentrated clan, helping establish the presence of eighty-five of the nation's 5,500 singing males at Lodge Hill, making it the largest population of the bird to be found in the whole country. This richness, however, soon led to a problem.

As a site that's been previously used by the military, Lodge Hill is technically designated as brownfield, the preferred land for further development and reuse. The MoD's intention had been to sell off Lodge Hill to a development company called Land Securities, whose stated aim was to build a new town of 5,000 houses on it. But as a result of the nightingale census, Natural England, the government's environmental advisor within the Department of Environment, Food and Rural Affairs, had little choice but to follow their own guidelines and safeguard the place, enlarging a protective SSSI designation that covered adjacent ancient woodland so that it also included Lodge Hill, making it the country's first site to be explicitly preserved for nightingales. Land Securities eventually withdrew their proposal as a result of the uncertainty. The government's Homes and Communities Agency then stepped in, but also backed out after a public inquiry, which would have openly highlighted the place's protected status, was triggered by the development plans. None of which prevented Kent's Medway Council from proposing in 2018 to build 2,000 homes there, a development which would necessarily destroy a significant proportion of Lodge Hill and its crucial nightingale habitat. For now, though, the place remained alive with song, as I was to discover with Owen.

For such a brash singer, the nightingale is a remarkably secretive species, monkish in its habits and cloaked by a camouflage of fawn-brown feathers. It prefers the dark inner chambers of dense vegetation to open glades of light. Only the russet-red flare of its tail occasionally unmasks the cryptic presence of a male when it isn't singing. 'The ideal habitat for nightingales is this umbrella canopy of thicket with surrounding edge effect,' said Owen as we stopped alongside a gallery of knotted hawthorn, 'but underneath the canopy is bare earth, because there's no light, so they can overturn leaves and find beetles.' Owen had begun to bring the species alive beyond its familiar song, reminding me that for all its remarkable music it is a bird with a range of adaptive abilities that carry a grace of their own. 'I saw a nightingale fly across the road once and it was carrying a year-old oak leaf,' he continued. 'And I found out, partly through finding a nest elsewhere in Kent, that they build it low down and then decorate their nest, both the base and the top, with oak leaves. Because the russety oak leaf is the exact same colour as the nightingale's tail.'

That predilection for secret abodes and visual obscurity is connected to the nightingale's decline, as the birds' preferred habitat of scrub and thicket disappears. Condemned by a cultural favouritism for tidiness and clean lines that has historically relegated scrub to the realm of the unsightly, such habitats are constantly at risk of being grubbed up or shorn to the bone, a problem also faced by life-sheltering hedges and floristically rich road verges. But across the sprawling spaces of Lodge Hill, scrub rippled and gleamed with the wing-beats of countless butterflies, dragonflies and bees. And in spring, returning nightingales lock in on these appealing patches of blackthorn, sallow, hawthorn and dog rose as if beacons in a storm.

These nightingale homes would be swept away if the go-ahead were given for the construction of human houses. The issue of housing has become a pressing one in contemporary Britain – skyrocketing prices, both to buy and rent, have meant that in many regions large numbers of people, including essential service staff such as nurses, firefighters and police officers, are pushed to the very margins of a locality if they're able to find somewhere affordable at all. A shortage of houses, combined with a large stock of empty ones (bought for either investment or as second homes) and a rising population, means that increasing pressure is placed on non-urban landscapes. But Owen was a pragmatist as well as an idealist. 'Look, we know there's going to be more housing. But we have to choose our sites carefully and protect the most important.' Owen gave me the example of Capstone Valley to clarify his point, another place of great attachment for him that's also been earmarked for potential housing. 'If you put me on a rack and said, *OK, Sweeney, it's one or the other, which one do you want?* I would save Lodge Hill.'

The reason for this is clear: Lodge Hill is simply unrivalled as a refuge. Adrian Thomas of the RSPB describes it as 'Heartland Nightingale' because of its density. 'This is a pretty consistent place if it's managed well,' said Owen. 'You've got the fundamentals of a nightingale hotspot, and as long as you manage the habitat as you should you're going to continue to get them.' Now and then we heard the bright brilliance of one singing and would stop to listen. It was nearing the end of June, and their songs had thinned to the point where only a few unpartnered males still sang, sending out their hopeful notes as the mating season sped away from them.

Although Owen lived on the other side of the Medway, Lodge Hill was very much his home. He would travel there to walk through the unveiling dawn to a liquid chorus of song. And on weekends he would ferry his grandchildren there after stowing a picnic in the car, encouraging them to run free during their visit. He wanted them to explore the natural world and their own imaginative realms in ways that only children have perfected, he said, with a freedom of curiosity that forges a deeper quality of engagement each time, so that they returned to this magical place with anticipation instead of muffled complaint. Through his love of Lodge Hill, Owen revealed how the spaces we encounter might be transformed into places of connection. He'd devoted his time to it with the same unstinting affection and concern more commonly reserved for friends and family.

Much of his dedicated efforts to protect the nightingale and Lodge Hill were bound up with great fondness and love for the woman he'd shared these wonders with. In 1998, at the age of fifty, his wife, Linda, had died of cancer, leaving a space that I could tell would never be filled. 'I was kind of wrapped up in that RSPB world with her and I think part of my motivation is I know that Linda would have done the same as me.' I realized as we walked the lanes and paths around Lodge Hill, the same intimate places that Owen had wandered for years in the dark to record the inimitable but thinning song of the nightingale, that his departed wife was with him in some indefinable but definite way. Seventeen years on from her death and he still poignantly began sentences in the plural before correcting himself, or told stories of his wife making dinner as though they'd eaten together only yesterday. 'She would have fought,' he said. 'In some ways it's a kind of tribute to her.'

I already had an idea of how its loss would affect him personally, so instead I asked Owen what it would signify in a wider sense if Lodge Hill were to be destroyed. 'The worst thing,' he said, 'would be the realization that if you can't save Lodge Hill as an SSSI, and we've got a national planning policy framework that says we should save SSSIs, then you're bust. If you can't save this place, there's no protection. The policy isn't working. Once they get it into their heads to do something, even if it's daft and other better solutions come up, they don't want to change it. We need some green spaces for quality of life. Our forebears who fought to keep Hyde Park and Regent's Park and St James's as green spaces, their work is at risk now because of these tossers who are in charge.'

*

Staying faithful to the precise date and place – even after Beatrice Harrison eventually moved house and the nightingales became the sole performers – that original BBC broadcast in 1924 marked the beginning of a yearly tradition that lasted until 1942. On 19 May that year, as sound engineers were about to go live to an expectant audience with nightingales on the airwaves again, a squadron of RAF planes loomed over the Surrey sky. Comprising 197 Wellington and Lancaster bombers, the squadron was flying east, towards Mannheim in Germany, on a bombing raid at the height of the war. Quickly realizing that a live broadcast of the aircraft could easily compromise the mission if being listened to in Germany, the BBC sound engineers immediately cut the feed.

Although that brief confluence of bombers and a nightingale was never aired, an archive recording from the day still exists. On one side of the disc can be heard the rising drone of the departing aircraft, while the other has them returning in the aftermath of the raid, minus the eleven planes that went missing on the mission. Both are threaded with singular and soaring song. Those few minutes when a nightingale, singing in search of a mate after its long and gruelling journey from Africa, shared the spring air of Surrey with a dense flock of bombers, laden with ordnance to firebomb a city, are poignant and haunting, the delicate beauty of one counterpointing the raw brutality of the other, the strange and dissonant braiding of nature and war.

I finally gained entrance to Lodge Hill's military base as part of a collective project organized by the charity People Need Nature. From the moment we began our obligatory safety induction at the gatehouse, the worlds of natural and military history appeared to coincide as on that recording. We were shown through a ring binder of explosive ordnance that might still be encountered onsite. It could have been a book of orchids, waders or wildflowers the way each of the images were depicted, but the security guard recited a checklist of 'species' that had none of their sensuous appeal: artillery projectile, anti-personnel landmine, area denial sub-munition, air-dropped high explosive. It was a field guide that focused awareness more than most, revealing the essence of the site's history.

Designed as a naval magazine for the storage of munitions in 1870, Lodge Hill was an active base for over 130 years. Being there was like watching archive film being projected onto the landscape, gathered together and sequenced by era. From grand Victorian vaults of elegant brickwork and arched windows to Britain's first anti-aircraft battery, built to protect the munitions stores in 1913 and still standing in ghostly ruins atop a defensive ridge, Lodge Hill takes you through successive ages within a matter of steps. And by the time you reach a replica street, screened by dense woodland and scattered with orchids and the nests of wild bees, you've arrived in a different place.

When the Troubles erupted in Northern Ireland during the late 1960s, Lodge Hill was transferred from the jurisdiction of the navy to the army. There a facsimile housing estate was built to train soldiers in guerrilla tactics, urban warfare and bomb-disposal techniques before being sent to the province. The scene was unnervingly authentic down to its smallest touches – the neighbourly back gardens where it was easy to imagine people chatting across fences over morning tea, the block of public toilets graced with *Ladies* and *Gents* signs, and the startling IRA mural of a Republican fighter painted on a wall at one end of the terraced houses.

Only a few hundred feet away, or one street over in the larger scheme of things, the base's Newry Road, signposted in the same manner as the parallel world that exists outside Lodge Hill, had been recast in the 1990s, dressed up with corrugated metal siding and fly-postered with fading images of Osama bin Laden and the Ayatollah Khomeini. Trying to conjure the mirage of a Middle Eastern city for Gulf War training purposes seemed strangely futile amidst the sheeting English rain, yet those posters of bin Laden and the Ayatollah, their eyes scraped away to the silver metal beneath, chilled all the same. Wherever you go in Lodge Hill, you feel as though you're somewhere else as well.

But there's also a chronological curiosity about the place to go with the geographical. I walked with Miles King through the grassland beyond the entry gates. Warm-hearted and welcoming, Miles had founded People Need Nature in response to a feeling that losses in the natural world were having a devastating effect on human health, spirituality and communal wellbeing. He sought to re-establish connections and hopefully repair some of the damage, noting that nature didn't need people as much as the other way round. An excellent ecologist with a particular affinity for plants, Miles began describing the larger context of this grassland. 'The reason why we've got all this dyer's greenweed here is because of the initial conditions from where we started.' Last farmed well over a century ago, the meadow had been absorbed by the MoD inside the perimeter of the base at that time, leaving it as a largely untouched buffer zone for the hazardous munitions magazines. As a result, that large, sloping grassland was a repository of older botanical wealth. A low-growing plant with thin, tendrilled stems, the dyer's green-weed was festooned with a glorious flourish of golden, pea-like flowers. It's another member of the increasingly large club of Red Data endangered species, having declined spectacularly in the past fifty years or so, primarily because of industrialized agricultural practices and the plant's inability to spread and recolonize easily. And yet there in Lodge Hill it painted the meadow yellow. 'Were we to take a piece of arable land now and start exactly the same processes that this land has been through over more than a hundred years,' said Miles, kneeling to peer at the flowers more closely, 'it would end up very different from this. The dyer's greenweed won't appear, because the countryside from whence it came has gone.'

Other species that are uncommon or in serious decline across Britain were also visible in the meadow as we walked. Increasingly rare grizzled skipper butterflies skimmed the flowers of creeping buttercup and stitchwort, and a brown-banded carder bee, a species that has vanished from most counties and declined by as much as 70–80 per cent since the 1950s, was swept up in a net by entomologist Steven Falk. As well as being important repositories of military history, sites with significant cultural value, active and former bases often exist as islands of diversity in a sea of increasing biological paucity. They're places that, in more ways than one, remember the past, frequently acting as home to disappearing creatures because they've been managed for other needs, kept insulated from the larger tides of livelihood and land use that have swept across the countryside. Not reliant on the chemical requirements of intensive agriculture or the economic pressures for growth and development, they're of our world and yet different. And sometimes that difference in intent inadvertently produces habitats especially conducive to wildlife. 'All these military sites are refuges that have soaked up the species that were common in the countryside at the time they were created,' said Miles. 'And those conditions are now gone.'

While in the presence of rarity rather than the common, there was a hopefulness about our findings at Lodge Hill, a recognition that places of outstanding biodiversity still exist in Britain, potential sites of source populations for a greater flourishing if we were to have the long-term vision to allow habitats beyond the gates to re-establish and thrive. 'Scarcer bumblebees speak a lot about landscape quality,' said Steven, holding the brown-banded carder bee in a plastic tube for us all to see. 'This is as important as a nightingale, because they need large amounts of the right flowers from spring until autumn across vast areas, so bumblebees effectively act as barometers of environmental quality.' He removed the lid from the tube and tipped the bee into the air. Its appearance was a sign of Lodge Hill's natural value and fecundity, a reminder that, while nightingales garner much of the public attention and acclaim when it comes to protecting places such as this, there is a significant spectrum of lesser-known species whose presence reflects the underlying health of the whole.

From the flower-spun meadow I'd heard a few snatches of distant nightingale music followed by silence, the kind of silence that H. E. Bates described as the 'breathless hushed interval' of their songs, but it wasn't until we'd dropped down through the rippling grasses that we finally heard one up close. It's a song that remains present around the base for a number of historic reasons; much of the periphery where Owen and I had walked only a fortnight earlier had been managed by the MoD through regular and rotational coppicing of its woods. They had their own reasons for doing so, but as a consequence they had created suitable habitat over an expansive area that drew nightingales from far and wide. And inside the base specific zones had been set aside for bomb-disposal training, areas that proved particularly conducive to the species. Clear-cuts had been mown in parallel lines through scrub where soldiers practised the craft of defusing, leaving unruly thickets to develop between them, unintentionally producing a checkerboard of ideal habitat for nightingales, a suite of dense greenery and clearings, a world of multiple edges where the bird could easily command territory, nest and feed in safety. 'The whole area was deliberately seeded with ordnance,' said Miles as we strode through a cloud of bees along one of the parallel green lanes, a long sunlit avenue where summer wildflowers and butterflies flickered in lucent profusion, 'so that your mine clearance teams could come in and find it. And of course, purely by accident, completely incidental to that activity, what they've done is create the best nightingale habitat in the country.' There is a serendipity to such places that we should be attuned to and cherish, the rich happenstance of our interactions with place. 'It's a dream of a nature landscape,' said Miles in response to the abundance of wild things. 'You couldn't create this from scratch.'

*

Around the start of the Second World War, a beautiful moth went missing from Britain. The small ranunculus – a cryptic mixture of pencil-greys and smudged charcoal flecked with orange and gold flashes – was once common and widespread throughout the south, but declined spectacularly during the late eighteenth and early nineteenth centuries until by 1939 it was finally no more. For six decades it was absent before a few migrant moths found their way over from the continent, turning up in Kent before naturally reproducing and spreading until records showed the small ranunculus making appearances in Cheshire, Yorkshire, South Wales and elsewhere. Although it was the moths that had excited keen-eyed homeowners in their back gardens, it's the larval stage of this species that tells its story of return most clearly. Dependent on wild lettuce species as its host plants, the small ranunculus moth is closely associated with brownfield, as these plants require disturbed ground in order to thrive. And so those old sites of industrial legacy and human toil – largely forgotten and culturally peripheral places, such as abandoned quarries, railway embankments and closed military bases like Lodge Hill – are responsible for restoring the small ranunculus to the greater landscape again, a renewal of life that brings the beauty of its tiny wings, splashed with an enigmatic pattern resembling lichens on weathered granite, back into the fold of our experience.

The colours alone, some would argue, say all that you need to know about the respective merits of greenfield and brownfield, the former undeveloped and made up largely of farmed areas, the latter the result of earlier industrial or commercial activity. Green is considered positive, progressive and uplifting, naturally related to the environment. It's the colour of spring grasses, flourishing forests and organizations committed to defending the natural world. Brown, however, has come to denote waste ground and eyesores in the landscape, barren, uneventful and ugly. And yet brown is the colour of the earth and soil that enables all that is green to grow. It's the colour of swallow nests patiently shaped with beakfuls of mud. It's the colour of bears padding through the darkness of our valley as small brown nightingales sing beneath the stars. And brown was the colour I was thinking about when invertebrate ecologist Sarah Henshall arrived to reveal a burgeoning world that might never have existed.

In the 1960s, a company called Occidental Petroleum began developing the coastal grazing marsh of Canvey Wick for an oil refinery at the confluence of Holehaven Creek and the Thames. The low-lying nature of the land presented an immediate problem, one that was resolved by dumping thousands and thousands of tons of river dredgings over the entire site until it stood proud of the river, having in places gained a layer of new ground as great as six metres in depth. Cylindrical oil-storage terminals were raised over it, connected by a network of roads strung with streetlights, and a mile-long jetty, still snaking into the Thames from Canvey Wick today, was constructed to siphon oil from overseas tankers directly to the storage drums through a set of pipes. By 1975, however, the oil crisis had lessened the project's viability to such a degree that the site was completely abandoned. For years Canvey Wick sat undisturbed until the empty and unused oil terminals were disassembled, leaving only the circular tarmac pads where they had stood as proof that they'd ever been there at all.

Sarah, who works for the environmental charity Buglife, showed me one of the old refinery roads, flanked by rain-flattened wildflowers strewn across sandy ground. All those countless tons of river silt and sediment had come alive over time and were now the single most important reason for the extraordinary profusion of natural abundance on the site. 'The beauty of this substrate,' she said, 'is that it's low-nutrient. It's got a bit of a saline character to it so the natural regeneration has been incredibly slow.' But what an extraordinary transformation it has been. That low-nutrient base favours wildflowers at the expense of trees, enabling a remarkable range of flora to co-exist with open ground ideal for their associated invertebrates. 'It was basically seen as a bit of a waste area until about the mid-to-late nineties, when there was a local group of naturalists who came here and couldn't believe the numbers of orchids they were finding. There were over a thousand spears of orchids in one area alone.' We stepped off the narrow road and slid sideways through a small pocket of silver birch, wading through water until a clearing of common spotted orchids lit the grey day like candles, spoking from the glade of grass and water in delicate shades of pink and purple.

I quickly warmed to Sarah's down-to-earth approach to showing me around, slipping and sliding like children at a mud bath. Beneath dour summer clouds and the constant splash of our puddling steps, the inherent beauty and significance of the site was palpable. It was a compact mosaic in the truest sense of the word, small pieces arranged to form a pattern, in this case the image of an invertebrate paradise. Sandy banks ideal for burrowing insects mingled with herb-rich grasslands; reed-fringed ponds, home to breeding dragonflies, were rimmed by sparsely vegetated gravels catering to ground beetles and spiders. It was this configuration of companion pieces, of tiny but intact biological shards, that made the site so significant beyond the existence of any one of them on its own.

When Buglife carried out a survey of Canvey Wick in 2000, it revealed that a staggering 1,300 insect species were living on its mere twenty hectares, a figure which has since risen to 1,400. 'It's within the top five sites in all of the UK for the number of rare and scarce invertebrates that it supports based on its size,' said Sarah, searching unsuccessfully for some of this profusion in the forlorn, waterlogged landscape. And Canvey Wick's brownfield, now theoretically protected as an SSSI and commonly referred to as 'England's rainforest', holds more biodiversity per square metre than any other place in the UK, the unintentional conse- quence of human action followed by a long fallow absence, an astonishing testament to natural resilience and recovery when suitable conditions and serendipity coincide.

Of those 1,400 different invertebrates, thirty of which appear in the Red Data Book of endangered species, one is the small ranun- culus moth, having sustained its remarkable renaissance and spread to this stretch of south Essex. But the moth isn't alone in making a compelling return to national life. When the original surveys were carried out, two species believed completely extinct in the UK were found to be happily living there. *Scybalicus oblongiusculus*, a jet- black beetle now named the Canvey Island ground beetle in honour of its chosen home, hadn't been seen anywhere in the UK since the 1920s. And after an absence of seventy-seven years, the Morely weevil was also rediscovered there. 'These things are turning up all the time,' said Sarah. 'These sites act as reservoirs and oases for things that used to be widespread, things like the brown-banded and shrill carder bee, the weevil wasps and the black-headed mason wasp, these things that shouldn't be really, really rare. They would have been in our wider landscape, never in huge numbers but they would have been on the edges of field margins and verges, or little patches of bare ground. And as we've shifted towards more of a monoculture within the agricultural system, these species have just got squeezed and squeezed and squeezed and squeezed. And now they're just found on sites like this.'

'The plants and the invertebrates are the cornerstone,' continued Sarah, 'they are at the heart of everything.' Without them, the rest of life's web quickly frays. And this great unravelling of invertebrate existence is already underway, as a 2019 study in *Biological Conservation* revealed in the starkest of terms. Although data is still limited to certain locales, the authors believe that 40 per cent of insect species are currently threatened with extinction, and that the planet's total insect mass is shrinking by 2.5 per cent each year. Alongside invasive species and climate change, one of the primary drivers of this catastrophe is the loss of habitat to intensive agriculture, a pressure compounded by the land being steeped in damaging pesticides and fertilizers. To halt such dramatic loss requires political and systems-level changes, but as much as anything it needs us to recognize and acknowledge the vital significance of insect life to the most basic functioning of the planet's life-support systems.

Of course, not all brownfield is a glorious assemblage of insect diversity. It's as varied in its properties and biological value as its celebrated greenfield relative. It can be ruined ground, or simply ecologically unremarkable because of the soil's high nutrient load or otherwise poor condition. Conservationists like Sarah aren't arguing for development to be halted on brownfield, but rather seek compromise and common ground. To be open to the *actuality* of a place rather than be swayed by a word. Ultimately only around 8 per cent of brownfield sites in the UK are believed to be of high ecological value, but those places are like rare gems, scattered about the land and in need of safekeeping.

The common threads of our conversation as Sarah and I watched bees and butterflies slowly emerge into a wet summer world were about connection and perception. When government policy stipulates that developers will be granted 'automatic permission' to reuse brownfield 'subject to the approval of a limited number of technical details', we found ourselves asking how you might shift the narrative of landscape and place when it's already been worked so thoroughly into the grain of a nation's culture? How do you enable wonder to ignite imaginations and minds when constrained by terminology that so spectacularly fails to convey the vibrancy and colours of Canvey Wick?

'It's about bringing people to these places,' said Sarah. 'Because if they haven't experienced a site like this, and spent a bit of time looking at different things, then it's a battle we're not going to win. *Springwatch* and *Autumnwatch* are fantastic programmes, but they need to show more bugs. They show all the fantastic, big, fluffy, spectacular things, but what can people actually go and see and engage with? It's probably invertebrates, probably bugs. Where they can come somewhere like this and start turning over logs and stones,' she said. 'We invited local councillors down one evening and they really enjoyed it. It took a little while but in the end, I remember, we were still here at nine o'clock at night and they were catching things and asking *What's this?* and *What's that?* They understood it a little bit more. Insects are flashy and sexy, just quite small.'

Canvey Wick felt distinctly different when I returned in the autumn, the dried-out terrain revealing the loose sand, gravel and shells of the Thames that had given rise to such peerless profusion of small and glittering life. Clouded yellows and red admirals fanned upwards from the path; dragonflies skiffed away like leaves on a river. Slotted between the grey spires and sprawling terminals of Canvey Island's petrochemical plants and the roundabouts and supermarkets of the town itself, the place shimmered like a dream in the warm, liquid light of the river. And it was constantly in use by locals that afternoon – birders tracking the hawking habits of a migrating spotted flycatcher, dog-walkers coming for a break and a breath of fresh air, and cyclists savouring lunch by the sea wall, sitting knee-deep in wildflowers as little egrets shoaled along the shore. It was clearly a haven for all.

A last riot of colour swept over the place, summer's combustive ripeness becoming the slow burn of the turning year. It was the tale of a successful season told through myriad tints: scarlet hawthorn berries and the pale yellow of a patch of mullein still in flower; wine-dark blackberries and the glacial blue sheen of sloes. I was reminded that you need to walk at a different pace in places like these; to attend to slowness for the sake of seeing more deeply, steeped in the richness of somewhere that almost never was. I nosed my way into a bank of everlasting sweet peas that were being combed by bees, and after a little time I found a brown-banded carder bee like the one we'd been shown at Lodge Hill. So rare and threatened, it gathered pollen with no concern for its scarcity, dressing itself in gold as if for an evening out. With no idea of just how close the end of its line might be, it circled the flowers as it always has, with an unchanging faithfulness, staying true to the habitats of its biological affection. As it dropped to the ground with its hoard of pollen, I noticed how the earth around it held myriad minuscule burrows. I sank to my knees to look more closely, to try to see with the levelling perception of an insect's height, peering with new admiration at this miniature world about my feet. Around each hole I discovered a tiny mound of moved earth, the countless toiling efforts of such small but ineffable lives.

*

Humans aren't alone in having complex relationships with place. Increasingly we're beginning to understand that animal responses to habitat and location can be similarly intricate, dependent upon a host of subtle and varied factors. Nightingales, for reasons yet to be fully unravelled, tend to gather in 'hotspots', places which support sizeable populations to the exclusion of similarly conducive habitat in surrounding areas. 'It's almost as if the established population draws in other birds,' according to Murray Orchard, a friend of Owen Sweeney's and fellow surveyor of the Lodge Hill nightingales. Whether it's a reflection of nuanced habitat needs unknown to us, or a social response to already successful breeding territory, this avian arrangement with place means that the intentional replication of habitat is a phenomenally fraught task. 'You might be able to plant habitat that to the human eye looks the same but you won't get nightingales. So once you lose those hotspots, the evidence is that's it. You don't regain them.'

He was talking about the mitigation plans that had been formulated by potential developers of Lodge Hill. Originally the idea was to offset the development by creating nightingale habitat on the other side of the Thames in Essex. Scientific opinion suggested that the space would need to be twice the size of the lost lands to allow for habitat to develop at different stages over time, meaning a vast and unrealistic piece of real estate would have been required by the developers just to begin with, the intention being that the nightingales, which overwinter in Africa and devotedly return to the same place each spring to nest, would somehow be relocated as one. Owen had jokingly wondered whether the developers intended to plant signs throughout Lodge Hill which said, *Nightingales, this way*. This was followed by an idea to create a number of small sites scattered throughout both Kent and Essex, something which Murray described as 'farcical'.

Development at Lodge Hill would set a precedent for other legally protected wildlife sites facing similar pressures. 'If this was to go ahead it would almost send a green light to developers to just go in elsewhere where there's SSSIs, thinking that they can just solve it all by doing this biodiversity offsetting,' continued Murray. 'To go somewhere else in the country and create another area to replace all this. And it's outrageously arrogant for the human race to think it can do that, because a lot of these areas have developed wildlife communities – birds, plants and insects – which happened over years and years and years, and there are so many subtle factors as to why they're there. They're not just areas of ordinary countryside, they're SSSIs because they've got special, complex communities and you just can't replace that.'

Behind the high Victorian fences and walls that have sealed Lodge Hill from public view for over 130 years is a place of unique and unexpected wealth, a mosaic of enormous historical value and bewildering natural profusion. It's not just a reminder of times long gone, but also a place of refuge and resilience in a contemporary sense, harbouring an abundance that has often gone missing from other landscapes. It may be brownfield by definition, but it's a site considerably greater than the range of meanings contained in that single word. And, in the case of a remarkable wild bird, it's a place of strange fortuity, where bombs and nightingales are once again entwined, enabling a species to thrive locally amidst its national diminishment. As we explored Lodge Hill I kept thinking of that recording from the war – how the conjunction of bombers and a nightingale evoked something other than their individual sounds customarily do. Together they produced a hymn to fragility, to all that is vulnerable and unrecoverable about these lives and environments, reminding us of how tenuous existence in this world always is.

'Beautiful as the notes are for their quality and order,' wrote Edward Thomas of the nightingale's music in 1909, 'it is their inhumanity that gives them their utmost fascination, the mysterious sense which they bear to us that Earth is something more than a human estate, that there are things not human yet of great honour and power in this world.' Despite considerable losses, and a planet that turns increasingly on the axis of the Anthropocene, there remains much in our surroundings to remind us that this Earth is more than just a human estate. It is what renders this world so compelling.

To lose the nightingale in Britain despite our best efforts for its preservation would be a pronounced and wide-ranging tragedy, an enormous natural loss that would leave the cultural life of the nation emptier after all that it has ever meant to our kind. But to aid in its national extinction by purposefully destroying one of its last and essential refuges would also carry an ethical implication. It would make us complicit in the effacement of a living creature from an ancestral part of its range. A song in our lives would have been silenced, and we would be both morally responsible and diminished by our own doing.

*

Regardless of the fate of Lodge Hill, a passionate and indispensable voice on behalf of nightingales has been lost. On 9 February 2016, just eight months after I heard him beautifully mimicking his favourite song in the thickets, Owen died in a hospice in Kent. But like the nightingales he so dearly loved, his was a voice that will linger with many into the silence. His indelible receptiveness to joy in the natural world will outlive his years on this Earth, having been passed on to many of those who spent time in his gracious company.

Near the end of our day together, Owen had told me – by way of apologizing for not being able to carry on any further as he'd have liked to, despite the fact that we'd already spent five hours walking and talking in the hot, sapping sunlight – that he'd been diagnosed with non-Hodgkin's lymphoma a few months earlier. His apology, and the exhaustion he must have quietly and selflessly endured in order to show me his special place and its endangered creatures, seemed to sum up the man I'd already grown extraordinarily fond of that day. He was generous and caring and kind. On the day before he died, Murray, his fellow bird surveyor, went to see him for the final time. 'He was amazingly on the ball. He was drifting in terms of concentration – he'd drift away for a while, but then he'd come back and be *right there*, and he'd be talking quite sharply about issues. Even then he was concerned about the nightingales and what was going on at Lodge Hill.'

A deeply religious man, Owen personally attended to the details of his own funeral at the church of St Thomas of Canterbury. His body was then transported in a wicker casket to the crematorium in Chatham, where he was accompanied towards fire by music, the songs of his beloved nightingales, recorded at Lodge Hill and played over the sound system as he made his final journey in this world.

5

The Sacred Reaches

We were deeply engaged in this improbable geology.
~ Patrick Leigh Fermor, *Roumeli*

It was all sky and stone as we neared the ridge, a circle of rising ravens above us. Revelling in the spring wind, they playfully cut through the air with the grace of dolphins shearing bright water. Trees had shrunk to shrubs as we'd climbed, their aspirations kept modest by the clasping upland cold. Angling sharply across the mountain slope, I tried making myself as small and unthreatening as I could on the recommendation of Vladimir Dobrev, sinking down into my clothes and speaking only when absolutely necessary. With each step we crushed a carpet of wild thyme, its heady scent trailing behind us in the sunlight.

Whenever there was a need to change direction, Vladimir pointed to our route without a word. After only a few hours in his company, I could already feel how at home he was in these mountains of south-east Bulgaria, his easy affability and naturalist's keen eye perfect accompaniments to his deft lightness of step. In his late twenties, goateed and wearing his long, dark hair swept clear of his face by a red bandana, he wouldn't have looked out of place at a beach party on Ibiza, but as I followed him along this exposed spine of the Eastern Rhodopis it was clear that it was to these mountains and their wild denizens that he belonged.

We reached a grassy hollow, where Vladimir motioned for me to wait. He unstrapped a collapsed tripod and telescope from his pack, then scrunched low to slink forward with the gear. From my angle it looked like he'd reached the lip of a crevasse, and I watched him glance over the edge before swiftly planting the telescope, rotating the focus wheel until a place somewhere below became clear.

'Your turn,' he whispered, beaming as he reached me. 'Just remember to be quick. No more than a few seconds.'

In the moment before I peered through the telescope, I saw how the ridge fell sharply away, forming one wall of a deep but narrow canyon. Closing my left eye, an extraordinary, prehistoric-looking bird filled the other through the lens. It was perched in a stone alcove on the opposing rock face like some ancient guardian of the abyss, the all-seeing keeper of the canyon. Secluded in its remote chamber, the Egyptian vulture stayed faithful to its nest while its partner sought carrion across the hills. Not big enough to be a cave, but too deep to be a ledge, its canyon niche was inset like a sunken window in the sheer wall. The telescope brought me near enough to the vulture that the bare skin on its face, wrinkled and egg-yolk yellow, gleamed like a glimpsed sun through the white clouds of its feathers.

The Egyptian vulture wears a garland of myth about itself; it's as much a metaphor of seasonal processes, or a symbol of the divine, as it is a living creature. To the Albanians it's the herald of spring, known as 'the horse that carries the cuckoo on its back'. In ancient Egypt, where it once nested on the pyramids at Giza, the bird was considered sacred, protected by pharaonic law for its cleansing properties and accorded the rank of deity through the vulture goddess Nekhbet, as well as being immortalized in the hieroglyphic alphabet as the letter 'A'. To the Muslims of Turkey and Bulgaria, the Egyptian vulture is known as Akbuba, 'the white father', in recognition of the legend in which it rescues the Prophet Mohammed from the grasp of a golden eagle. To express his deep gratitude, Mohammed granted eternal life to the Egyptian vulture, turning its plumage white in honour of its wisdom, purity and bravery.

In the midst of magnetic animal encounters, 'a few seconds' can often be difficult to gauge: time broadens like a rain-swollen river. The vulture turned towards me, a white light of sentience amidst the arid crags. I pulled away from the telescope, knowing how critical it was not to outstay my welcome. As it shrank to a pale speck on the canyon wall I became aware that it wasn't just the vulture that lent the experience its charged and hypnotic quality, but the way it cleaved to its isolated nest. It dwelled in a world of stone and stark precipices, living apart from other animals and beyond the reach of most things. For a flicker of time on that ridge, it felt as though I'd peered into another, more rarefied, realm.

*

Not everyone finds vultures attractive. For some they trigger a repulsion, premised on the perception of them as dirty, fetid and ugly. Condemned by the primitive strangeness of their faces, they're made even more unappealing by their scavenging instincts. Even our language has had a deleterious effect on the consideration of vultures, making their name synonymous with a rapacious or predatory person who preys on or exploits others. But theirs, for me, is a beauty found beyond the perimeter of the conventionally aesthetic, an appeal that combines utility, evolution and appearance in a marriage of refined ecological need. Feeding almost exclusively on carrion, vultures are the great cleaners and purifiers of the environment, a rubbish-recycling system with wings. Throughout many parts of the world they are instrumental in clearing away the carcasses of dead animals, nullifying any potential bacterial hazards associated with decomposition and drastically reducing the risks of disease, particularly in hot climates, where the spread of viruses, infections and pathogens can be rapid. They deal with death, often in close proximity to human activity and settlements, with an artful simplicity, consuming the expired flesh, organs and tissues of each fallen creature and processing them so that they are returned to the environment through their faeces, neutralized of any potentially harmful effects. Sometimes gathering in large numbers around a find, a wake of vultures, as they are aptly known collectively, can reduce a carcass to bones within minutes, left there to bleach and bake clean in the sunlight.

Such was the intimate understanding of the vulture's cleansing capacities that the Zoroastrians of Iran and India – followers of an ancient Persian religion who revere a supreme being called Ahura Mazda – developed the practice of 'sky burials', seeing vultures as essential components in the process of purification. Considering the dead body to be *nasu*, meaning 'unclean' or 'polluted', the Zoroastrians practised excarnation, leaving corpses openly exposed to these birds after death. This custom can be traced back to at least the mid-fifth century BC through the writings of Herodotus, while from the early ninth century AD specific places were built to host the ritual. Known as 'towers of silence' in English, and typically positioned on prominent hills, the buildings resemble circular fortifications. Inside each of the squat, spherical towers is a raised stone floor that is open to the sky, sloping gently from the perimeter to an open well at the centre which acts as an ossuary for the bones. The platforms are inscribed with three concentric rings – the outer one designated for men, the middle for women and the inner for children. Believing the cardinal elements to be sacred, the Zoroastrian ritual of excarnation is a way of making certain that earth, air, fire and water remain uncontaminated by the unclean body. Instead of lowering the deceased into the earth or cremating them in fire, thereby rendering those elements impure in the process, the body is ritually washed and dressed in white muslin while prayers are said over it. It is then conveyed to a tower of silence, where it is laid out in the appropriate ring of the platform and stripped of its covering. As wheeling vultures lower through the air and begin to feed, Zoroastrians believe that the deceased's soul is released and allowed to ascend to heaven, aided on its cosmic journey by the intermediary birds. Active towers of silence are still found in India, where they are known as *dakhmas*. The most significant are on Malabar Hill in Mumbai, where the city's Parsi community of Zoroastrians own fifty-four acres of the forested slopes, the site of sky burials for well over three hundred years.

The Parsis, however, currently face a defining concern: India's catastrophic vulture crisis. In a majority Hindu nation, where 96 per cent of an estimated 500 million cows die in the open rather than in an abattoir owing to the animals' sacred status within the religion, vultures are indispensable to the ecology and health of the environment and its people. The fine balance of this beneficial reciprocity was tipped dramatically out of kilter in the 1990s when

India's vulture population, comprising 40 million birds spread across nine different species, was suddenly and inexplicably almost entirely wiped out. It wasn't until 2003 that scientists uncovered the cause, tracing the scarcely believable number of deaths to diclofenac, an anti-inflammatory veterinary drug that had been approved for the treatment of cattle in 1993. While safe for the animals it was intended for, it turned out to be catastrophic for the vultures that ate their carcasses, triggering acute liver failure and rapid death.

Numbers of the white-rumped vulture, the country's most common, fell by a calamitous 99.9 per cent. Population trends for the Indian vulture, the slender-billed vulture and the Egyptian vulture were similarly stark. These compound losses unleashed terrible consequences: water supplies were contaminated by rotting and decomposing bovine flesh, and populations of opportunistic species such as rats and feral dogs ballooned in response to the sudden banquet. Scientists estimated an increase of 5.5 million in the country's feral dog population between 1992 and 2006, leading to an additional 38.5 million bites to humans. Statistically, there are 123 deaths from rabies for every 100,000 bites in India, and so the scientists asserted that the disappearance of the vultures was directly responsible for 47,300 fatalities in that fourteen-year period. The absence of vultures has also been implicated in a sharp rise in cases of anthrax and plague. And for the Parsis of Mumbai, it has meant the almost certain end to their tradition of sky burial.

Despite the banning of diclofenac in 2006, the Indian vulture crisis remains one of the most comprehensive environmental, medical and cultural catastrophes ever to have hit the subcontinent, its effects both long-lived and wide-reaching, reminding us how seemingly innocuous human interactions with the natural world can upset the scales of balance, resulting in consequences that are profoundly life-altering in the starkest possible sense.

*

In April 2014, scientists from Yale University and the Zoological Society of London published a list of avian species in *Current Biology* that was exotic and sobering in equal measure: the one hundred most unusual and endangered birds on the planet. Employing a variety of metrics, including prevalence of habitat, evolutionary uniqueness and risk of extinction, the scientists sifted through the world's 9,993 bird species to discover and name the most singular and imperilled amongst them, compiling a register called EDGE, an acronym for Evolutionarily Distinct and Globally Endangered. The list seemed a strangely beautiful incantation to me, both an inventory of things unseen and a potential archive of the extinguished. Scrolling down the list was like reading a long poem of wonder and loss, the names alone summoning a rare kind of magic on the page: waved albatross, Juan Fernandez firecrown, masked finfoot, Sulu bleeding-heart. And there, in the middle of the assembled birds, was the one species on the list that I'd ever seen in the wild: the Egyptian vulture.

Victorian travellers and naturalists had documented the Egyptian vulture in a wide variety of Greece's landscapes from the 1840s onwards, even discovering their nests on the larger islands, as well as in the vicinity of Athens, something wholly unheard of today. By the time I arrived in the country in the year 2000, the Egyptian vulture had long slipped from the height of commonness; seeing them had become a rare and geographically restricted phenomenon, as they no longer inhabited large parts of their former range. A Balkan-wide census carried out in 2012 showed there were only twelve pairs to be found in Greece, which made those encounters with them all the more poignant – the way they gleamed magnificently over northern meadows, gliding off on still wings and paling into far white specks, like the last glimmers of stars at daybreak. And it turned out that only ninety pairs remained in all of the Balkans when attempts began that same year to halt the momentum of the bird's decline.

Named after the vulture's Latin binomial, *Neophron percnopterus*, the Return of the Neophron project brought together Greece and Bulgaria as primary partners in a series of efforts to save the species in the region. Funded as a LIFE project by the European Union, these collaborative actions also included Albania and North Macedonia as associated partners in the region. The environmental groups in charge, the Bulgarian Society for the Protection of Birds (BSPB) and Greece's Hellenic Ornithological Society (HOS), faced an enormous task, considering how little was known about the Egyptian vulture and the specific challenges it faced. While the birds continued to fare relatively well in France and Spain, the central European population had entirely vanished in the mid-twentieth century, meaning no bridge existed between the two groupings to potentially reinvigorate the Balkan territories. The project partners recognized that to have any meaningful impact on the decline of a species which roams far and wide it was essential to cross borders of human invention, co-operating politically and culturally across countries that mean little to a migrating bird. For the Egyptian vulture in the Balkans is a bird of the flyway, one of the invisible aerial routes that avian species utilize to steer themselves north or south with the seasons, bringing them into contact with unique pressures dependent on their location at any given moment. Leaving the Balkans by way of the Bosphorus Strait at Istanbul, the birds thread together Europe and Asia via the Middle East, riding high currents of air onwards into Africa on their autumn journeys, routes that they'll retrace come spring in the northern hemisphere.

These migrations can be ruinous. In some areas of Africa, the Egyptian vulture is hunted for body parts. When consumed, they are thought to transfer magical powers from the bird to the person, superhuman abilities associated especially with vision. At the Port of Sudan, until decommissioned after persuasive efforts by Birdlife International and the Return of the Neophron teams in 2014, uninsulated power lines had been responsible for the deaths of hundreds, if not thousands, of Egyptian vultures since their erection in the 1950s. Across the Middle East the bird must overcome a barrage of bullets from illegal sport hunters, while in the Balkans it faces the twin threats of poaching and poisoning, all adding up to a series of struggles that would test the most resilient of species.

The future of the Egyptian vulture in the Balkans is further compromised by the bird's slow rate of reproduction. At the end of its first summer a juvenile vulture will travel to Africa, where it will spend two to three years living on the fringes of villages before returning to the Balkans to breed, showing a remarkable degree of philopatry by honing in, just as nightingales do, on its precise place of birth. It's not until the eighth or ninth year, however, that an Egyptian vulture is regularly successful at rearing its own young, primarily due to a lack of experience in nest-building and caring for its chicks. Even at that stage, if it makes it that far, only 40 per cent of Egyptian vultures raise two chicks, the remainder of them just one. Capable of reaching twenty-one years of age in the wild, the species' population was functionally viable when numerous individuals offset the slow breeding cycle, but now that those large numbers are simply no longer present in the Balkans, the loss of even a single adult bird can be catastrophic. It pulls loose another of the already frayed threads that keep the birds attached to the region. Victoria Saravia, the project manager for the Greek portion of the programme, described to me what they'd found of the bird's past in the landscape of the present: 'We would talk to these old grandfathers. They all knew the bird and they really loved it. And they would tell us, *Τα χάσαμε τα πουλιά, χαθήκανε. We used to have them everywhere. The sky was full of them and now – oh, it's years and years and years since I last saw one.*'

*

I woke early to beat the fevered heat of the Greek plains, the kind of humid blaze that leaves you listless and soaked to the skin by mid-morning. The silhouettes of Meteora were dimly etched against the night sky. As a crack of light appeared in the east, a startling cry broke the last of the true darkness while I sat on the balcony of my guest house. Other wolves joined the first until a chorus of mysterious howls funnelled upwards like smoke between the towering pinnacles, reflected and echoing off the encircling stone drums. While the wolves moved off before the arriving light, the stone pedestals and prominences of Meteora took shape in the silence of their leaving, as if they'd been called into presence by that wild and plaintive song.

A car pulled up beneath the balcony. Faint light scrolled from the edge of the horizon as a bear of a man in his mid-twenties emerged from the driver's door. Over the course of that day, and the occasions we've met since, I came to understand that Dimitris Vavylis is a man whose heart is more than equal to his stature, his concern for the wild species of this world both intense and compassionate. He'd recommended we start while it was still dark, the temperature due to soar above 40°C that day in the starkly exposed landscape. Wearing a baseball cap and a thick bush of a black beard, Dimitris was one of an increasing number of young Greeks I've met who are confronting the bleak prospects of their country with a reflective and uncompromising honesty. Noting that external factors have unquestionably played a role in the nation's precarious situation, he talked openly and easily about the chronic corruption and nepotism that had historically held his society back. But while there was a resigned weariness to his words, he exuded the same generosity of spirit and make-do grit so common amongst his people, the very same characteristics that had made such an impact on my wife and me when we were welcomed with gracious hospitality in the village where we still live, for ever endearing us to this country.

Working for the HOS on the Return of the Neophron project, Dimitris was responsible for its implementation in and around Meteora, one of the few remaining sites in Greece where the Egyptian vulture precariously clings to existence. An avid bird-watcher and wildlife photographer who had recently graduated with a degree in biology, Dimitris had originally felt conflicted about turning his hobby into a job, keen instead to work the land and expand his nascent plot of goji berry trees, but his initial experiences with the Egyptian vulture convinced him to continue. He's since become profoundly attached to the birds on his watch, monitoring their activity, keeping an eye out for possible threats and ensuring his charges have plenty of safe meat to eat by topping up the 'vulture restaurant', a feeding station in the hills where they gather.

Spending a day with Dimitris was a lesson in connectivity, in the way humans remain bound to the natural world through myths, rituals, habits and stories, despite the undeniable rift that has been opened between the two. 'It's a very beloved bird in Meteora – it's an angel of spring,' he explained. 'They have a saying for the Egyptian vulture, it's τυροκόμος in Greek, that means "cheese-maker", and χοντρή μαρκάτ' in the local Vlach language, which means "fat yoghurt". So they say that the Egyptian vulture has come and soon we'll have cheese and fat yoghurt. It reflects the improvement of weather, a sign of hope that the difficult period for surviving in the countryside is over.' Tragically there are fewer and fewer opportunities around Meteora to renew that relationship with the bird each spring. Local to the place, Dimitris has witnessed the disappearance in person. 'When I started birdwatching back in 2006 or 2007 I always saw an Egyptian vulture when I drove through Meteora, but now I almost never do.'

What has traditionally drawn the vultures to Meteora are the same staggering cliffs and towers of stone that have transformed the landscape into a place of resonant reflection. It was too early for the first tourist buses and so we had the place to ourselves still, winding up through the soaring silence of stone, the astonishing landscape gradually revealed in the golden and rose hues that break like waves across the Greek plains at dawn. The nearest anyone has come to unravelling the origins of the remarkable rocks of Meteora – meaning 'suspended in air' in Greek – was the explanation given by German geologist Alfred Philippson. In 1897, he suggested that a river had once run into an ancient lake that covered what is now the plain of Thessaly, depositing in the same place where Meteora has risen its rippling debris of silt, gravel, mud, pebbles and stones. Some 60 million years ago the estuary of the river was an alluvial fan that opened and spread from its point of entry into the lake. Over the course of thousands of years the layers of the fan deepened, eventually being compressed by the immense forces of water and earth into conglomerate – a type of sedimentary rock composed of the pre-existing stones that the river had washed into the lake – that was concreted together by hardened sandstone. When a massive earthquake emptied the lake by cleaving open a channel to the Aegean Sea, the deltaic cone at the end of the river was raised from the lake bed into the sky. Loose sandstone was rinsed away by rain and the stone pillars were further worn into their present sinuous forms, pocked and riddled with caves and fault lines by wind, weather and the subsequent movements of the Earth.

The stones are beguiling in their shapes – an entrancing sky-scape that continually lifts the eye from the surrounding plain to peer upwards into the vaulted air. It must have been this same sensation that enticed the first hermits to live precipitously on the rocks. From as early as the ninth century, Orthodox hermits retreated into seclusion in Meteora, somehow ascending these sheer faces of stone to live inside the clefts and fissures of the cliffs. By the fourteenth century the hermitic community at Meteora had become so large that monasteries were founded on the high pedestals and plinths. As a measure of how bewildering the ascents – let alone the construction – would have been, St Atha-nasios Meteorites, the founder of the first monastery, the

Transfiguration of Christ, was said to have reached the top on the back of an eagle. And before our day was done, Dimitris would tell me that when rock climbers – using all the modern equipment and technology available to them in the twenty-first century – finally ascended one of the highest and most demanding pillars they found tortoises roaming its grassy top, believed to be the descendants of those placed there by monks as potential food sources during long seasons of solitude.

Dimitris stopped the car and we dropped down a dry, crackling path through a forest until we settled in a gap between plane trees, a window through which we could see a crack in the rounded stone prominence ahead of us that resembled an eye only just opened at dawn, still heavy and squeezed thin by sleep. A quick scan with my binoculars and I made out a pair of Egyptian vultures at the edge of the stone fissure, primordial and magnificent in their cloistered nest. It was Dimitris's favourite place in the area, he said, and as the sun pulled free of the hill I could easily understand why. Sunstreams pierced the dell where we stood, as if we'd sunk into a submarine world where light was now filtered and fanned outwards by water. Insistent young kestrels called with fledgling urgency as they circled with their mother above the trees, and a black stork stood as still and distinguished as a commemorative figure on a plinth. The Egyptian vultures watched over the space like pharaohs, peering from the lip of stone with the untroubled eyes of native sovereigns.

Dimitris, though, soon drew my attention to a sad imperfection in the scene, a flaw merely hinted at in the way the two vultures stood at the edge of the stone cavity instead of being tucked further inside. 'Their chick was twenty days old when it died,' he said, 'possibly from some kind of fungus in the nest, as it was an unusually wet period of summer.' His voice was stoic and reconciled to the loss, but I could hear the timbre of sorrow in its pauses. All of his hopes for this nest, one of only two with a pair of adults in Meteora in 2014, along with the birds' natural desire to continue the lineage of their species, were dashed for another year. Where only minutes earlier it had felt as though the two vultures commanded the space with unruffled authority, they now projected an acute vulnerability. Helpless against a wet summer, there was still a whole season ahead of them shorn of the intended purpose of their stay.

*

Unpicking the meanings of communication between non-human animals can be remarkably difficult. Often their exchanges are conducted in cadences beyond our realm of comprehension, or are transmitted through patterns so subtle as to largely evade our skills of detection. Con Slobodchikoff, an Emeritus Professor of Biology at Northern Arizona University, has studied the calls of prairie dogs in the western United States for three decades. In that time, he's determined that the animals are capable not only of warning others in their clan of distinct predators through specific calls, but also of conveying their speed, size, shape and colour, even reworking the structural aspects of the iterations to refer to something previously unknown to them. It is Slobodchikoff's claim, after all those years of patient and meticulous listening, that prairie dogs have acquired true language.

While humans are primarily accustomed to understanding language as a verbal or aural system, one that embraces sound as the nexus for conversation, everything from subtle human body contact and sign language to the waggle-dance of bees constitutes a form of ordered communication, or a language. In animal species whose sense of smell or touch is often far more sensitively calibrated and refined than our own, it's possible that we just don't register what might well be communication. Egyptian vultures traditionally gathered in large numbers in the southern Balkans at the end of each summer, congregating from dispersed territories, as though each had followed a tributary until reaching the main branch of a river, amassing at certain recurring places prior to departing to Africa for the winter. As birds that exhibit a remarkable degree of intelligence and capacity for tool use – renowned for employing sticks to untangle from fences the sheep wool they use to line their nests, and for picking up stones in their beaks to crack open the tough shells of ostrich eggs – there's no reason to believe that these late-summer gatherings weren't sites of sophisticated communicative exchange. They appear to have been critical to structuring the vulture clan and keeping groups of adults and juveniles clasped together for the duration of the voyage, tracking their southward course around the rim of the eastern Mediterranean before fanning out into North Africa en route to Chad, Sudan, Ethiopia, Djibouti, Niger and Nigeria. But like those speakers of vanishing indigenous languages that no longer have a reason to converse as there are so few remaining who can listen to their words, these assemblies – as many as 143 birds were recorded at the Kalambaka rubbish dump near Meteora in August 1979 – have gradually petered out. And it seems that something vital has been lost in the unravelling, some essential interchange or reciprocity of knowledge that has had devastating consequences.

While past records show that Egyptian vultures almost exclusively used to depart the Balkans via the Bosphorus, many of the young are no longer faithful to that ancient, proven route. 'Juveniles often die at sea,' Vladimir had told me when I'd visited the area around Madzharovo, the heartland of the Egyptian vulture in Bulgaria, and peered at the adult in the nest cavity being monitored by the BSPB for the project. 'One of the reasons is because they don't have the guidance of experienced adults – so they just set off south on their own.' And rather than following the known coastal route that would enable them to refuel and rest along the way, utilizing thermals that rise off the land in their flight, they tend to strike out immediately over the Mediterranean – as though the allure of that direct route can be sensed on the winds, but without hint of its attendant perils. 'It doesn't seem far from Crete,' Vladimir had continued, 'but without any experience it can be.' Of the ten juvenile Egyptian vultures that the Bulgarians had satellite-tagged the previous year, only one of them was still alive. Nearly all the others had perished at sea.

On the project's website you can learn about the lives and journeys of Asparuh, Berenice, Heraclis, Ikaros, Katerina and Red Cliff, all young vultures that struck out across the Mediterranean and eventually drowned after crashing, exhausted, into the waves. The traced trajectories of these birds are tragic – simple, coloured lines representing all their misguided migratory desires and the hopes of the project suddenly stopping like an unwound watch on the screen.

The naming of these vultures isn't meant to anthropomorphize wild animals, but to aid human engagement with them. Nor will it, on its own, halt the terrible loss of the species in the Balkans. While names are by no means the only way into wonder, something which can also be occasioned simply by contact, appreciation and emotional connection, they *are* an important method of bringing people closer to the natural world as it spins steadily towards oblivion. Without names, whether species or individual, we're only able to access a surface beauty, just as knowing the name of your lover takes a human relationship beyond the basic realm of sexual attraction. I can admire the astonishing aerial grace of a bird by observing it, but without a name I would be oblivious to the fact that the arctic tern undertakes the longest migration of any species on the planet, annually tracking between the Arctic and Antarctic on its season-turning journey. Not only does it span the poles in its peregrinations, it also follows a zigzagging course in order to take advantage of prevailing winds, nearly doubling the shortest direct route of 19,000 kilometres between them. These birds live in the light of two summers, seeing more sunshine than any other creature on Earth. Wonder needn't be lessened by the act of naming, but can instead be enlarged by the opportunity. If not utilized solely for the ticking of lists, or for purposes of compartmentalization and ownership, naming can trigger a sense of fascination, concern and care for an animal's fate. A word or two on the tongue that brings us closer to things that so often seem far.

In her essay 'Good Grief', Lydia Millet writes of the importance of naming in relation to the extinction crisis, noting that the very last of so many species, known as an 'endling', is remembered not because it was the terminal point on an evolutionary trajectory interrupted by humans, but because it had a name. She gives Martha, the last passenger pigeon, and Lonesome George, the last Pinta Island tortoise, amongst others, as examples. 'It's partly because they had names that these animals are able to be mourned. We're a species that loves individuals best . . . I bring up love because to save what's left we need to love it, and more

than that we need to *know* we love it . . . And to know we love it
we need to name it.' A name can be both potent and propelling;
and, crucially, it can be the start of a story. So often narrative is
more persuasive than statistics in getting many of us to pay attention. As engines of connection, stories enable us to register the
weight of the world, bringing us into contact with other lives,
allowing the possibility of empathy to be seeded.

There is a need and a place for both forms of positive interaction with the natural world – naming and non-naming – either
separately or combined; the key, ultimately, is the quality of the
connections we wish to make, opening the way, as in the case of
the Egyptian vultures of the Balkans, to see extinction differently.
Not as an abstract catastrophe devoid of anything to latch on to
other than an overwhelming numerical absence, but as a concrete
and felt diminishing, the colossal loss of diversity, species and
wild plenitude that occurs not with a sudden and insensible overnight disappearance, as if an entire species had never existed at all,
but incrementally, through each and every perishing of a single,
distinct individual. A loss that is compounded by the countless
other deaths and departures that go unreplaced in the world
around us.

*

The sun scalded us when Dimitris and I stepped from his car at
the side of a rising road, setting up a telescope to peer towards the
monastery of Agios Stephanos, its pale stone and russet-red roofs
gleaming in the stark light. Our focus wasn't on the monastery,
but rather on a space some thirty or forty metres beneath it on the
sheer face of vertical stone. The large cavity in the cliff had been

home to a single Egyptian vulture that had been unable to find a mate that season. We took turns with the telescope, uncertain whether we could see a bird through the midday spill of haze, and each time I had a look I was further fascinated by how the world of the monastery and the vulture's nest existed in such close parallel, separated by so small a gap on that unlikely stone tower. The vultures, monks and nuns of Meteora were inseparable from the essence of the place, seeking something in its high and other-worldly spaces that appealed to an inner need or longing. It was a landscape that spoke a language recognizable to them all.

Humans have long had a tendency to connect the higher reaches of the planet with sacred space, those soaring landscapes inscribed with divine stories. Whether it's Mount Kailash in the Himalayas of western Tibet, considered sacred to Jains, Buddhists, Hindus and the indigenous practitioners of the Bon religion, or Mount Olympus in Greece, the country's highest mountain and the dwelling place of Zeus, Hera, Apollo and the other Olympian gods of the ancient Hellenistic world, the high peaks and pinnacles of the planet have greatly inspired human imagination and spirituality. For a remarkable number of sacred systems, mountains have been revered as the distilled essence of their worldview, connecting the planet's elevated spaces to their foundational dreams and beliefs.

In the state of Odisha, in eastern India, live the Dongria Kondh tribe. The 8,000-strong indigenous community makes its home in a series of hamlets strung out across the Niyamgiri hill range, a landscape of deep undulating forests, rippling mountain streams and cavernous gorges. The lives of the Dongria Kondh are largely subsistence-based, spent tending the fertile slopes and harvesting wild bamboo, jackfruit, honey, mango and pineapple, along with cultivating orchard crops of sweet papaya, orange, ginger and banana, all of which are traded and sold in local markets. As well as the villages of the Dongria Kondh, the Niyamgiri hills host sloth bears, leopards, elephants and tigers in a mosaic of resounding diversity.

In Odisha's primary language, Oriya, the name Dongria Kondh means 'dwellers of the hills'. The tribe, however, refer to themselves as Jharnia, meaning 'those who live by streams'. Hundreds of perennial waterways percolate through the hills, replenishing the forest and providing water for drinking, bathing and cultivation for the tribe. The Dongria Kondh consider themselves to be the protectors of those streams, as well as of the forests and hills of their homeland. Their relationship to the entire hill range is both sacred and symbiotic. Animist in their fundamental beliefs and philosophies, the Dongria Kondh ascribe deities to nearly all aspects of the natural world, each of its constituent elements and interconnected parts thought to have spiritual significance because together they make life possible and permit their society to flourish. In exchange for these gifts they honour and protect that wellspring of fertility where they've lived for centuries, their religious system forbidding the desecration and pollution of the local, sustaining environment, enabling it and its wildlife to thrive. The reverence they hold for the hills in whose shadows they live is drawn explicitly from the belief that their god, Niyam Raja, makes one of them his abode, named Niyam Dongar, or 'mountain of the law'.

This relationship has an existential consideration as well as a spiritual one: the bauxite-rich and forested mountaintops act as enormous sponges during the monsoon season, preventing flash floods from destroying villages, then slowly releasing the water throughout the dry season. Without the mountains there would be no streams; and without the streams there would be no way for the tribe to exist there. So sacred and essential is the mountain to the members of the tribe that the cutting of trees on its slopes is taboo, the customary laws of the Dongria Kondh premised on principles of restraint known as *niyam*. As these traditional rules revolve around respect for nature and the limits of what can be taken from the environment, the proposal in 2003 by Vedanta Aluminium – a subsidiary of London-listed mining company Vedanta Resources – to build an aluminium refinery and an open-cast mine in order to extract the bauxite from beneath the Niyamgiri hills felt like a profound and visceral desecration. It amounted to the physical abuse of everything the Dongria Kondh hold sacred.

The state government, however, seeing the extraction of an estimated 70 million tons of ore from the mountains as an investment that would bolster economic development, formally signed a memorandum of understanding with the company. Assuming they would be granted the right to mine the hills, Vedanta went ahead and constructed a smelter and refinery on the plains below them, displacing a neighbouring tribe who now live primarily on handouts in a purpose-built colony. The toxic sludge from the processing of bauxite, commonly known as 'red mud', is pumped into storage ponds on the land where the tribe previously lived. The Dongria Kondh, having seen what befell their neighbours, have resisted every move made by Vedanta since then, fearing that their land, livelihoods and the dwelling place of their god would be destroyed by the mine. 'We worship the rocks, the hills, our houses and our villages,' said one member of the tribe in a Survival International documentary, which was made to raise awareness of the battle his people faced. 'The mountain is our temple and our God.'

Despite the tendency amongst major world religions to ascribe the role of creation to one or more godly beings, in global terms – culturally, economically and philosophically – our relationships to the natural world of that creation and all its interconnected communities and systems of complex organisms lean towards damage and abuse. And yet we assign a lofty degree of custodianship, propriety and respect to the human constructs intended to honour the divine, as though the churches, synagogues, mosques, chapels, monasteries and temples of our own creation were intrinsically more valuable than the world itself, deserving of greater veneration than the nature that many of those sacred systems uphold as the works of one or more supreme creators. As animists, however, the Dongria Kondh hold the living planet to be the fount of the sacred, revering the actual world of creation rather than human artefacts. And so they naturally seek to preserve what they see as nature's divinity in precisely the same way that devout Hindus or Christians would protect seminal sites of worship and devotion. An application to destroy St Paul's Cathedral in London in order to dig an open-cast mine beneath it to extract rare earths and economically valuable materials would be thrown out by a government without hesitation as rightfully absurd. A proposal to level the astounding monasteries of Meteora in order to mine the stone pedestals they perch upon for their constituent minerals would be met with overwhelmingly fierce resistance and be swiftly dismissed by any court. And yet these examples have equivalency for the Dongria Kondh: the natural sites in their immediate vicinity resonate with exactly the same intensity of spiritual significance for the tribe as do those built sites for other religious practitioners. The sense of protectiveness accorded to spiritual places, for it to be truly grounded in the enlarging meaning of the sacred, must be extended equally to them both.

When the Indian Supreme Court gave the go-ahead for forest clearance and opening of the mine in 2008, the Dongria Kondh took up an even greater active resistance. They blockaded the rough roads that Vedanta had bulldozed through the jungle, setting up barricades that prevented the company's workers from reaching their sacred mountain. They conducted sit-down protests in neighbouring towns and symbolically closed Mahatma Gandhi Street in the state capital, some 600 kilometres away. They marched en masse to the aluminium refinery gates in a show of force that included other tribes and supporters after their plight had gained greater attention through Amnesty and Survival International. Accusations of harassment and intimidation of tribal members dogged the company as it pushed forward with its plans, but the Dongria Kondh were yet to unveil their most dramatic act of defiance. On 27 January 2009, more than 10,000 tribe members and supporters linked together to form a seventeen-kilometre human chain around the Niyamgiri hills, encircling what most mattered to them.

In 2010, following the mass actions and international attention, the Indian Minister for the Environment rejected Vedanta's proposals on the grounds of violation of tribal rights and environmental protection. In 2013, not satisfied with the result, the state of Odisha, on behalf of Vedanta, took the case to the Supreme Court again, which ruled that the company must seek consultation with, and approval from, the Dongria Kondh for the use of their lands, selecting twelve villages where a referendum would be held. Those village councils, known as Gram Sabhas, voted resoundingly against the use of their mountains for mining, finally ending a decade of anxiety about their potential loss and enabling the Dongria Kondh to continue living as they have always chosen to, tending and harvesting the lush, stream-filled hill country of Niyamgiri, where the god of their people resides in its sacred crown.

*

Like his biblical namesake, Lazaros had miraculously lived. Rescued from the poison coursing his bloodstream just as his internal organs had begun to collapse, he'd been raised from the dead and restored to the skies again, unexpectedly granted a second chance. In the midday hush of the searing summer months we peered up at his nest. It was unusually low, set some five metres above us on a deep lip of rock in a naturally curved amphitheatre of stone. Stacks of baled hay belonging to the shepherd whose sheepfold we stood inside rose from the ground to the nest ledge. 'I clearly remember the first Egyptian vulture I saw for the project,' said Dimitris. 'It was here, under the nest of Lazaros, together with the shepherd.' He took me through the bird's resurrection story. 'I knew that this was their nest but the birds weren't back yet. So the shepherd approached me and stayed with me for an hour as we talked, and then he said, *Here they are, they're coming*. The shepherd had only one eye, but he could spot an Egyptian vulture from miles away. Because he'd known them since he was a child.'

Not long after Dimitris had seen him for the first time on that April day in 2012, Lazaros was poisoned in Meteora, having consumed laced bait set out for other animals in the landscape. 'He was saved by another shepherd,' said Dimitris, clearly moved by the help given by local people. 'He found Lazaros and drove him to Trikala, about half an hour away.' There the shepherd located a vet who stabilized the bird with sufficient anti-toxins that he could be sent on to a wildlife hospital in Athens for rehabilitation. From then on he was known as Lazaros. The opportunity was taken to place a satellite transmitter on his back while still under sedation, and the vulture was released in Meteora, set free by the shepherd who'd saved his life. The vulture's mate was never found, presumed dead from the same lethal bait, and so Lazaros spent the summer alone on the empty nest before departing on migration.

'I waited the whole winter for Lazaros to come back,' continued Dimitris, 'and one day I was speaking with a colleague about a new nest that possibly had a pair of vultures, and he said, *OK, you lost one and you have a new one. What did I lose?* I asked him. *Oh, you haven't heard the news? Yesterday Lazaros was poisoned.* And it was a big shock to me. He was the first vulture I'd seen and now he's not here. That was the point when I actually realized what we have to do, how hard it was going to be, and that maybe there is no hope.' Lazaros had survived only to return to Greece the following spring, and, within days of his arrival, be poisoned again, some 200 kilometres from Meteora. Only this time he wouldn't rise like before.

Wherever in the world it is used, poison crumples a creature. It slackens skin and steals shape from a living thing, like wind dropping out of sails at sea. It demeans all that was elegant and complex and persevering about an animal, transforming it to a husk of skin and bones. All this in a matter of minutes, and sometimes much less. Even if there's an intended target for their deeds, poisoners can't completely control what they're killing. The deaths are indiscriminate because that's the nature of the tool.

And while the last agonizing moments of an animal's life unfold in a forest or field, the person who's set the scene will be long departed, their conscience, if not their hands, always cleansed by distance.

To counteract any already ingested poison – which might have been set out specifically against wolves, foxes or feral dogs – Dimitris carries a bag of atropine with him at all times in the field. But he also has another tool in the fight against illegal poison. Funded by the Return of the Neophron project and BirdWING, a conservation organization working on behalf of birds in northern Greece, Kuki is a handsome German shepherd dog which, along with her sister, Kiko, is specifically trained to detect the scent of poison bait and the carcasses of stricken animals. Seeing how Dimitris and Kuki worked together on a demonstration run revealed a clear bond between the two, though he's mindful not to view Kuki as a pet, needing to maintain an objective distance for the sake of her training and the success of their joint mission.

Having hid a piece of poisoned bait in the meadow, Dimitris released Kuki. She cantered through the long grasses like any young and excited dog in a park, as though waiting for a ball to be thrown to her. The key to Kuki locating poison is one of proximity: she needs to be in roughly the right vicinity to begin with. There is no magic formula able to guide her from her kennel to the precise spot of its presence, but with Dimitris's knowledge of recurring sites, together with crucial tip-offs from farmers, wardens, shepherds and other residents, she stands a good chance of uncovering what is often a tiny and easily missed deliverer of death in the landscape.

I watched her circling the meadow like a figure skater building up speed around the periphery of a rink, then narrowing the potential target area, turning inwards as if in preparation for a jump, and finally coiling towards the centre. She leapt in the air when she discovered the bait. Swiftly stowing it in his rucksack, Dimitris then rewarded Kuki with a dog biscuit. Day after day he walks the landscapes of Meteora doing exactly this in order to help save the very last of Greece's Egyptian vultures. 'It's a silent servant of people,' he said, deeply angered by the unintentional treatment the bird receives from a small minority, 'and we don't understand it. It cleans our environment and wants only food, and yet we give it poison.'

*

The monasteries of Meteora are astonishing. Not only in the rich patina of centuries-old frescoes that adorn the churches' walls, arches and cupolas, but also in the staggering nature of their creation. They cling to the sheer cliffs as if extensions of the stone, the brickwork and masonry fitted seamlessly to the ancient, existing forms. They are a perfect example of affinity with place, built with such extraordinary and imaginative skill. Until the 1920s and 30s, when steps were eventually cut into the stone towers, the only way of gaining entrance to the monasteries was via a ladder that was raised up whenever the monks felt threatened, or to be wound upwards in a rope net by a windlass operated from the ascent tower. When an abbot was once asked how often the rope was changed, he was said to have replied: 'Whenever it breaks.'

In his book *Roumeli*, Patrick Leigh Fermor writes of his journeys in Meteora in the 1950s. By then he was already describing a vanishing world. The great monasteries – totalling twenty-four at the height of their magnetic influence amongst the Orthodox – had been in decline since the 1800s, and by the time Leigh Fermor stayed at St Varlaams, perched on a lofty eyrie of a plinth, there were only small numbers of monks and nuns who remained cloistered in the Thessalian sky. Describing the incremental decline of the monastic tradition, the abbot of St Varlaams told Leigh Fermor that in the old days there was 'a hermit in every hole in the rock, like hives full of bees'.

Since then the fortunes of the monasteries have radically changed. While even fewer monks and nuns are in residence today than when Leigh Fermor visited in the 1950s, Meteora has become one of Greece's premier tourist attractions. Listed as a Unesco World Heritage Site, the complex of religious buildings draws visitors and pilgrims from around the world to these sacred rocks. One afternoon I found a path that swung clear of the monasteries across a hill of burnished grasses smouldering golden under the sun. A succession of old and knowing tortoises kept me company on the way. I walked out along piers of dark stone, looking across the distant plain shimmering in haze. I passed the ruins of earlier hermitages and monastic cells, their long-abandoned shells clinging to the edge of canyons like bats. Alpine swifts, peerless in their artful swirl about the high crags, danced at the tapered edge of the sky and ant-lions flared from the grasses like blown glass, their translucent wings lifting and spinning, glittering helicopters of light.

For all that we rightly revere the stupefying monasteries of Meteora, there is something equally wondrous, extraordinary and enlarging about the living world around them. It is replete with marvels. To encounter those ant-lions, alpine swifts and tortoises as they followed their own paths through that beckoning landscape was no less exalting an experience for me than seeing the hermitages and monasteries. While not, strictly speaking, a religious man, it's the natural world that brings me closest to expressions of the spiritual. Something as simple as standing in a vast prairie landscape, squeezed small between endless seas of grass and sky while meadowlarks sing from the wind-murmuring bluestem, can be numinous in its overwhelming effects. And while I can attempt to describe such deeply felt sensations, there are no words I know of, in any combination or sequence available to me, that can adequately compress their totality into language. These are experiences born essentially of mystery, when the porous border between human and non-human lets in light, allowing an acquaintance with the impalpable to take place. Others might describe such resonances as wonder, awe, or even the divine, but at the heart of all these human words is found a reverence or great respect for things outside of ourselves. If we were to accord the living world the same veneration that we reserve for human monuments to the sacred we would inhabit a more enriching creation, a more vibrant, mysterious and potentially spiritual realm.

*

Dimitris and I sat in a quiet corner of my village taverna, where a sluggish blue cigarette haze hung in the air from those turned indoors by winter. It was late afternoon, early January. The already dark streets and cobbled lanes were slick with ice and snow, the lake at the foot of our valley a hard grey shield of frozen water. It was a world away from the weather of Meteora and the fierce heat of my July visit over two years earlier. After five years the Return of the Neophron project had finished the week before. In that time Dimitris had witnessed the further unstitching of the Egyptian vulture's threaded presence in the landscape and lives of the country, the all-but-unstoppable decline of one of the region's most singular species. 'To be honest, the future of the Egyptian vulture in Greece is really dark,' he said.

Only a decade earlier, in 2006, the Meteora population alone consisted of ten pairs. Now the rocks supported just a single pair and one solitary male, while only five pairs survived in the entire nation. The numbers across the rest of the Balkans weren't quite as stark, but they couldn't be considered encouraging either. In total there were thought to be some seventy active territories in 2017, reduced from approximately ninety at the beginning of the project. A successor programme was soon due to begin, building on the significant amount of knowledge gained during the five-year period, particularly with regard to the specific, but different, threats faced by the Egyptian vulture in the regions it traverses. Along the bird's flyway, stretching from eastern and central Africa to the Balkans, each area would be charged with tackling their own geospecific issues in the hope of ensuring a safer passage through the travails of poaching, migration and power lines. For the Balkans, where it's estimated that over 2,300 vultures across the four species that live there have been poisoned in the past twenty years, the focus was sadly clear.

'You just need one poisoning incident and you can now eliminate half the vulture population of Greece,' said Dimitris. The two anti-poison dogs – Kuki and Kiko – have together found seventy-seven poisoned baits in just the small parts of the country they patrol. They've also recovered ninety-six dead animals, primarily dogs but also cats, foxes, martens and wolves. The dogs have saved the lives of countless animals by being able to lead their handlers to the bait before it killed again. And although there's no way of knowing for sure, they could very well have saved the lives of Egyptian vultures with their efforts too. But these daily forays in search of poison have taken their toll on Dimitris. 'You have to bury them all of course,' he sighed. 'It's supposed to be the job of the forestry service but I've buried around sixty animals. A shovel is just part of the job equipment. And this year, at some point, I said, *I'm fed up with death*. Spring is the hot season for poison, so every day I was burying bodies, and it was really frustrating. But if you have a poisoning incident, if you decide that you're bored, or you're tired, then more animals will die, so you can't just stay home.'

He looked away for a few moments, quiet and considering something beyond my knowing before eventually returning his eyes to mine. He suddenly seemed shy, as though aware he'd let his guard down. I shifted tack and asked him what kept him going when it felt like there was no hope, what lent him the strength to carry on in the face of such losses. 'Nature gives you hope,' he replied. 'You go out and you see something beautiful and you gain strength from it, and you say, *OK, it's worth protecting it with all your power*. Many times I'm tired. I might have been in the field for sixteen hours and then received a call that there's an injured lesser kestrel or something. And many times I'd say, *OK, fuck it.*' Dimitris began to laugh, his eyes restored to a bright and mischievous shine again. 'But I can never really say *fuck it.*'

Meaningful change is slow, but Dimitris has already been witness to some of it; the incremental shifts that over long periods of time may, possibly, result in an alternative tradition being forged. 'I think we've changed the mentality, at least in the core areas where we've worked. I have relationships with many shepherds and local people, and they sometimes tell me that they have problems with wolves, but that they won't put down poison any more.

You need to sit down with these people – they're not aliens, just different people.'

Dimitris is also clear that, in a larger sense, leaving our appreciation for wild animals until they have become scarce is catastrophic. 'You only appreciate something when it's rare,' he said, echoing the magnitude of attention focused on the vultures of India now that they're simply not there. 'We have to start appreciating the common things.' This is something that Victoria Saravia confirmed in terms of the Egyptian vulture when she said, 'I think we arrived too late. That's my impression. We should have done it ten years ago. And maybe, just maybe, we would have had some options. Nobody understood the real emergency of the problem. That the decline was so, so, so steep.' Dimitris translates this lack of notice for the common into something universal. 'Maybe it's not only conservation but some matter of attitudes in life. Because we have the same problems in human relations. You don't always appreciate your friends because you take them for granted, or your partner, or anyone else.'

These links between people and the natural world are what feed Dimitris's view of ecological issues. He sees them through a different lens than some ecologists I've met, steering away from the dichotomy of 'us and them' while analysing a deeper suite of causes for the rupture between the human and more-than-human world. 'We have lost species, almost all species, because of human ego,' he said. 'Human ego and stupidity have killed the Egyptian vulture. But this is why I love conservation: it's about politics and changing minds and attitudes. And my dream is to see Egyptian vultures again at Meteora, to stand by a monastery and see them flying by.'

6

A World Within Water

If there is magic on this planet, it is contained within water.
~ Loren Eiseley, 'The Flow of the River'

They moved each fragment of coral as if they were archaeologists at an ancient site, setting down slivers and shards with careful and considered precision. Surveying the options remaining open to her, one of the girls clasped a grey tubular piece in her small brown hand, suspending it in mid-air while she weighed up the possibilities. With her decision finally made, the girl – about eight or nine years old – moved that smooth hovering hand of hers and placed the coral down in the upper right quadrant of the board, clearing away her opponent's piece with a swift flick of her wrist. Her adversary, a year or two older, picked up an oval fragment of her own coral and studied the game with pensive intensity, the world around the two of them having fallen away from their concerns.

The shore was swollen and shelved with coral, bleached and broken fragments naturally detached from their underwater reefs by a combination of storms, currents and the infirmities of old age. The two girls had scooped a handful as their pawns, using one of them like chalk to score a concrete breakwater with a roughly rectangular grid. It had been spliced with diagonals, where other pieces of coral adorned the intersecting lines, like charms on a bracelet. As the sun sank away from the Indonesian island, leaving the girls tangled in a falling net of gold, they sat astride the cement sea wall playing a game called *maintambahtam-bah*. For several minutes I watched them play as the daily ferry from the mainland returned across the glittering blue strait, spilling residents of Bangka Island onto the pier. There were still people here who had never travelled to the mainland in their entire lives – less than an hour away, but another world from their experience as islanders. Dozens of other boats were being tended to along the shore; they were small, slender craft, which would ride about a foot above the water. Intended to hold only a few people, they were decorated in a striking range of colours: carrot and cranberry, lemon and mauve, emerald and aquamarine. Called *ketinting* by the residents of the island, these outrigger canoes are characteristic vessels of the tropics, ideal for a place such as Bangka, where no roads have yet penetrated the landscape. These boats, similar to the canoes that were first used by the early Austronesian societies of South-East Asia in the exploration and colonization of the wider archipelago, are called *bangka* in the neighbouring nation of the Philippines, the same name as the island and a reflective echo of their importance to the extended people of these expansive seas.

As I sat in the narrow craft that would curl me around the coast, the sea flashed by just below the hull line and I trailed my hand in its liquid blue warmth. Other voyagers hailed us as they passed over the strait, all suffused with gold and rose from the slanting sun. The sharp refractions off the water creased their eyes to narrow lines. For these people the sea was their anchor, the central element around which their lives were spun. It provided provender and was a medium of conveyance; it was connective and yet separating; it was the colour of their days.

*

The Coral Triangle is a roughly three-sided span of Western Pacific waters that is home to the most concentrated and astonishing assembly of marine lives on the planet. Taking in territorial waters belonging to Indonesia, Malaysia, Papua New Guinea, the Philippines, Timor Leste and the Solomon Islands, the Coral Triangle is an Amazon rainforest of pelagic biodiversity. While covering some 5.7 million square kilometres, which is just 1.6 per cent of the planet's oceanic surface, the triangle hosts over 600 different corals, or 75 per cent of the world's total number of coral species. Over half of the planet's coral reefs are found within its boundaries, along with the largest area of mangrove forests on Earth. And more than 3,000 fish species reside within these seas, from the whale shark – the world's largest fish – to the most minuscule of luminous reef inhabitants. It is home to dugongs, a strictly herbivorous marine mammal related to manatees and sea cows, beautifully coloured sea slugs called nudibranchs, manta rays and coelacanths; it is home to pygmy seahorses, spinner dolphins, moray eels and banded sea kraits; and it is home to six of the seven extant marine turtle species. This vibrancy of life is packed together like a tin of sardines, in a region of island-studded seas that is also home to some 120 million people, many of whose livelihoods are critically dependent on this remarkable marine presence. Reflecting the rich biodiversity found within these waters, over 2,000 languages and dialects are spoken across this span of equatorial seas, their distinctive words, concepts and meanings mingling with the varied and living aquatic world.

Reaching Bangka Island, which rises near the geographical heart of the Coral Triangle, had taught me something important about the nature of this vast region. For it was largely a seascape I passed over rather than a series of landscapes. Solid earth is clearly only one component of Indonesia, an archipelago of some 18,000 islands, stitched together politically but separated, for the most part, by enormous spans of water. And relatively few of those islands amount to any memorable size: for each Java, Sumatra and Sulawesi there are hundreds of minor islands; for every Bali and Lombok there are thousands of islets. And it's this expansive tracery of land amidst sea that enables pelagic species to thrive to such a spectacular degree, life-seeding mangroves and coral reefs encircling each island like bracelets slung around a wrist. In their book *Reef Fishes of the East Indies*, Gerald Allen and Mark Erdmann point out that this 'multitude of insular environments has fostered the evolution of an amazing wealth of reef fishes, unsurpassed anywhere on earth'.

The flight from Jakarta to Manado, a city situated on the northeastern tip of the large island of Sulawesi, was a journey of some 2,200 kilometres – roughly the same distance that separates London from my home in northern Greece but one that covers less than half of Indonesia's latitudinal span. And for the vast majority of the nearly three and a half hours that I spent peering through the window we were suspended over a cobalt floor, an entrancing tilework of wave-tipped, sun-glossed water. Tiny islets resembled eyes, each wearing a turquoise ring of liner where light permeated the shallow water, enabling reef and sand to shine.

A pod of whales, dark against the ocean blue, briefly provided a reference point in the seemingly endless firmament of sea.

*

'The ecosystem on this island is very unique and also very complete.' Ulva Takke spoke with a warm timbre to her voice and an unpretentious immediacy. Born in South Sulawesi, Ulva had migrated from the hills of her native landscape northwards to this satellite island off the tip of North Sulawesi. 'I'm highland people, not island people,' she laughed. In her late thirties, Ulva was one of those people whose laugh could turn the mood of a room, a trait passed on to her three young daughters who were chasing each other around the outdoor dining area of the small dive centre that Ulva ran with her husband, Owen. 'But when I came here for the first time,' she said, 'I was amazed by the coral reefs and the fish.'

Bangka Island is tiny, a mere forty-eight square kilometres of buckled green hills in a huge blue sea, but like all islands in Indonesia that are less than 2,000 square kilometres it is lent greater stature by the state's 2007 law on the Management of Coastal Areas and Small Islands, which stipulates that mining and other extractive industries are forbidden in places of such size. The law was in line with the philosophy of Indonesia's then President Susilo Bambang Yudhoyono, who, in 2009, went on to inspire the leaders of five adjacent states to found the Coral Triangle Initiative, a multilateral partnership that sought to address a variety of issues facing their joint maritime territories, including climate change, food security and marine biodiversity. The initiative's founding document, signed in the city of Manado, just thirty kilometres across the strait from Bangka Island, included rising concerns about the 'serious level of degradation to the uniqueness, fragility and vulnerability of marine, coastal, and small island ecosystems within the Coral Triangle region'. On Indonesia's small islands the law gives explicit priority to conservation, education and training, research and development, sea farming, tourism, environmentally friendly fisheries, organic agriculture and animal husbandry, but in the case of Bangka Island, as in so many other places, from the Hoo Peninsula to Mavrovo National Park, these legal provisions have so far had little effect in preserving its small island ecosystem or stemming intrusions on its integrity and cohesion.

'From the first time that I heard there would be mining on this island I said to Owen, *No, that's impossible. If it's really happening, I'll burn my passport and go away from here*,' said Ulva, laughing as soon as she recognized the impossibility of the latter without possession of the former. But her concerns quickly returned. 'I know there are very clear protection rules about small islands and that it's forbidden to mine on them, but more and more I see that it's not like that. When we go to Halmahera [a region of Indonesia to the east of Sulawesi], far away from here, with a lot of small islands, it's like . . .' Ulva's voice trailed into silence and Owen filled in the end of the sentence for her, 'mining, mining, mining'.

Owen's clear blue eyes matched the analytical precision of his thinking. I asked him what the mine proposed for Bangka, already partially constructed despite its apparent illegality, would mean for the 'complete ecosystem' of this small island if it were to begin operation. 'The type of iron-ore mining they'll do here,' he replied, 'is to open the land, take away the forest, drill holes, stick dynamite in, break the rock, and then just take the rocks, load them onto the ships and go away.'

His words were a stark description of modern strip-mining. Unlike the hand-hewn bell pits of Britain's ancient woodlands, locally destructive to the soil profiles and organisms of the forest floor but enabling recovery over time, current technology means that whole mountaintops can be removed or islands whisked away for their inherent mineral properties. So devastating are contemporary extractive capabilities that the American writer Erik Reece has described the landscapes of Appalachia, where coal is taken from the summits by blowing up the wooded earth and trucking entire mountaintops away on newly laid roads, as resembling a 'highway system on the moon'. We can now vanish things that would once have seemed inviolate.

Bangka's mining saga began in 2008, when PT Migroko Metal Perdana (MMP), a subsidiary of the China-based Aempire Resource Group, was granted an exploratory permit by the regional authorities to survey for iron ore on the island. By 2012, as decisions rose through the ranks of a decentralized administration, largely uncoupled, in practical terms, from national oversight, the mining company was granted mineral rights to 2,000 hectares of the island, not far off half of Bangka's entire land mass. It was then that the island revolted, local people joining forces with dive resorts and environmental organizations to sue MMP, hoping to have their permit revoked under the 2007 Small Islands Law by claiming that the mining operation would devastate Bangka's sensitive ecosystem, fisheries and tourism industry. When their case was thrown out by a court in Manado, the group, spearheaded by Ulva, appealed to the High Administrative Court in Makassar, which ruled in the campaigners' favour in 2013, rescinding the mining permits in the process. The decision, appealed by MMP, eventually made its way to Indonesia's Supreme Court, Ulva and others shuttling back and forth between their island home and the far capital, forging connections with anti-mining NGOs and additional environmental groups while making pleas for the enforcement of the law. The Supreme Court, in 2014, dismissed the mining company's application for an appeal.

Despite the court ruling, the then Minister of Energy and Mineral Resources granted a mining operations permit to MMP, while the district head of North Sulawesi gave permission for preliminary extraction activities to begin. At the same time, ways of altering the spatial plan of the island were being explored, a move that sparked another legal case by Bangka residents in the Supreme Court. They won this one as well, though the result had little effect on the ground. In 2014, MMP's mining equipment arrived by ship, and the company quickly turned their attention to transforming the landscape at the core of the site. Regardless of the court decisions, the mine seemed to have an avalanching momentum of its own, until, in early 2017, just a few months before I travelled to Bangka, and under pressure from the island's campaigners for legal enforcement, the Supreme Court reiterated its ruling, sending a letter of execution to the regional authorities requiring them to comply with its demands for all mine-related activities to be halted. While I'd expected to find a joyous and relieved atmosphere amongst those who'd fought to preserve this rich place, the situation on the island, if not in the courts, was still clouded with considerable uncertainty. Only the week before I arrived, rumours had begun circulating that construction work at the site had recommenced. And there'd been reports of intimidation and an attempt to confiscate the camera of a visiting Jakarta-based campaigner.

A part of Bangka is viscerally missing, torn away to leave stark lacerations through the island's greenery. Simon Foote, the owner of the dive centre I was staying at, offered to take me by boat past the mining site; no sooner had we come parallel to it than a man emerged from an outbuilding, hopping onto a moped and following us closely along the coast. The earth was rust-red where great swathes of jungle had been devoured by machines. Whole hills had been hollowed out, reshaped into roads, parking bays and platforms, where three industrial storage tanks had been erected. Buildings had sprouted in place of trees: row after row of concrete blocks to accommodate administration offices, employee barracks and equipment stores. Our view of the site was untrammelled, a clear pathway from the sea up through the ravaged hills, where a thick band of once-obscuring mangrove forest about two kilometres in length had been bulldozed into the ocean. Following the mangrove's obliteration, cargo ships had dumped a payload of boulders onto the adjacent coral reef to form the foundation for a landing area and jetty ample enough to receive mining equipment, lorries and industrial conveyor belts. Ulva and Owen had shown me before-and-after footage of the reef taken while scuba diving; I've rarely seen a more stark depiction of difference, the vibrant and intricately interlaced world of a thriving coral community laid waste to by the bombardment. The rocks and sediment had ruined what was living, either swiftly crushing or starving it of needed light, to be replaced by a barren shroud of inactivity. This incursion, though, was relatively small. In time, if the entire project were to be realized, close to half of Bangka would be surrendered to the mine, all the silt and sediment of the excavation works sluiced from the broken hills until they smothered the surrounding reefs, making the island unrecognizable.

While islands have long been set apart in both a physical and imaginative sense, for those who dwell on them, an island's separation from the mainland, the defining feature of its existence, is increasingly coupled with grave anxieties. The sea that embraces them, once the hallmark of their otherness, has come to signify exposure to a series of external threats. Because of an overheating climate, innumerable islanders now exist on the frontline of rising, ravaging seas, and many live at the mercy of extractive industries, especially in archipelagos like Indonesia's, where the proximity of all that ocean enables the transport of mined ores and other valuable seams of materials from their land masses with fluid ease. These are people and places on the cusp of pronounced and irreversible change in our lifetimes. 'Islands are invulnerable until they're breached,' wrote Julia Whitty in *Deep Blue Home*, her illuminating work about the wonders of the oceanic world. 'And then they're as fragile as mirages.'

*

I threaded the mangrove forest on a watery path of my own making, stepping even more carefully than before after learning that what I'd taken to be seedlings were in fact the trees' breathing tubes, or pneumatophores, sticking up from the mud and silt like caveless colonies of stalagmites. Encircling the island, this living barrier of trees is critical to protecting the coastline against storm surges and wave erosion. As a refuge of calmer, protected waters, mangroves also act as giant nurseries for many crabs, fish species and even sharks, making them essential for both marine biodiversity and the livelihoods of tropical fishing communities. And together with sea grass, the food source of the endangered dugong, mangrove forests, according to a 2016 study led by Daniel Alongi, store around 3.4 billion metric tonnes of carbon dioxide in Indonesia alone. Their ability to sequester it makes them, per hectare, amongst the most efficient carbon sinks on the planet. And yet, despite this plethora of ecosystem functions, which are of enormous human benefit, mangroves continue to be lost at a staggering pace. Each year it is estimated that 1–2 per cent of Indonesia's mangroves disappears as a result of development, tourism, agriculture and shrimp farming. Those missing mangroves at the mine site were another rent in the enormous circle of shielding trees.

The roots of a red mangrove rise in great, woven arches, effectively acting as stilts, suspending the tree's leafy parts above the inundations of water. When the tide completes its rise, that tangle of knotted roots will be completely submerged in salt water until the sea eases out again. Mangroves have adapted in order to live in some of the harshest environmental conditions that it is possible to imagine for the growth of trees, grounding themselves in the bleak prospects of a salt-soaked and low-oxygen coast, their home a place of swamps and waterlogged, tidal mud. Not for them the temperate lowlands of Britain's great ancient oaks and beeches, or the stream-rinsed slopes where the Balkan lynx roams. Instead they cling to the very margins of terrestrial possibility, outsiders staking claim to a radical periphery. To exist in this salt habitat and have their roots submerged twice a day, two phenomena that would rapidly end the lives of most trees, mangroves have developed ingenious methods to aid in their survival, including those breathing tubes that I'd walked across, harvesting essential oxygen from the air at low tide. Some filter salt that's been absorbed through their roots by secreting it out via glands in their leaves, the bright green surfaces encrusted with white crystals. Others utilize cell-sized pores called lenticels, which permit oxygen to enter through roots, leaves, branches and trunks while closing up like clams at high tide to prevent the tree from drowning.

I searched the canopy until I found a long, dangling shoot,

resembling a cross between a vanilla pod and a French bean, but about four times the size. It was a mangrove seedling, tethered to its parent tree. To aid in the success of their progeny, many mangrove species germinate their seedlings, called propagules, while still attached to the tree. There they grow, umbilically fused. When fully developed, this long green pod will drop out of its parent's embrace, beginning a long journey to find a place of its own. In order to increase the range of the tree's genetic pool, seedlings rarely root within the vicinity of their relatives, instead floating horizontally out to sea. There they are carried by currents; they're driven by winds. As the seedling voyages it slowly begins developing roots and shifting its position of buoyancy from the horizontal to the vertical when it locates brackish water, preparing itself for touch-down if coastal conditions are auspicious. If, after some days, it has failed to successfully root, the seedling is able to re-establish buoyancy, continuing its journey in a horizontal position like one of the island's canoes, capable of sustaining its travels in a dormant state for up to a year, a long-distance seafarer searching for home. It is an exemplar of nature's great persistence.

I headed for higher ground as the tide began to rise. So, too, I noticed, were others. Around my feet crawled hundreds of miniature hermit crabs of the most beautiful hues – pistachio, pewter, wheat and pearl. I knelt down and watched how their tiny legs engaged with the sand and flicked grains behind them, their shells no bigger than a fingernail. Theirs was a slow procession, having to contend each day with clambering over a line of wrack. In his evocative short story 'The Shell Collector', Anthony Doerr writes how the tides plough 'shelves of beauty onto the beaches of the world'. The poetic resonance of these strandlines, however, the furthest extent of the tidal incursion, where water deposits a ribbon of found things – shells, stones, coral, driftwood and seaweed – has sadly been added to in recent decades by an altogether more ominous and devastating component: a shelf for our disposable societies.

I conducted a rough inventory of the beach, randomly selecting a stretch about four metres in length along the line of the latest tide. Within a few minutes I'd identified juice containers, solitary and unmatched flip flops, yoghurt pots, sun-cream bottles, cosmetics tubes, sweet wrappers, oil cans, jerry cans, water bottles, coffee lids, multicoloured straws, shampoo sachets, empty Kleenex packets, tubing, hoses, plastic bags, both plain and labelled with the names of companies and shops, a doll, nappy packaging, keychain fobs and water cups, single-use types with a flimsy, pull-off lid. While plastic was the common denominator – as well as the base substance of the innumerable fragments whose origins I couldn't determine – it was the sheer volume of the detritus that stunned me, as though another kind of reef were being formed, a shoreline conglomeration nearly as diverse in manufactured species as a coralline reef is in natural ones. Some of the hermit crabs clambered higher up the shore, having scaled the debris, an obstacle that ancestors of theirs, as recently as only a few decades ago, would never have known.

I grew up with plastic, both in the everyday sense of witnessing its increasing prevalence in our lives in the 1970s and 80s – from my beloved Lego sets and replica model of the Millennium Falcon to lunchboxes and Atari computers – but also through my father's livelihood. He ran a plastic injection moulding company that serviced and sold the machines that were fed the raw ingredient from which plastic was then shaped into objects of human choosing. I vividly remember visiting his company's stand at a trade show in Toronto while just a boy and being allowed to dip my hands in great bins of granules, the pre-production constituents of plastic, millions of tiny pellets of synthetic or semi-synthetic organic polymers and compounds, most commonly derived from petro-chemicals, which are then mixed and blended with a variety of additives, many of which are potentially toxic, including fillers, plasticizers, colourants and stabilizers. The granules can be cast in a painter's palette of colour choices, customized for anything from children's toys to parts for the space shuttle. I sank my hands again and again into those bins of bright grains, feeling for all the world like I was lifting the most beautiful cupped sand from a shore and letting it fall through my fingers, an image that, decades later, seems disturbingly apt, since so many of the items fashioned from those long-ago felt fragments have ended up coating the coastlines of the world.

For all its unquestionable usefulness for the human race, a convenience that's turned out to be irresistible to us, plastic places an unearthly burden on the rest of the living world. From sea turtles with drinking straws jammed tight inside their nostrils to the sperm whale found dead on a beach in southern Spain in 2018, its intestinal system ruptured by twenty-nine kilos of largely plastic detritus, our use of the substance increasingly harms wildlife precisely because of the qualities that make it so appealing a material. Its durability after being shaped under intense heat, becoming virtually indestructible once hard, means that most of the plastic that's been produced since its popularization in the 1950s is still in existence, virtually unchanged since the day of its making.

A month before I arrived on Bangka Island, a study led by Jennifer Lavers and Alexander Bond of the University of Tasmania's

Institute for Marine and Antarctic Studies had revealed that Henderson Island in the South Pacific, an otherwise isolated and uninhabited coral atoll in that great blue space, listed as a Unesco Heritage Site in 1988 in recognition of its unique ecological qualities and range of endemic species, has the highest density of human-made debris anywhere on Earth. Nearly 38 million pieces of plastic had been found on its shores. This figure, however, was no sooner tallied than immediately obsolete, as each day some 13,000 new pieces float ashore. Much of the waste wasn't even visible, 4,500 pieces per square metre being buried to a depth of 10 centimetres. All in all, either on the surface or embedded beneath sand, 17.6 tonnes of plastic weighted the otherwise pristine island. According to the study, this total accounted for a mere 1.98 seconds' worth of annual global plastics production, another figure, amidst spiralling rises, that was inaccurate the moment it was determined. Statistics like these can numb the mind. Like the fact that every minute one million plastic drinks bottles are bought around the world. Or that, if placed end to end, the 480 billion bottles bought in 2016 would reach halfway to the sun.

The photographer and film-maker Chris Jordan wrestled with this conundrum of scale when he travelled to Midway Island in the North Pacific. Throughout his career Jordan has deftly depicted the debris of human consumption, photographing vast, nearly inconceivable hills of discarded mobile phones and towering walls of crushed cars in scrap yards. But his journey to Midway introduced a living element to his evocations of excess. Some 600,000 Laysan albatrosses breed on wave-washed Midway. Although one of the most remote islands in the world, rising well over 3,000 kilometres from the nearest continent, Midway sits near the bullseye of the Great Pacific Garbage Patch. Trapped by the circular currents of the North Pacific Gyre, this ocean region has become infamous for the monumental volumes of plastic litter that gather there, the vast majority of it either floating on the surface or drifting in the upper layers of the sea, where marine life is at its most profuse. It endlessly swirls in the currents, a visible tribute, roughly three times the size of France, to the far-reaching influence of humankind. And for the albatrosses of Midway, this rubbish tip of ours is lethal.

Laysan albatross chicks are dense bundles of brown and grey fluff studded with obsidian eyes. Sitting on the nest where they hatched, the young are reliant on their parents for growth, the long, gracefully winged adults sweeping and gliding over the buckled waves of the Pacific as they forage for food. Returning to the atoll, they regurgitate meals of flying-fish eggs and half-digested squid that they've sieved from the sea's surface into the beaks of their hungry and restless young. But in doing so, the parents also proffer unintended items to their offspring, pieces of plastic scooped alongside food from the ocean. Indigestible to the chicks, this deadly stew of human junk gathers in the bellies of the young birds. While many are still able to take to the skies at six months of age, tens of thousands of them are grounded. It is these birds that Jordan photographed: creatures condemned by the human world, elegantly built for air but weighed down by so much plastic waste as to be anchored to the Earth by chains. Slowly perishing from starvation, suffocation or puncture wounds to the stomach lining, their bodies litter the atoll like the washed-up plastic on Henderson Island, eventually rotting down from the innards out, where a harrowing image takes shape.

Each dead albatross leaves behind an imprint of accusatory and condemning power, as haunting as the chalked outline of a traffic victim after the body has been removed from the road. Nested inside the bowl of bones and frayed feathers is the evidence of their killer: a compact heap of plastic. Like macabre funerary offerings, many of the items found inside the withered-away bellies of the birds are immediately identifiable, familiar to any one of us: bottle lids, cigarette lighters, toothbrushes, beer-can ring loops and straws. Everything else is fragmented to a pointillist design, just the chips and shards of much larger objects, broken ever smaller by the pounding surf until their scattered, nebulous presence drifts through the water like appealing plankton. Jordan made a critical aesthetic decision not to move or disturb a single piece of plastic but to photograph the birds as he found them, stark and shocking, with the irredeemable weight of our world fully upon them, afterwards diligently counting up the individual pieces found within a single corpse, a tally that would regularly rise into the hundreds, especially disturbing when the chicks were no more than a few months old on the drawn-out day of their death.

We have largely ordered our modern world in such a way as to avoid emotional and intellectual contamination between cause and effect, our transactions and exchanges taking place in an imagined void or vacuum, where precious little overlap with the living planet is perceptible. The commonplace presence of plastic, the convenience and ease of its disposal, and the difficulty involved in being witness to its continued existence beyond our personal use of it, sanitizes its ultimate destination. And that destination can now be anywhere at all, even to the deepest part of the planet's oceans, confirmed in 2018 when a plastic bag, like any plastic bag we carry our shopping home in, was discovered at the bottom of the Mariana Trench, eleven kilometres beneath the surface of the sea. In 2019 chemical additives used in the production of plastic were even found in the eggs of northern fulmars breeding in a pristine corner of the remote High Arctic. And when the journey of a single plastic water bottle can last some 450 years until it completely degrades, potentially travelling across varied ecosystems and imperilling a range of wildlife en route to its eventual end, there is much we are insulated from through that physical and imaginative detachment. It then becomes expediently easy, as with all decisions that ask of us a critical change in habit, to turn our backs on account-ability, something the American writer Guy Davenport sums up with just three words, a phrase that could be applied to nearly all of our environmental crises: 'distance negates responsibility'.

Increasingly the impact of plastics on the natural world is being publicly raised, but for me the most disquieting and powerful aspect of Jordan's albatross photographs is the way in which he bears wit-ness to its effects with such devastating intimacy. 'I discovered that grief is not the same as sadness and despair,' he said about his work with dying and dead albatrosses. 'Grief is the same as love. Grief is a felt experience of love for something that we're losing, or that we've lost.' There is nothing to distract within the frame of his compositions beyond the remains of the bird and its plastic ballast, and the cumula-tive effect over many images is to draw a harrowing relationship between those two unavoidable things – death and a synthetic material – compressing the connection between them to incontestable fact. He has gone out into the world and brought back verification of agonizing human impacts, shrinking the distance that negates respon-sibility. To see that equation in such startling proximity, the ruinous links between our world and theirs, is to confront what I would call *furtherance*, the notion that our actions can spool out far beyond us – sometimes for the better, quite often for the worse – continually coming into contact with the living world, regardless of how remote it might sometimes seem. Each year 700,000 tons of plastic fishing gear is discarded at sea, either intentionally cut loose or accidentally snagged and torn free, becoming floating death traps called 'ghost nets'. In 2004, divers around the San Juan Islands north of the Puget Sound discovered a midden of bird, fish and marine mammal bones one metre deep beneath a discarded gillnet suspended between underwater rocks, still killing years after its abandonment. While empathy and connection are essential to the preservation of wild places and species, so too is the narrowing of that gap between decision and responsibility if our concern for the non-human world is to be sufficient to stimulate and transform emotion into action, to turn philosophy into practice, to convert words into legislation and a different way of living.

I left the hermit crabs to their strandline of shelved plastic, remembering the words of Sally Huband, inveterate beachcomber of the Shetland coasts where she lives. 'There are so many plastic bottles on these shores that I no longer bother to check if they contain a message; the cumulative message is loud enough.'

*

The people of Bangka are subsistence fishers, harvesting only a few fish at a time. None of their catch is shipped to the mainland for market, but is instead exchanged between themselves, swapped with neighbours for root crops, a variety of greens, pineapples, coconuts and pigs. Typically they ply the waters alone, where they can be seen throughout the day, solitary figures in their vivid boats, the swell of the glossy waves making it seem at times as if the *ketinting* has vanished, leaving just a man sitting far out and lonely at sea. They'll sometimes attach a large palm leaf to their fishing line, the wind carrying it like a kite, jiggling the hook enticingly through the teeming water. Bangka's coral reefs and mangroves are essential to the fecundity of these fishing grounds, to this way of life passed down through the generations, so when the extent of the mining plan eventually came into focus it aroused deep concerns amongst the islanders.

Around 2,400 largely indigenous people live on Bangka Island, scattered over four villages. Other than the sea, their primary means of subsistence is through the harvesting of jungle products to supplement their kitchen gardens, particularly cashews and coconuts. All day I would see people walking the shore or rising up through the jungle with woven bamboo baskets on their backs, topped up with coconuts that they'd macheted from the trees. Where smoke houses had been erected from bamboo, coconuts smouldered in huge heaps to dry and preserve their flesh, a grey haze drifting upwards like mist through the trees. Islanders also find employment with the small-scale dive operations on Bangka, acting as boat captains, cooks, divers, cleaners, technicians and guides. But the sea, foraged with their own particular form of sustainable harvesting, is still the primary pull for the island's people.

Though remarkably beautiful, their slender fishing canoes remain small and vulnerable vessels, no match for anything more substantial should conflict ever arise. And yet when the mining company first tried landing equipment on the island, crossing the strait in a large cargo vessel, the fishermen of Bangka set out to repel them. They rallied and spread the word that a boat was headed their way, convening offshore by the intended mine site and using their low-slung outriggers, and considerable bravery, as a barricade. Arranging their canoes nose to tail, dozens of small craft were somehow able to hold the line, sealing the landing spot and preventing the ship from unloading. When the company's cargo vessel next returned, it had the Indonesian police as an escort.

Although Bangka's story has been presented in the international media as though the entire island is united against the mine, this is extremely misleading, even if the narrative appeals. Time and again I heard how the mine had savagely ruptured Bangka's otherwise cohesive society, introducing rancour and dispute into long relationships of good standing, as the mining company sought to gain a foothold through extravagant offers and promises of opportunity, despite their work having been ruled illegal. The mine has seeded mistrust on all sides, and Bangka is now an island divided when it had never been one before. Ulva knew families that had been splintered down the middle into opposing camps: pro- and anti-mining. And I would hear from people in the village of Lihunu that there were members of the community who decided which church service to attend depending on whether the day's pastor was a supporter or an opponent of the mine. One whole village had committed to radical resistance, while another had swiftly sold its land and been relocated higher up the hills.

Ulva, however, had been seeking common ground. In 2012 she and Owen founded Suara Pulau, an NGO whose name translates as 'Voice of the Island', to encourage greater community development through workshops in kitchen gardening and marketing of local products, alongside environmental education for Bangka's children. 'Each village has common needs and common things that they can work together around, such as water,' she said. Her work had brought her into contact with all facets of the debate, and so I asked Ulva what she thought the mine would mean for the subsistence nature of the local economy.

'The mine will ruin the nature here,' she replied. 'It will take

away the forest. The company is buying the land from the islanders, so if the islanders don't have land any more they can't have a
plantation. Which means they can't eat, basically, because people
here live from their own land. They live from the land and from
fishing. So if you break nature, if you take away their lands, then
there's nothing for them to grow. And the run-off from the mining will go into the sea and you'll get a lot of sedimentation. The
soil will settle down on the reef, the reef will die, and when the
reef dies the fish will disappear. So the second source of food for
the locals, fishing, will disappear as well.' Environmental conflicts
are never solely about the natural world, but influence and perme-
ate the social landscape as well, affecting communities whose lives
are embedded both culturally and economically in a place. They
reveal, in the most profound way, just how tethered to local
topographies so many people are.

I asked Ulva what the fishermen were ultimately fighting for
when they blockaded the site with their boats. 'For their children,'
she quickly replied. 'They've said to me, *We've been living here for
generations and this island has fed us and made us big, and so we
believe in this island. And when people want to come and destroy it,
we're going to stop them. We want this island for our children and our
grandchildren and our great-grandchildren in the future. And if it's
destroyed, it's our sin that we allowed it to happen.*'

*

Strong and muscular, Otny Thomas stood like a figurehead at the
prow of the boat. He had an angel tattooed on his back, and a
large centipede inked in a coiled and wavy line around his navel.
He'd eagerly borrowed my binoculars, having never before

experienced the rapturous magnification of glass, and was already pointing out to me brahminy kites and great-billed herons in the far distance. In his mid-thirties, and originally from the small neighbouring islet of Pagga, Otny now lived on Bangka. Welcoming, friendly and fun – a man of the beach as much as the island or sea – he was unshakeably focused when dealing with his technical tasks on the boat, or in preparation for leading a dive. Passing me the binoculars, he began suiting up, sweeping back his black thatch of hair with a hand, two small patches lightened by henna to a copper glow, a silver cross swinging from a long chain around his neck.

Once ready, he went through the dive with those around him, running through various signals for the marine species they might encounter. He folded his hands together in a variety of ways to silently name seahorse, frogfish, crab, angelfish, shark and nudibranch. Everyone who dived with him remarked on his extraordinary ability to locate the smallest of things underwater. Hand signals and safety checks completed, Otny gave the sign for 'OK' and tipped backwards off the edge of the boat, each of the other divers following him into the water. I let them clear the area and then plunged in.

Sea-sway, sun-drift, water-light. Schools of silver fish spilling like shimmering silt through a river. Wave shadows mirrored and rippling across an undulating bed of soft corals, the tug of the sea fanning a million tiny polyps like meadow grasses in a summer breeze. Bodies banded like wasps, Moorish idols glided and glimmered, each one trailing a snaking white streamer from its dorsal fin. A blue tang, lapis and lemon yellow, gleamed beneath me. Dazzling and luminous hues rose to either side, built up into dense, overlapping neighbourhoods of breathing beings, creating a

fantastical underwater city, where both architecture and residents
are alive. I floated over whole seascapes of bewildering coral
shapes: magenta rosettes, delicately abraded with crystalline stems;
a suite of circular discs like an array of radio telescope dishes scan-
ning deep space, each one delineated by radial slices resembling
the rays of the sun; a fuchsia pillow pitted with the crater holes of
an elaborate sponge, multichambered and tenanted by small shining fish striped blood orange and cream; an encrustation of
amethyst plates, stippled with countless pale pillars. The coral reef
rippled and dipped with long valleys and hidden glades, their
sweeping vistas broken by steep, crenellated bluffs, where domino
damselfish, black and white and striking, danced on the lip of the
crevasse without any fear of falling. I swam through a shallow
gorge that opened onto a vista of stag coral, as if all the deer antlers
mounted on the walls of country estates had been piled together at
the bottom of the sea. From deep wells of water fluttered flights of
butterfly fish, large and buoyant but as laterally thin as their namesake's wings, lavishly done up in summer tints: lemon, tangerine
and apricot. The arms of large sea stars, cornflower blue and lux-
uriously splayed across coral beds, quivered in the current.

An intense sense of compression was attached to this trancelike
realm, its immersion in water magnifying it to such a luminous and
limpid degree that each of its components was revealed as a complex miniature world, intricately beautiful in both design and
behaviour. A mere metre or two of reef summoned a whole continent of terrestrial features to mind. The bleached and stony pieces
of coral that the girls on the breakwater had played with bore little
resemblance to their living kin, having washed up as just the hard
grey skeletons of their former selves. Underwater, in a vale of
light, the coral reef rose and stretched like a kingdom of

unimpeachable pageantry, invested with mobility, colour and lucency. It was like dropping into a psychedelic dream, some mind-altering fantasy of forms so stupefying as to feel suspended not solely in water but within the current of a baroque imagination.

A coral reef is home to a considerable number of constituents, and yet this enormous span of submerged beauty would have begun with individual, free-floating, hard coral polyps, tiny animals that are related to jellyfish and sea anemones. Finding a suitable rocky surface to attach themselves to at the edge of the island, these coral polyps initiated the process of reef construction, each one secreting a calcium carbonate sheath to act as the animal's protective dwelling. As it grows, the polyp slowly lifts, sealing off the lower floor of its house and building a new one on top of it, a process continually repeated until a high-rise of closed chambers form the stony base material of the reef. Rarely is this structural work done in isolation, however, as most coral is colonial, a living and thriving community of animals coalescing into a coral head. Each compound organism can be composed of hundreds or even thousands of identical polyps from the same species, either the clonal buds of parent polyps or sexually produced through a cloudburst of spawn. These creatures largely seek shallow seas, where the light of the sun pours unimpeded through water, their individual housings cemented together for greater stability. There, in symbiosis with a type of algae, called zooxanthellae, that lives within their cells, the hard corals, found on the reef in a multitude of co-habiting species alongside soft corals, sponges, anemones and sea fans, are able to exist in such nutrient-poor seas. The algae acts as the coral's agent for photosynthesis, contracted out to process sunlight into nourishment. A coral reef, like the assembly of starlings off the coast at Brighton, exists only in aggregate – it functions and thrives through cohesion. This amplitude emits a distinctive crackling, the ever-present underwater sound of a healthy living reef, all its creatures and components, all its multitudinous expressions of existence, continually in the process of becoming.

The interconnectedness of this world within water became abundantly clear to me when I swam back to the boat, anchored over deeper sea. A lone coral cone rose from the sandy depths, a miniature version of all these volcanic islands strung out across the Indonesian archipelago. Fish clouded its colourful interstices, gathered in swirling, tenebrous masses around the vermilion, teal and emerald coral heads, where pearlescent thimbles studded their surfaces. It could have been a streetlamp on a summer night, its beam pulling in all the myriad moths and winged insects of the surrounding landscape, soothing them from the dark to dance in mad profusion about its crown of light. All around me, where the sands stretched away, I could see little more than a handful of fish sliding through the dim spaces, but the tower of living coral shimmered and heaved with them, circling, finning and darting around it as though a god they were honouring with their attentions. A staggering column of connected creatures, it was a murmuration within the living sea.

Later, back on the boat, I asked Otny about the threat posed by the mine to these thriving coral reefs around the island, remembering the stark video footage I'd seen with Ulva and Owen.

'It used to be a beautiful coral reef and great for diving,' he said, referring to the one on which boulders had been dumped by the mining company. 'Now it's destroyed. There's nothing.'

The afternoon sun sparkled over the endless blue waves, warm spray pluming into air.

'I hope the mine stays closed,' I said.

'It will stay closed,' Otny replied, his eyes fastened resolutely ahead of us.

*

Coral reefs account for less than 1 per cent of the ocean's undersea surface and yet are home to a quarter of all marine species. Supporting an estimated 800 million people throughout the world, they are also worth, in strictly economic terms, some $375 billion per year in goods and services through the provision of fisheries, coastal protection and tourism. And yet, just like islands, they are as fragile as mirages when breached, encircled themselves by numerous threats, including overfishing (whether for food or the tropical aquarium trade), dynamite and cyanide fishing, careless or unscrupulous tourists who break pieces from the reef, mining, sedimentation from development, climate change and plastic.

A study led by Joleah Lamb in 2018 revealed the extent to which the plastic debris I'd discovered on Bangka's shores, a dire and damning scene replicated across the coasts of the world, was gravely affecting the ability of coral reefs to flourish. After assessing 124,000 reef-building corals in a comprehensive survey of 159 reefs in the Asia-Pacific region, researchers estimated that 11.1 billion individual items of plastic were snagged on those extraordinary underwater gardens, a number they believe will rise to 15.7 billion by 2025. Each one of those discarded plastic bottles, bags, straws and lighters that elude an effective waste management system has the potential to journey through the seas and add to this sum. And the penalty paid by coral for its eventual arrival is severe.

According to the researchers, incidences of sickness on corals were increasingly attributable to plastic, the material acting as a carrier of pathogens that trigger the outbreak of disease on a reef. Bacteria, particularly in the genus *Vibrio*, are responsible for the devastating white syndromes, a class of small lesions that can cause tissue loss and the death of an entire coral colony. 'The likelihood of disease,' the team's findings state, 'increases from 4 per cent to 89 per cent when corals are in contact with plastic.' Each coral organism is stressed through a combination of 'light deprivation, toxin release, and anoxia, giving pathogens a foothold for invasion'. With increasing amounts of plastic travelling from our hands to the oceans, the coral reefs of the world are being gradually weakened just when they have to contend with the violent volatility of climate change.

Confined primarily to tropical seas where the water temperature ideally ranges from 23°C to 29°C, coral reefs are supremely susceptible to the human-caused heating of the oceans. When water temperatures climb much beyond the corals' comfort zone, the polyps experience severe environmental agitation and expel the zooxanthellae algae that exist inside their cells, meaning there's no longer any symbiotic mechanism for the transformation of sunlight into food carbohydrates. As the algae are also responsible for the pigmentation of the generally translucent polyps, the lack of zooxanthellae leaves the coral white, ghostly and haunting, transfiguring the reef's glorious chromatic vista into an eerie zone of stark and sterile bleakness. While corals can remain alive for a period of time during these bleaching events, they will eventually die of starvation if unable to reabsorb the algae. Mass bleaching events instigated by the warming of the seas – such as the one that decimated Australia's Great Barrier Reef in 2016 – are now happening about every five years, instead of every twenty-five to thirty years as in previous decades. This increased frequency means that even the fastest-growing corals struggle to recover. On top of this, corals must also cope with an increasingly acidic ocean, the result of carbon dioxide from the atmosphere dissolving into sea water. As the proportion of carbon dioxide contained in the oceans rises – primarily the result of fossil fuels being burned – a series of chemical changes means that there are fewer free carbonate ions available for corals to utilize in the construction and maintenance of their calcium carbonate dwellings, a problem also for other calcifying creatures such as oysters, clams, sea urchins and nautiluses. Such is the severity of the threat posed by the climate crisis that many marine scientists believe that by 2050 as much as 90 per cent of the world's coral reefs could be gone.

All of which makes the reefs of Bangka Island and the surrounding seas too important to lose. A study in the vicinity of the island in 2018 revealed that these particular coral communities appear less susceptible to climate change than others. If they can be protected from plastics and development, they might be the only ones to survive into the future. 'Even global changes haven't stressed this area too much,' said Marco Reinach, an Italian marine biologist who'd lived on Bangka for some years. 'It's important to maintain this place because it's the only one in the world. You don't have another Coral Triangle somewhere, there is only this one.'

Marco has fought to protect Bangka Island against the mine from the very beginning, helping with efforts to restore the bulldozed mangroves and conducting sedimentation studies of the damaged reef to compare with undisturbed sites.

'The sedimentation in front of the mining site, especially in the rainy season, was up to twenty-five times higher. And the quality of the sedimentation was completely different. The good sites had only coral sand and tiny fragments of coral, but the other was 90 per cent mud that covered all the coral. The only thing I know for certain at the moment is that they haven't started mining yet and they've already fucked up some kilometres of coast. For the island it will be, more or less, the end of Bangka as we know Bangka today. Of course, Bangka will not disappear totally, but it will change completely. I think after ten or fifteen years you wouldn't recognize it any more.'

I asked Marco how we might approach the ocean differently, to make amends for having, to some degree, culturally ignored its condition in favour of prioritizing the concerns of land. 'We cannot consider the land and the ocean,' he said. 'We must consider the Earth, and the Earth is one. It's like me considering you without your head. You cannot take out one or the other wouldn't survive. Don't see the ocean like the ocean. See the Earth and try to do something for her.'

*

While Rachel Carson is primarily remembered for *Silent Spring* – her devastating account of the damage done by DDT to the natural world, wiping out large numbers of winged creatures as the sprayed insecticide accrued in birds' bodies, resulting in paper-thin eggshells that were easily crushed by a nesting pair – she was also a consummate marine biologist, deftly describing the wonder and complexity of the maritime world in a trilogy of books that wove poetry and precision through the skin of water. The world's oceans were her first love. In *The Sea Around Us*, published in 1951, she wrote this of islands:

The tragedy of the oceanic islands lies in the uniqueness, the irreplaceability of the species they have developed by the slow processes of the ages. In a reasonable world men would have treated these islands as precious possessions, as natural museums filled with beautiful and curious works of creation, valuable beyond price because nowhere in the world are they duplicated.

Valuable beyond price. It might seem an elusive and romantic notion in an increasingly corporatized world, the structure of economies both industrial and developing harnessed to the engines of extraction and commodification, but at times human societies have shown a concern for the natural world that reflects a more enlightened and inclusive approach, such as the Small Islands Law that the Indonesian government implemented with considerable sensitivity to other valuations of marine ecosystems. It was a vision born of a belief in something beyond price, too valuable in its own right to be sacrificed solely for human material gain. But for philosophy to rise above rhetoric, however progressive its guiding principles might be, requires the enactment and enforcement of such creeds, honouring the underlying commitment they entail. Without it, words are just the chaff that's been winnowed from wisdom.

There existed on Bangka the clear sense of an ending. If iron-ore mining was allowed to proceed, despite the court decisions and actions of local communities, this place and its encircling ecosystems would be emptied of its natural and cultural meaning. Without its mangroves and coral reefs, the community would wither and leave, and the island would be shorn of its soul. From such home grounds as these flow the base materials of human consumption. In the case of mining, there are mountains and islands throughout the world that are scoured, shipped and shaped into desirable items – iron ore transfigured to steel for our vehicles, gold fashioned into beautiful jewellery, rare earths moulded inside mobile phones. We hold some of these places and their people in our hands when we text, or nip out in the car to the shops, when the light catches a ring on our fingers. But while Bangka Island had made the international news because of the prominent environmental organizations advocating its cause, most places do not. For every Bangka there are hundreds of threatened islands scattered about the seas that receive no attention at all, unheard of or forgotten except by those who dwell there.

The distance that negates responsibility is the same distance that divides people from one another, easily disenfranchising whole communities through their physical and political isolation. Out of sight and out of mind, their stories go unheard, fading away on those vast spans of sea. According to JATAM, an organization that advocates on behalf of Indonesian communities threatened by mining, 1,890 of the country's 9,721 mining licences are in violation of the Small Islands Law, meaning that the stories I'd been hearing on Bangka were just fragments of a far larger narrative of loss. 'Everybody has to help,' Ulva said, explaining the reason why their legally successful challenge had gained traction. 'The only way is if you fight together, as a coalition. It cannot be just the villagers from an island.' She paused for a few moments before continuing. 'They will disappear, and nobody will ever know.'

Perhaps this is the deeper, more enduring meaning of Bangka, irrespective of whether the mine opens or not. 'I don't know if in the end we will win this battle,' said Marco, 'but I would like it if Bangka could be an example for many other places.'

It's been the only island so far to win a case against mining in the Indonesian courts, proving that *possibility*, at its most fundamental level, requires but the smallest of beginnings, something to adhere to or assemble around, like those original coral polyps in the earliest days of a reef, solitary, searching and adrift on the sea's currents, seeking a toehold to create something stronger through cohesion. Islands require of us an effort of collective will. Very little of the plastic I discovered on Bangka originated on the island itself, as its inhabitants are few in comparison to the finds. But ocean currents and tides enable that debris to travel there from almost anywhere in Indonesia and other parts of the world. The profusion of plastic waste and the rise in ocean temperatures as a result of climate change means that we are all, despite the separating seas, now connected to islands, because they're not truly islands any more. The sea – for so long a barrier – has now become a bridge.

As I prepared to leave Bangka I met a young environmentalist who told me that rifts were slowly being mended on the island. 'After the last court verdict,' said Hendra Pangandaheng, 'some people on the island have changed their minds from being pro-mining. They've seen that ordinary people can fight against big companies and they've gained strength from that. There was a big celebration after the recent verdict, and several people who used to work at the mine came and joined the party because they have relatives and family who are anti-mining. And the village leader, who'd always been opposed to the mining company, said, *Let's forget the pros and cons and remember that we're all from this island.*'

7

A Rose of Defiance

'I'm gonna call all these roses "Defiance".'
~ Pete Baillie, allotment holder

To know fully even one field or one land is a lifetime's experience.
~ Patrick Kavanagh, 'The Parish and the Universe'

Of the following two places, one will be saved, the other destroyed.

*

From where I stood at the centre of Glasgow's North Kelvin Meadow, waves of shadow and light flashing across the four-storey tenement flats stacked up around its edges, the essence of Patrick Kavanagh's words rang true. Not in the sense that the children who were slipping through a slim stand of trees in a game of tag would necessarily spend their entire lives there, but rather that this place – a small field of green in the middle of the city – had the ability to engage individuals deeply at every stage of life. I'd seen people from infancy through to old age pulled into its absorbing spaces like iron filings to a magnet. It was a place that addressed a multiplicity of needs and wishes – even ones you might not yet be aware of. Only that morning, two silver-haired ladies on a neighbourhood stroll had stopped to see what I was photographing; introduced to a common spotted orchid, one of dozens that put in a wild appearance on the site each summer, they knelt to admire the roseate speckling across its pale pageantry of petals. 'I've never seen an orchid outside a florist's before,' said one of them, rising with a rapturous smile.

North Kelvin Meadow covers a mere 1.4 hectares of urban space, situated on the border between the well-heeled West End and the considerably poorer working-class district of Maryhill. But what does a figure like 1.4 hectares mean when it comes to the actual *span* of a place within the human experience, the way it uncoils inside a life or is threaded through a community? Only eleven years old, her smooth skin the same colour as her name, Olive Mojsiewicz lives across from the meadow. She's bright and engaging when I speak to her, and deeply attached to this small patch of land that has effectively become an extension of her home. 'It's really safe here, like my house,' she said when I asked how she felt about the meadow.

To walk the diagonal path that roughly bisects it, connecting its northern and southern entrance points, takes Olive a mere 209 steps. And it requires only 430 steps for her to circumnavigate the perimeter path, which seems negligible when you begin totting up your strides on a city street. For Olive, though, this number of urban footsteps carries her into a world of compressed and vibrant natural variety. First, there's the community orchard – apples, plums, cherries and pears swelling with Glasgow's summer rains and sunshine. Her steps then take her past wooden barrels that have been sawn in half and packed with soil, where the heady scent of thyme, rosemary and mint swirl on the air as she brushes them with her hand. She passes that spotted orchid, slowed for a moment by its delicate glow, before continuing on past communal compost boxes and meadow flowers dizzy with bees. She walks alongside raised beds tendrilled with runaway squash vines and studded with leafy broad beans, before the path eases her into a thin ribbon of trees. There she leaps over one of the earthen mounds that have been heaped up and padded firm by a group of teenagers, acting as DIY jumps for their bike track. Then on past the fire pit, where evenings crackle with flames in the company of friends and food, slipping into a glorious stand of silver birches, the gleaming white columns like pillars of snow-light. Known as the Children's Wood, where a mud kitchen lets kids rustle up recipes from earth, bark and leaves, this area of trees in the meadow is visited by twenty-three different schools for classes, hosting outdoor learning activities, including Forest School courses and readings by children's authors. Leaving behind the cooling shade of the birches, Olive strides into bright sunlight again, back where she began only 430 steps ago. 'I like coming here because you can be free,' she said, handing me a badge emblazoned with *Love our Land*, 'because normally, at our age, most people just go into town and shop, and just go on their iPads and stuff, but here you can do whatever you like.'

This route of hers, though, wouldn't always have taken a child on such a multifaceted journey. The space where today's North Kelvin Meadow and Children's Wood thrive was once part of a stitched landscape of fields that made up this district of sparsely populated North Kelvinside in the mid-1850s. By the end of the nineteenth century, however, most of those green spaces had been built over and stacked with the elegant sandstone tenements and civic buildings that continue to be the focal point of Glasgow's rich architectural heritage. But looking closely at a map from 1894, you can still make out a field, roughly rectangular in shape and tucked near a deep bend in the River Kelvin. Over time this field would come to enjoy spells as a racetrack, cricket pitch and billeting station for American, Norwegian and Polish troops during the Second World War, when two barrage balloons were tethered to its ground as bomb protection for the nearby headquarters of BBC Scotland. By the end of the war, and then owned by Glasgow City Council, the site had been converted into a municipal football pitch with adjoining tennis courts for a local school. It was entirely surfaced with red blaes, the baked and hardened clay that commonly forms the surface of athletics tracks when crushed and pressed firm. The playing field was still in use when the school became a college, but within a few decades it had been abandoned by the council and allowed to fall into disrepair, despite regular visits by local families and children at play.

'Although the council owned the land, they hadn't been on it for twenty-five years,' said Douglas Peacock, referring to the quarter-century period prior to 2008, the year in which so much changed in the fortunes of this field. 'They wouldn't do anything on the land; it wasn't in their interest to do anything on the land. So they let it run down. There was a sofa bed about here, a fridge over there. The hut was something out of *Trainspotting*,' he added, pointing to a brick shed at the southern end of the meadow, which had once been the girls' changing rooms. Alongside the boys' rooms, long since gone, it was the only building this piece of land has ever seen, its bricks now painted sky-blue and lavishly decorated with flowers, trees, butterflies and a pair of twin suns. 'The foil, the syringes, the Yellow Pages that the guy hadn't bothered putting through people's doors but just tossed into the building. It was a heroin shed. So yeah, why wouldn't you sell it? Jesus!'

In his early fifties, Douglas is a central figure on the meadow. He's an engaging conversationalist, primarily because it feels as though he's given considerable thought to the issues under discussion, carefully sifting through viewpoints to weigh up the pros and cons of any concern. This might stem, at least in part, from his work in the financial sector, analysing the benefits and risks of investment, balancing perspectives. It also means his opinions are firmly grounded when he eventually airs them; since 2008, when he learned that the council intended to sell off the land for 120 luxury flats, to be built by the property developer New City Vision Ltd, this skill has been rewarded countless times. Local residents had no say in the matter; they were only consulted over which of four development proposals they preferred. As for the loss of communal recreational space, however derelict it had become under the mismanagement of the council, there was no mention of it whatsoever. Dismayed by the lack of meaningful public consultation and angered by the lack of affordable housing on offer in the proposals, Douglas decided to reach out to the many neighbours he didn't know.

'I thought, *Fuck it, I'll do a wee questionnaire*. I'll just go to all the people around here and ask them to answer the ten questions and, crucially, put their email address down on it and their name.' His queries concerned the plans for luxury flats and the corresponding loss of public space, and from this initial decision of his, like Olive's first step or two at the start of the perimeter path, leading her into a whole province of possibilities, grew the revitalization of an entire place.

'I had a lot of the questionnaires come back, and every single one wanted to keep the open space. And I thought, *Well, I'd better tell the council.* And they said, *Well, we don't care, it's getting sold.* So I contacted all the people through their emails, told them the results of the survey and that the council wasn't interested, and asked them what they wanted to do. So we had a campaign at that point, and we started by cleaning it up. The land was as you see it today in many ways, but it had litter on it, broken glass, stuff like that. We filled sixty or seventy black bags of rubbish. And we had many, many clean-ups. We really cleared it up for a good year, again and again and again.'

The transformation was striking. Other than two metal towers – once the football pitch floodlights, now painted and strung with coloured lightbulbs – there was little sign of the meadow's previous incarnations. You could enter at either end and feel suspended inside a singular green world, its interior seemingly out of all proportion to its actual physical size. 'One of the principles of the land was no fences, no borders,' said Douglas. Long grasses billowed and bent beneath the weight of seeds, fruit trees flourished, and silver birches needled a brilliant blue sky. The meadow hummed with activity throughout the hours, a place sufficiently revitalized through the volunteer efforts of local residents that it won a national community award, one aimed at recognizing attempts to heal and benefit a neighbourhood on a collective level. And while Glasgow's Labour council still intended to dispose of the site, despite the accolades and visible rejuvenation, it was, in the end, bat boxes and raised vegetable beds that provoked the municipal authority's ire.

'Two men in suits showed up at my house and said, *You've been summoned to court,*' said Douglas. His name had appeared on an email that he and Karen Chung, another Kelvinside resident, had circulated to see whether there was any interest in erecting bat boxes in the meadow's trees and building a communal raised bed for growing vegetables. For this they were both taken to court by the council. 'That was enough for them. It set them off.'

I would later learn that the judge had asked what exactly a bat box was. 'A box for bats, my lord,' Douglas had said.

'Oh, perhaps I should have been able to work that out for myself,' replied the judge.

'It was like something out of a film,' continued Douglas. 'I was fucking shaking. And the judge just said, *You have done no harm; you have done only good. But you're on someone else's land, the council's land, and they've asked you to get off. Now you're going to have to get off.*' As the legal case was specifically built around the issue of bat boxes and raised beds, the judge forbade Douglas from having anything to do with either of those actions on the meadow. 'So I had to turn my back when other people did those things,' he said, laughing in the meadow's sweet summer air.

*

While I would visit Farm Terrace Allotments numerous times, there were only two constants that I could rely upon when arriving. First, that Sara Jane Trebar's hair would be a wonderfully different colour from the time before. And second, that her spirit of resistance would be as unbreakable as ever. In her early forties, and formerly a teacher of English as a foreign language, Sara Jane and her husband had taken on a plot at Farm Terrace in 2009, shortly after the birth of their first child, keen to nourish their budding family with the healthy harvest they were hoping to coax from their small parcel of earth. Before them the plot had been tended by an elderly man called Patrick, who'd had to relinquish it when he became suddenly ill. 'The shed was still locked,' said Sara Jane when I first met her, the new tenants having never known the old, 'so when we managed to open it up we found all of this. And we've kept it pretty much as it was.'

She creaked open the wooden door for me, and in the dour March light I could see Patrick's worn blue gardening coat, a flat cap, old weathered tools and a small round mirror hung from rusted wire on the back of the door. A personal history enveloped the shed, and yet Patrick's was just a tiny fragment of the site's larger past. First a quarry, and then a sewage farm – which helped explain the rich density of the soil and the uniquely terraced design, its 128 plots being laid out on three long lengths of shelving land – Farm Terrace Allotments have been in existence since 1896. Which meant that in 2015, when I saw Patrick's left-behind belongings, 119 years of personal, social and gardening history had accumulated and accrued in the place.

Set in the shadow of Vicarage Road Stadium amidst the dense, multi-ethnic neighbourhoods of west Watford, Farm Terrace's late-nineteenth-century origins can be traced to the heyday of urban allotment provision in Britain. An attempt to atone for some of the inexcusable excesses of the Enclosure Acts, which removed people from common lands they'd had the right to use for generations, allotments began life as rural affairs, intended to provide poor agricultural labourers with the opportunity to grow food and thereby offset meagre wages. But economic and demographic shifts during the industrial age meant that allotment land was increasingly allocated within areas of built-up housing. In time, allotments became a common feature of the urban landscape, proving particularly popular amongst miners, railwaymen and shipyard workers. They were places of proud, working-class identity and culture, and vital to those whose wages were low and working conditions grim. Such was the importance of the allotment to these communities that the 1925 Allotments Act enshrined the right of anyone to a plot, stipulating not only that local councils were legally obliged to provide them but that they could be disposed of only with ministerial consent.

'The story of the allotment,' wrote David Crouch and Colin Ward in their book *The Allotment*, 'remains that of one of our long-term relationships with the land. It is also a story of the change in the city and the country. It is also an alternative to the supermarket, the car-park and barren fields.' Allotments are as much a part of the modern landscape as of the old. They remain quintessential signatures of vernacular British culture – idiosyncratic, co-operative and popu-list. They are edgelands of blended opportunity, hybridized worlds of communal individuality, where people and nature rub close on sites of lively and harvestable creativity. Even the commonplace sheds, invariably constructed of second-hand or salvaged materials, lend each one a uniquely weathered outlook, an architectural personality closely aligned to the whims and designs of its owner.

These days allotments resonate with a wide range of ages, entic-ing men, women and whole families to devote their spare hours to the hopeful tending of the earth. And yet, despite their social leg-acy and contemporary relevance, allotments are being lost at a startling pace, unravelling the fabric of urban life. Between 2007 and 2014, only four of 198 applications to close allotment sites were rejected by the Secretary of State. Despite legislation designed specifically to preserve them, all the rest were razed.

'It was an enormous shock when the letter arrived,' said Sara Jane, 'because the allotments weren't supposed to be part of the plan.' She was referring to the Watford Health Campus Scheme, which brought together Watford Borough Council, West

Hertfordshire Health Trust and Watford FC. Although known about since 2007, the original masterplan had seemingly assured that the allotments would be protected at the heart of a large-scale regeneration of brownfield in the immediate area, a development intended to be primarily of benefit to the nearby Watford General Hospital through the addition of new facilities. But with the arrival of a letter in 2012 from Watford's Liberal Democrat mayor, Dorothy Thornhill, Sara Jane and other plot-holders learned about the possible closure of the allotments, after two prospective developers claimed that the campus would 'greatly benefit from additional land near the hospital, which will improve design and the viability of the project'. When the revised masterplan was published later that year, Mayor Thornhill stated that the allotment site, which had statutory protection, would now be required in order to make the development viable. But rather than new hospital facilities to go alongside the 600 houses and flats, retail outlets, car parks and green areas, it transpired that the hospital trust had no specific plans for the use of the allotment space and was, in fact, in considerable debt, making enlargement unlikely in the near future. More and more it seemed there were other plans for the allotments.

'If it's really going to be a hospital,' said Sara Jane, 'then we all agreed we'd leave. You can't argue with that. But once it turned out that it was most likely to be houses and a car park for the football club on the allotments that changed everything.' The mayor herself admitted that the allotments were now needed for financial reasons, saying, 'If we don't use the allotments we will have to build more houses to make up for the loss of money.' She would later confirm that it wouldn't necessarily be hospital facilities built over the allotments, either. 'So yes it may be a car park on the allotments, it may be seventy family houses. With the allotments out it gives us a blank canvas for the whole of the site. We have just got to move on and get on with turning this into something that is fit for people to live in and not this blot on the landscape that it is now.'

'They think that we're just being awkward,' said Sara Jane. 'But we're not the owners of this land, and we don't see ourselves as the owners. We are not saving it just for ourselves, we are saving it for future generations.'

By the time I began visiting Farm Terrace in 2015, the Communities Minister had twice ruled that the council could dispose of the allotments. And twice the plot-holders had appealed his decision, winning their case in the High Court on both occasions after spirited campaigns, one of which culminated in taking a little piece of Farm Terrace to the pavements outside London's Courts of Justice, complete with baskets of freshly harvested crops and placards reading 'Give Peas a Chance'. Sara Jane understood that these efforts of theirs could have enormous implications for allotments throughout the country, many of which face similar threats, as the 2014 update of the Allotment Act under which they are protected states that they can be disposed of only if 'exceptional circumstances' exist, a term that has never been legally defined with any precision. Watford Council, determined to strip the historic allotments from the town's landscape, and having sufficient funds to mount continual legal challenges, submitted a third application for their disposal shortly after losing the most recent court battle. This was the immediate threat Farm Terrace was under during the course of my visits, and the campaigners were preparing for another legal case to try to preserve what the mayor had described as a 'hideous, derelict site'.

Swinging open the gates to the allotments, I step with Sara Jane into a burgeoning green world. An extravagant lushness has taken hold of Farm Terrace in the June sunshine. Strawberries blush scarlet beneath skirts of leaves. Flourishing potato plants sparkle with starry white flowers, their invisible knuckles of spuds swelling within the concealing soil. Clematis vines explode into discs of stunning colour. Standing inside the perimeter of the site, it feels as though the surrounding town has faded, muffled to a thin, background murmur.

If Sara Jane is the heart of Farm Terrace, then Vincenzo Santarsiero is its soul. A small, sweet-natured man of eighty, Vincenzo spoke with the thick Italian accent of his origins. Arriving in Watford as a nine-year-old boy, he'd eventually gone to work at the town's hospital. His plot, he told me, had been critical to helping support his family, providing nearly all of their vegetable needs for much of the year. It also enabled Vincenzo and his wife to maintain their heritage and traditions, canning vast quantities of tomatoes as passata, and bottling and preserving whole or cooked vegetables in abundance. His plot was an entire farmers' market of perfection. Hundreds of heads of lettuce prospered in long green rows; early cabbages pushed upwards as bowls of dark, crinkled leaves; and courgette plants erupted into great umbrellas, the first of the shining fruit sheltering below. As a fellow gardener, I had a good idea of the time, energy and dedication Vincenzo must be committing to his plot's digging, sowing, thinning, weeding, watering, pruning, manuring, composting, staking, tying and harvesting. And he'd been tending to this bounty for forty-three consecutive years.

'You work, you move, you become strong,' said Vincenzo. 'The blood circulation works, the brain works, everything works.' He spread his arms to embrace the goodness all around him. 'This is a hospital.'

'They're really important,' said Stephen Windmill of the allotments, 'particularly in this sort of area – Victorian housing, very little back garden space – and it's a place to get outside. You know, for kids to come and mess around. And you're connected with the soil. It's that connection with the land through growing things. And this is home territory for me,' he said. 'My family has been in that road for ninety years. And my grandad, many years ago, had a plot on this site.' Some of the place's long history finds its way to the surface each year, revealed with a lifted spade. 'I have a little pot at home,' said Stephen, 'where I put all the clay pipes that I've found here.'

So much of the communal spirit of resistance present on Farm Terrace is down to Sara Jane. Without ever really intending to, she's become a galvanizing force for the defence and celebration of allotments, not just in Watford but throughout the country. Even with an offer from the council of £1,000 per plot, a sum most see as a bribe to get them to vacate the site before the court's judgment, the remaining gardeners are committed to staying. 'You can't re-create what we have here,' said Sara Jane. 'Once this allotment is gone, it's gone for ever. It takes so much with it. And you're taking it away from people who don't even know they want it yet.'

*

'We start here,' said Douglas, at the southern entrance to North Kelvin Meadow, 'and we take our adult heads off, put on a four- or five-year-old's, and see the land through that. So for some adults, they'll go, *Grass needs cutting, the bushes are a wee bit big, it's not quite the same as the Botanic Gardens*. But if you're a four- or five-year-old, then you're looking at this as an adventure. *I can do something with this*. All of a sudden you have them on a journey.'

Such imaginative journeys are of increasing relevance as the footfall of children's travels within the vicinity of home dramatically dwindles. Much has been written about the transfigured daily routines of people in the twenty-first century, but an article by David Derbyshire from 2007, called 'How children lost the right to roam in four generations', sums up the contracting circumference of childhood in a way that is particularly unsettling.

The Thomas family had lived in the vicinity of Sheffield for close to a century, and Derbyshire used that long-term local tenure to chart the radius of a child's wanderings, the distance the respective generations allowed them to travel unsupervised as part of their daily lives at the age of eight. At that age in 1926, great-grandfather George Thomas regularly walked six miles from the centre of Sheffield to his favourite fishing spot in the Rother Valley, while also walking to school every day. George's son-in-law, Jack Hattersley, turned eight in 1950; he was allowed to travel unaccompanied the mile-and-a-half to a nearby wood, as well as walking to school on his own. Jack's daughter, Vicky Grant, who happened to grow up close to Smithy Wood in Chapeltown, turned eight in 1979. She'd had the freedom to bike with friends around the housing estate where she lived and to travel to the nearby park, while also walking to school and to the local swimming pool half a mile away. Her son, Edward, however, is only allowed to walk on his own to the end of the street, a distance of 300 yards. Each day he is driven to school by his parents.

The wandering radius of those four eight-year-olds is depicted on a map of Sheffield by circles of varying sizes. They're like a set of Russian nesting dolls – smaller and smaller worlds of local experience slotted inside the next. If such shrinkage were to continue unchallenged, a child would ultimately be left with just her home to roam. 'Over four generations our family is poles apart in terms of affluence,' said Edward's mother, 'but I'm not sure our lives are any richer.'

This sharp contraction of experiential space has made the existence of such places as North Kelvin Meadow and Farm Terrace Allotments critical to the wellbeing and formative experiences of children. They represent spaces of freedom, enabling encounters with nature, people and place that are serendipitous and intimate, and vitally important to a child's development. 'It's amazing just to be able to bring the kids down,' said Sara Jane. 'What it does is it gives them the opportunities that we all had when we were young, being able to go off and explore.'

Oliver Rackham recorded four kinds of loss in the landscape: the loss of beauty, freedom, wildlife and meaning. I'd like to add one more, a loss both cumulative and overarching, knotting the other four into an ever-lengthening rope of disappearances: the loss of connection. The gradual severance of our relationships with the natural world stems, at least in part, from a lack of experience with it in our immediate surroundings. As numbers of starlings, butterflies, water voles and brown-banded carder bees dwindle, so too do the opportunities for a relationship with the natural world. The fewer the patches of bluebells glimmering each spring in ancient woodland glades, the scarcer the prospects for kindling connections to such wild and sustaining beauty. And whenever a place is destroyed, all that possibility is taken away with it, robbing people of an incalculable potential.

There is a kind of abundance that receives too little attention in the wider discussion of ecological plenitude – that of the nearby, the local, the immediate. Semi-natural places like North Kelvin Meadow and Farm Terrace Allotments may not be replete with the full spectrum of wildlife, but they still have the power to light a path to a lifetime of care and concern for the natural world, all traceable back to the initial wonder and enchantment illuminated within their small, confiding spaces. It's for this reason that the Conservative government's removal of the term 'Local Wildlife Site' from a 2018 review of the national planning policy framework – meaning England's 42,000 such sites, a land area equal in size to the whole of Devon, could potentially be left without any protection – is such a ruinous and corrosive idea. Relatively few of us live in such vast and compelling landscapes as the Hoo Peninsula, and many others lack access to the more far-flung and secluded parts of the country, for reasons of affordability, accessibility and time. In fact most people reside in cities, where places such as a meadow, an allotment or a quiet local wildlife site, in which robins, greenfinches, ladybirds and red admiral butterflies flourish, are just as important to those living nearby as the more capacious landscapes of national renown are to those able to enjoy them.

In *The Thunder Tree*, his important book about childhood and urban wildlife, the writer and naturalist Robert Michael Pyle explores an idea he calls 'the extinction of experience'. Growing up in Aurora, Colorado, he understood how the issues of local contact with wildlife and larger environmental concerns were tightly bound. Without the first, the second might never arise. As the locally common becomes increasingly rare, a 'cycle of disaffection' ensues, resulting in children growing up with less and less intimacy with the natural world. 'As cities and metastasizing suburbs forsake their natural diversity, and their citizens grow more removed from personal contact with nature, awareness and appreciation retreat. This breeds apathy toward environmental concerns and, inevitably, further degradation of the common habitat.' While the protection of rare species is imperative for biodiversity's sake alone, it mustn't come at the expense of the small, the common and the familiar. As Pyle rightly asks, in what is probably his book's most memorable and resonant line, 'What is the extinction of the condor to a child who has never known a wren?'

'The teenagers who get up to mischief here,' said Douglas one day in the meadow, 'I love them because I always think – and maybe I'm completely wrong and they'll end up in prison – but I actually think they'll be the park rangers of tomorrow.'

*

'What sparked it, to be absolutely blunt, was incandescent rage.' Ian Black had crossed the meadow with Jim Divers to join Douglas and me. His silver hair swept back from his face and hanging loose on his shoulders, he wore a white jacket with the words *Bob Feist Invitational Team Roping Classic* stitched in red letters on the back. Ian had been the lightning rod for an earlier attempt to revitalize this forgotten urban space; as his flat adjoined the meadow, he'd witnessed the slow withering of its care up close. But the final, inexcusable act of dereliction for him was the removal of the field's goal posts. 'It was intended as a lesson to us,' he declared, recollecting the day in 1993 when the council abandoned any last pretence at maintaining the site. 'They came out, the council guys, and knocked down the goal posts with sledge hammers. They literally moved the goal posts.'

Ian had a knack for drawing you into his tales, his smoothly timed flair for the dramatic polished between the offices of *The Herald*, where he'd been the newspaper's senior book editor, and the convivial pubs of Glasgow.

'*What are you doing?* I shouted to them. *It's nothing to do with us,* they said. *You go and take them away,* I said, *or you'll leave all those sharp bits, with kids around.* So finally me and a few other people moved the goal posts again. We got a skip, and we put the goal posts in the skip. And I said, *What we should do is plant some grass.* The guy I bought the grass seed from came round and I said, *Are you absolutely certain this will grow through red blaes?* He had a wee look about the land and said, *Sir, this will grow through fucking concrete!*'

Earlier that day Douglas had pointed to a man carrying bin bags through the meadow. 'That's Jim,' he'd said. 'He's so important for the land. He's a stalwart.' Unknown to many who use the meadow, Jim has collected bags of dogshit and rubbish from a designated spot and carted them out to the roadside bins for eight straight years. This daily task, unasked of him and carried out without any fuss or payment, is his way of contributing to the shared place, investing his time in helping to hold it together for all. His actions summed up something that I'd noticed on both the meadow and the allotment site – how communal space has the capacity to elicit selflessness from the people who share in its concerns. To pull us into wider affiliation with the world.

A tall, thin, live-wire of a man, Jim had spent his working life as a plumber. 'Some people say, *Aye, but all the poo,*' he said, referring to his role in the meadow, 'but if you've been a plumber you dinnae mind. I've been in most of the bathrooms of the area, remember.' His sharp grey eyes shone behind gold-rimmed glasses. Like Ian, Jim was in his seventies and now retired. While they'd witnessed considerable change to this city of theirs, they retained hope that environmental awareness, greater social justice and transparent, equitable democracy were yet to come.

'I think society has a history of moving from one generation to another,' said Jim, 'and we're fortunate enough that the present younger generation are taking over from us.'

'Aye,' agreed Ian. 'To you, from failing hands, we pass the torch.'

Places such as these are our contemporary commons, spaces of communal connection and political engagement. The tragedy of the commons is not so much that users act out of individual self-interest and thereby harm the good of the many, but that these vital shared spaces are deemed to be of so little value by many who hold power. The effacement of the commons is to everyday societal life what the removal of grace notes is from a score. The constant, unrelenting pressure of development, delisting, deregulation and destruction leaves a simpler, leaner and less refined land than before. 'You've got a prototype here for a new world everybody's wanting,' said Jim. 'A prototype for cities and countryside.'

Whether this vision would ever materialize into anything more durable than a dream was still to be seen. Glasgow City Council's decision to sell North Kelvin Meadow to a developer was called in by the Scottish government in 2016, triggering an inquiry headed by a reporter from the Department of Planning and Environmental Appeals, which would ultimately decide its fate. The inquiry would establish the merits of both the meadow and the proposal for high-end luxury flats – now reduced to ninety in a revised building plan – and the final say on the matter would be made by a Scottish minister on the advice of the reporter. After eight years of transformation – both of the land and of the lives that revolve around it – the three men knew that the dream, still so fragile and formative, could all be over in a flash.

'I'll be on it day one, if they raze it, with a sack of seeds,' said Ian. But Douglas spelled out his fears as we left the meadow.

'They'll have the money to put up the fencing. And to be honest with you, within twenty-four hours this will be bulldozed, and then you've got nothing to fight over any more. A bulldozer will just come straight through, boom, boom, up and down. They haven't built anything; they've just razed it to the ground. That's all they have to do.'

*

'Heaven on Earth,' said Pete Baillie as we walked a path between plots at Farm Terrace. 'A million, million times I've used that expression.' A greenfinch punctured the summer thrum with its nasal drone and the congealed murmur of insects spread like treacle through the air. A whitethroat scratched out a line of song from a bramble cane. 'You wouldn't want for anything better. Just look at it.'

A *Sign for Victory* poster was pasted on the glinting window of his shed. It was the catch-phrase for the allotment campaign's petition, echoing the wartime resolution to 'dig for victory'. From 1939 onwards, citizens had been encouraged to bolster self-sufficiency by producing food wherever possible. Allotments became focal points for wartime cohesion, their spaces instilling a sense of resilience and potent pride that was arguably as important as the provisioning of food. Front gardens, golf courses, school playing-fields, tennis courts and public parks were converted to plots, as was the moat in front of the Tower of London. And places like Farm Terrace – their potatoes, cabbages, cauliflowers and leeks helping to feed a nation mired in war – were frontlines as imperative to hold as those across the Channel.

Seventy-two years old when I first met him, Pete was born in the middle of that war, amidst the dark days of rations, blackouts, air-raid sirens and bombs. 'I'm Watford born and bred,' he said. 'And the wife grew up just over there.' He pointed beyond the nearest terraced houses. 'She used to come down here with her friends when the allotments went right through, right past the hospital car park to Willow Lane.' His words reminded me that shifting baselines don't apply only to the abundance of the natural world in our remembering, but can include the dimensions and depth of places themselves. Until he'd mentioned it that morning, I'd had no idea that Farm Terrace Allotments had once been so much larger. 'What's left is about a third, maybe 25 per cent, of what it once was,' he continued. 'And it's been nibbled away, nibbled away, nibbled away.'

Wearing a broad-brimmed canvas hat and paisley braces, Pete pulled a spade from his shed and set to work loosening the soil around some of his early potatoes. 'The community spirit here is phenomenal,' he said. 'And it's international. We've got Australians, Chinese, Italians, French, Watfordians.' The enriching cross-fertilization of cultures was encapsulated in the crops being grown. Pete had cultivated what was easily the most pungent oregano I'd known outside of Greece; rubbing a few leaves between finger and thumb, I was immediately transported to the hills of home. While I revelled in its scent, Pete had moved on to inspecting his broad beans. 'My broad beans are the best in the world,' he said, 'because twenty-six million blackflies can't be wrong!'

Pete was a master of homebrewed wine, though – fruit and vegetable vintages fermented from allotment ingredients. 'You just brew 'em up with a bit of yeast and a bit of sugar and let nature do the rest.'

'When our lawyers came down to the allotment from London,' said Sara Jane, 'the top barrister was going, *Have you got any more of that runner-bean wine?* There's like twenty-five-year-old Scottish whisky there, and he was like, *No, I'll have some of Pete's home brew please*.' We all laughed in the simmering sunshine, enjoying another node of connection that this place had enabled.

'That's father-in-law, Bernard,' said Pete as we walked towards two fruit trees. 'He's got a pear tree. And here's his wife, Dorothy, ten feet away.' Her apple leaves sieved light into dancing fractals beneath the boughs. After his in-laws had been cremated, Pete and his wife decided they'd plant fruit trees in their memory. 'Instead of taking flowers up to the crematorium all the time,' he said, 'we've got life here.' I could tell in the way he spoke about these paired trees, naming them for me rather than simply describing their symbolic meaning, that they were more than just memorials to his departed in-laws. They were a way of keeping their spirits close.

All too often such green spaces are deemed politically expendable, earmarked for development and assigned a value solely monetary in measure, calculated at the expense of the considerable emotional, physical and psychological relationships already brokered there. But connections to the living world run deep, sometimes only revealed when the possibility of loss becomes real. This is what happened in Sheffield when the local Labour council entered into a Private Finance Initiative arrangement with the contractor Amey, signing a contract worth £2.2 billion over a twenty-five-year period in exchange for the maintenance of the city's pavements and streets. The agreement resulted in a dubious tree-culling programme, its finer details kept secret by the council until a Freedom of Information request revealed the aim of felling 17,500 of the city's 36,000 roadside trees. According to the council, the trees were condemned because they fell foul of the so-called '6 Ds', meaning they were dead, dying, diseased, dangerous, damaging or discriminatory (impeding wheelchairs or prams from being used on the pavement). Tree experts rejected this view in the vast majority of cases following independent surveys, but it still resulted in thousands of vigorous and beloved trees being unnecessarily levelled. And when the contract was finally revealed in full by the *Yorkshire Post* there was no mention of the '6 Ds' or the engineering solutions that the council had claimed it was seeking for any threatened trees. All it essentially included was a focus on 'minimizing future maintenance requirements and nuisance' by replacing the felled trees with saplings, a strategy geared entirely towards increasing profits rather than the consideration of the overall health of the city's environment and its citizens' welfare.

The felling brought to the surface the intense affection many of Sheffield's residents have for their local trees. They gathered around their favourites, including the Chelsea Road Elm, one of the few survivors of Dutch elm disease and home to a colony of rare white-letter hairstreak butterflies, and the Vernon Oak, a magnificent, statuesque tree that pre-dates the road it anchors. They sought to defend the memorial trees of Western Road, planted in 1919 in honour of the former pupils of the local school who had died as soldiers in the Great War. And yet, the council still couldn't understand what all the fuss was about. Cllr Neale Gibson tweeted the following on 17 October 2017: 'Enough paper, time and money had [*sic*] been wasted on the subject of Street [*sic*] trees. I want to debate issues that really effect [*sic*] people's lives. Employment, care, housing, traffic, policing, litter, homeless [*sic*], these issues are far more important.'

For too long we've accepted the notion that there are issues 'far more important' than the natural world. Which isn't to suggest that employment, housing, traffic and policing are of lesser worth, but simply that there needs to be a greater balance and understanding when it comes to the value that nature – in all its varied permutations, from clean air and water to functioning ecosystems and wonder – has in relation to constituents' wellbeing. It's the very foundation from which we rise.

'We're custodians, that's all,' said Pete. 'They really don't get that.' We'd continued exploring his plot, strolling past rows of beetroot, carrots and leeks, admiring tubs of luscious rosemary and mint. 'I'm just an ordinary guy. I worked up the road at a printer's. After work, down here to work and water, then home. Or meet the wife and spend the evening down here. It gets us away from west Watford, it gets us away from the road and all the traffic noise.' We ended up at a spectacular arbour of roses that he'd tended for years, sweetly scented and crimson in colour. 'I'm gonna call all these roses "Defiance",' he said, standing there in his broad hat and braces, a determined grin on his face. 'I mean look at 'em – magnificent, absolutely magnificent.'

*

A chorus of voices lifted like mist from the silver birches. Six women sang in a circle in the Children's Wood, the trees wet and shining with summer rain. While the language was unknown to me, the music had about it a striking blend of poignancy and joy.

Gorgeous and elegiac, their voices pulled me towards the wood, where I leaned against a tree to listen. I would later learn that they'd been singing a Finnish song called 'Lapsuuden Toverille', or 'To my Childhood Friend'. One of the singers, Riikka Gonzalez, translated its words for me:

> *A maiden as beautiful as a flower grew up in her father's cottage*
> *She used to be my best friend, but she wanted to see the world*
> *I will never forget her.*

It was the Sunday before Juhannusjuhlat, the Finnish midsummer, and North Kelvin Meadow had been transformed through music, food and community to a place of celebration by the Finns of West Scotland. All morning people had been arriving, raising shelters of canvas sheeting in the trees, clearing out the fire pit and arranging logs and tree stumps in tiers of grained seats, ferrying potatoes to be roasted in the glowing embers. The canvas sheeting was soon needed when the day turned wet. But despite the snapping squalls of rain, there was no dampening of the celebratory spirit: the women's songs gave shine to the dull shield of sky and everyone was welcome to the hot Finnish food and drinks being generously poured and passed around. It was one of those festivities that result from a blend of cultures, the mingled traditions being the enriching consequence of Finns like Riikka living in Scotland. The transposition of this typically rural celebration to the site of a Glasgow meadow sparked a series of conversations about the possibilities of place: how it can just as easily convey you elsewhere – *she wanted to see the world* – as ground you in one spot.

In *Wisdom Sits in Places*, his thoughtful study of Western Apache connections to the land through place names and narrative, Keith

H. Basso describes places in their culture as being 'portable possessions' – a concept akin to Gill Moore's idea that a place can dwell
inside you – going on to say that, 'When places are actively sensed,
the physical landscape becomes wedded to the landscape of the
mind, to the roving imagination, and where the latter may lead is
anybody's guess.' For Douglas the meadow was a place of restoration and resilience; for Ian it was a place of community bonding and
the spirit of defiance; for Olive it was a place of friendship and
freedom; and for Olive's mother, Kristin, it was a place that con-
jured other places in time.

Knowing the meadow through the eyes of her daughter as
much as her own, Kristin was familiar with its spaces on two levels, as though seeing it through a pair of bifocal lenses. And owing
to her work as an artist and lecturer at the Edinburgh College of
Art, she showed me around in a way that no one else could have.
Where others saw nature, restoration, playfulness and community, she perceived textures and surfaces, the radiant geometry of
shapes. 'It sort of transports you elsewhere,' she said as we stood
at the edge of the Children's Wood. 'At different times of the day
it's totally different. Coming through in the morning, sometimes
there's a very fine frost or a very light kind of mist, or you're
walking through and seeing all these spider webs, glistening. And
just having that, it's like an awakening every morning.'

This resonance with the meadow pulled other places to the
surface for her. 'My work is quite often about creating substitutes
for the places I can't get to, which for me is actually eastern
Europe.' Her family's origins, prior to the Second World War,
could be traced back to the borderlands of contemporary Poland,
Belorussia and Lithuania. 'And I'm always looking at these
birches, and that's probably the thing that transports me most of

all. When I see a birch, in evening light, I'm thinking about train journeys. So I keep wondering whether it's only me who does that, or do other people do that too? Do they use it to think of these other spaces? Because I realize my grandfather did that in the Scottish Highlands, because he couldn't go back to Poland. And I think he sought out the place that was most like the places of his youth, which was, in fact, a bit like Aviemore. And that's where he used to take my dad and his brothers.'

When Kristin's Polish cousins had visited Scotland the summer before, one of them had immediately understood the emotional and psychological significance of the meadow and wood. 'It's a place,' they'd said, 'that can be anything you want it to be.'

That evening, before musicians began playing around the fire, flame-glow flickering across the faces of festive residents squeezed together on the circle of logs, I approached a group of teenagers. They were huddled on the grass around bikes, thin wisps of smoke from roll-ups rising between them as they shared cans of beer. There were nine or ten of them, all seventeen or eighteen years old.

'So where would you be if you couldn't be here?' I'd asked.

'The streets,' said a boy and girl simultaneously. 'We'd just hang about alleys and stuff,' continued the girl. 'But you can't hang about Glasgow safely at night because it's just, like, dodgy.'

'It is dodgy,' confirmed another of the boys.

'But here it feels safe. It's a nice wee bit of nature and a nice community,' added a girl to my left.

'And how would you feel if the meadow was lost to the development?'

'Sad,' four or five of them chorused as one.

'This is like the only place that you would talk to us like everyone else,' said a girl who'd been quiet until then.

'People always avoid young people where it looks dodgy, but here everyone talks to us.'

'It feels like you're allowed . . .' started one girl.

'. . . to be yourself,' finished another. They all laughed together. They'd lost some of their initial shyness in speaking to me, and the words began tumbling out.

'It's almost like your own private back garden.'

'But with random people!'

'Because you can do what you want to, it's not like the Botanics or something, where you're not allowed to touch anything.'

'There's a kind of freedom that comes with the place.'

Douglas had told me about the inclusivity of the meadow – how its connective and communal space engendered a sense of belonging. 'The secret of the land is this: the dog-walkers think it's their land, the kids think it's their land. If you were to ask them, everybody thinks it's their land, to be honest. And that's good, because they'll look after it. Even the drinkers take their empty bottles with them.' Unlike the resurgent politics of nativism, which frames belonging around a fallacious belief in blood and soil identity, places such as the meadow and allotment site give space to a far more inclusive, honest and ultimately valuable notion of attachment and affinity, one that isn't predicated on longevity or racial origins but is instead based on the value of presence, community and solidarity.

*

Despite the number of worked plots being significantly reduced by the council's deliberate closure of the waiting list, there was still an overwhelming sense of wellness about Farm Terrace.

Marion Harvey was ideally situated to understand the place's considerable impact on the community. A dietician at Watford General Hospital, she had a plot at Farm Terrace on which she kept bees, while also helping manage an adjacent plot under the aegis of the Dietetic Department. 'The word *opportunity* springs to mind,' she replied when I asked her what she felt the essence of Farm Terrace was. 'Opportunity for community integration. An opportunity for local people to come together more frequently, particularly to encourage elderly people who are living alone, to make those community connections. We have a number of primary schools around here with no green space at all,' she said. 'Let's teach the children, let's have an educational section of this allotment where you can have people growing things. Let's have, for example, an elderly day-care centre. Let's have people coming in and meeting people.'

In her early sixties, Marion was on her way to church when we met, but she was keen to stop and share her thoughts about the extended benefits of this place. 'When you think of what's going to be the biggest impact on the health services in the next thirty years, it's going to be the impact of the older population and dementia; it's going to be the impact of obesity and type 2 diabetes. And all the things that they lead on to, all the health issues associated with them, the heart diseases, the rheumatic diseases, the lack of mobility. So there's a huge link between diet and lifestyle and the health of the nation. But we have all this potential here.'

Having lost none of their many beneficial reasons for being – especially when the use of food banks in Watford rose by an alarming 40 per cent between 2013 and 2015 – the allotments need to be at the heart of any truly original and cohesive vision of

West Watford's regeneration. For what better signal could be sent in a nation in which obesity, diabetes, social exclusion and mental health issues are widespread than the valuing of inner-city spaces where communities coalesce to grow food in stimulating green space? What better way of incorporating a long-standing place into the very fabric of renewal than by forging stronger ties between the health benefits of allotments and the neighbouring expansion of the hospital? What better way of anchoring a regeneration than by supporting the ways of being well that are already in place; to make compromise a part of the process for the benefit of all? 'We have made it very clear that we would go as far as 50 per cent,' said Sara Jane, reluctantly willing to sacrifice to the development half of the allotments, already winnowed down to a fraction of their original footprint, if that was the only way to retain some of their positive value for local people.

Cities face critical issues surrounding health, and the need for varied green places within their borders has become ever more acute as the pressure of rising populations is coupled with funding cuts from central government. In the south London borough of Southwark, the local council began a controversial programme to reopen Camberwell Old Cemetery in 2014, after it had been formally closed for several decades. To make space for reuse where burials had already taken place, the works have destroyed not only a large number of gravesites and memorials but also a large part of the self-seeded woodland that had emerged in the intervening time. It was a small but vibrant oasis in the midst of the city. During the campaign to retain the woodland, I was sent a letter from a local resident, one that resonated with the story Charlie had told me about the importance of Hopwas Wood for his mental health:

I have a mental illness. Specifically, I have Post Traumatic Stress Disorder. For some years now . . . life has been very hard for me. Formerly an optimistic and productive person, I have been dealing with a condition that makes me, to put it simply, frightened most of the time, frightened badly: a person living in a world that feels profoundly threatening . . . These woods are, in reality, a psychological, near-medical resource for people like me – and there are many people like me. Mental illness is common; a common estimate is that 1 in 4 people will suffer it at some point during their lives. Most of us are normal dutiful citizens who make a great effort not to be a burden on others. One of the things we have to deal with in this effort is the fact that medical science is still at a point where many of our illnesses are not curable. We have to manage them ourselves, and we do our best to manage them. Please do not take away a place that makes it possible for us to do so.

David Ridsdale had seen what can happen to people when such nurturing, life-affirming places are merely threatened, let alone destroyed, reminding me how the National Trust report on the neural underpinnings of place discovered a strong connective link between place and positive emotion. David's Farm Terrace plot is as much an exhibition as it is a garden, utilizing sculptures and varying yearly designs to fashion a space that is artistically striking as well as edible. He and his partner, Daniel, grow flourishing herbs out of old boots and arrange a sunken array of bottles to serve both as gleaming borders and magnifiers of the slow-to-warm sun. The summer colours are set out in spring, the seeds sown in specific patterns so that several months later a stunning constellation of shapes and shades takes form – arching, spreading, spiking and beautifying. But as much as I enjoyed talking to him about their upcoming season of designs, there was something else on his mind that day.

'He's been a Watford man all his life,' he said of a neighbouring plot-holder. 'Love him to bits. Total working-class Labour his whole life, and he'd come and go, *290 days*. He was counting down the days until retirement. And it was a hundred days until retirement when they pulled this shit on us,' he said, referring to the original notice in 2012 that Farm Terrace would be disposed of. 'And he lost ten years of his life. Oh my God. His allotment was the most beautiful, welcoming space. He had two plots, one was full-on old-school garden, the other was trees and grass, so his grandkids could play. And you'll see it now, and you'll just look at it and go, *It's so run down*. And it's his spirit. We physically watched his spirit drain away.'

When those letters were first received in 2012, some of the plot-holders simply lost the will to carry on; they were fearful that investing further time, love and energy into their pieces of earth would only lead to a greater degree of loss. 'Lots of journalists ask me, *Why are you fighting so hard?*' Sara Jane had once said to me. 'And the honest-to-God truth is, not for me necessarily, but for my community, and, in particular, the old boys down at the allotment. It's a nail in their coffin if we lose. There's no two ways about that.'

'Three-and-a-half years ago, I was drifting,' said Pete by his plot one day. 'And I was drifting slowly but surely somewhere I didn't want to be. I didn't know where I was going. I could see the finishing line and there was nothing. And along came me first grandchild, and now I've got two. And I don't even think where I'm going now, because I know: I want to bring my grandchildren down here.'

*

It was my last evening in the meadow. Clear summer skies lidded the city as I sat in the grasses with four Kelvinside residents, sharing a bottle of wine. A young couple clapped their books closed and folded their blanket into ever smaller squares of blue. Further off, the teenagers I'd chatted to the previous night sat in a circle with their bikes, laughing with one another in the windless evening. I could make out youngsters and their parents in the wood, squealing between trees in a game of tag.

The inclusive atmosphere and mood of the meadow reminded me of Farm Terrace the week before. The spirit of the communal was strong in both, and it raised for me the question of what 'community' means at a time when many societies appear increasingly polarized and riven by ideological differences. While visiting Farm Terrace I'd sifted from countless discussions the presence of radically different political perspectives within the assembly of allotment holders, a fact particularly apparent in the run-up to, and aftermath of, the Brexit referendum. Around North Kelvin Meadow I could sense underlying disagreements between those who wished to retain the quieter space of the rejuvenated meadow as originally envisioned and those advocating for a more active, educational arena geared towards a full calendar of organized events and activities. There were tensions between dog-lovers and those without animals; between advocates of the meadow and those of the wood. Such differences should be a healthy reflection of diversity in society, providing the foundation from which tolerance, understanding and mutual exchange can arise and be nurtured. But, in an age when the echo chamber of social media and newspapers' editorial lines can easily affirm and amplify our ideological biases and leanings, the word 'community' has, to some considerable degree, been simplified. It's been thinned of its intricacy and nuance, streamlined in order to convey a sense of agreeable and all-encompassing harmony. It has become shorthand for the type of frictionless unity that is often idealized but rarely real.

At its very heart, community is the consequence of collective commonalities, but also, critically, of compromise. It's about coherence *despite* differences, finding common ground over which to move forward together. As the writer B. K. Loren puts it, 'I think community has little to do with like minds. It has to do with very differently minded people finding a way to get along because we all live in, are connected to, and share a sense of place.'

A fox streaked from the Children's Wood across the dimming meadow, ghostly, fleet and glowing, the trigger for silence to fall around us. A pair of bats circled above. I could still vaguely make out the corner of spotted orchids, where moths and other night insects would by now have convened after following a subtle path of scent over the grasses. Foxes and human families, moths and mothers, boys and bats: they were all inseparable elements of these places, all part of the deep connections that had been forged between local people and urban landscapes. Where true vision exists, it can be radically transformative in character, creating space for myriad possibilities and an upwelling of joy.

We don't speak nearly enough of joy, as though its levity were somehow a burden. But for me that is the defining feature of both places, visible, shared and catching, surfacing in small, private moments, or corners of common greenery – a blue butterfly bringing a radiant smile to a young girl's face by landing on her hand, an old man lifting from the earth the first fresh carrots of the year, a Finnish summer song in a Scottish stand of silver birch. Hopeful, energizing and sustaining, that joy spreads out through the braided network of lives and communities, bringing people into connection with one another and fostering a sense of agency, duty and care. Each place a hinge on which so many things open.

*

> We were the last plot-holders on site today. When I stood outside plot number one at 3.30 p.m., plucking up the courage to walk off site for the last time, looking at the devastation that was left behind, I found it really hard to hold back the tears, especially as today was the forty-fifth anniversary of Dad getting this plot. We even decided to close the main gate together for the last time as no one else can understand what it means. The only highlight for Dad today was the little robin who regularly comes to visit his plot coming to say his final goodbye. I can't help thinking that maybe even God was crying tears today (through the rain). I am tired, emotional, hungry, aching all over, soaked to the bone and covered with Farm Terrace soil. Just like I was all those years ago as a little girl helping her Dad.

Vincenzo's daughter, Rosangela, wrote these words after saying goodbye to Farm Terrace in November 2016. Two days earlier, the plot-holders had lost their final battle in court to save this beloved place. Upholding the ruling of the Communities Minister on behalf of Watford's council and mayor – who had never even met with the plot-holders on site, despite numerous invitations – the judge ruled that 'exceptional circumstances' dictated it should be built over. As Sara Jane had long feared, there was no attempt to define what 'exceptional circumstances' might mean or amount to, opening up the very real possibility that any developer, in conjunction with a local council, could categorize their proposal for the razing of allotments as an exception. Sara Jane, Vincenzo, Pete, Marion, Stephen, David, Daniel and the others were given just forty-eight hours to remove what they were able to save from the site before it was lost for ever. After 120 years of continuous use – surviving two world wars, twenty-seven different prime ministers and the disintegration of the British Empire, having been founded in the last years of Queen Victoria's reign – it was a callous and shabby end. But then Watford's mayor and councillors have never been capable of seeing in it what others did, dismissing its importance out of hand, and perhaps out of convenience. The gardeners uprooted all that mattered to them that they could conceivably cart away: barrowing home winter cabbages, cauliflowers and parsnips; gathering tools, clothing and almanacs; lifting potted herbs, bulbs and perennial flowers. All the stories held by the earth were left behind. 'It feels a bit like grief,' said Sara Jane, learning of the decision, a feeling that only deepened when, in 2018, the developers finally bulldozed the site, churning all of its remaining sheds, orchards and vegetable plots into rubble and mud, ready to be paved with concrete.

A month after the Farm Terrace verdict, the Scottish minister responsible for ruling on North Kelvin Meadow decided against Glasgow's council and the site's prospective developers, thereby preserving the inspiring communal efforts of the Kelvinside community. Although Glasgow was sunk deep in the darkest part of its winter, I could easily imagine the party that would be held outside that evening, bringing together all those who'd fought with such dedication and resolve to sow the seeds of possibility throughout an urban landscape.

8

The Sum of a Place

Passion is lifted from the earth itself by the muddy hands of the
young; it travels along grass-stained sleeves to the heart.
~ Richard Louv, *Last Child in the Woods*

'They always say the best way to see the Gwent Levels is with a microscope or a helicopter.' I was walking through the stunning June meadows and dense willow copses of Magor Marsh Nature Reserve with Sorrel Jones, a conservation officer for the Gwent Wildlife Trust. 'You've either got to get right in and go, *Look, this is amazing down here*, or you've got to get up high and see this vast, extraordinary landscape from above.' On her back Sorrel carried her son, Iestyn. Although I didn't know it at the time, being with Iestyn that day as he irrepressibly pointed at cygnets and mallard ducklings in the marsh was to be only the first of many encounters with children on the Gwent Levels, something that became so uncannily common by the end of my stay that the place has become synonymous with childhood in my mind. With the aid of their renewing curiosity and enlarging capacity for wonder, these children helped me see the place through different eyes.

Beguiling beneath wide estuary skies, the levels are mesmeric.

They shape-shift with the weather as you walk them, borrowing the magical sea-light of the Severn Estuary when it's struck by sun, or turning as dark and dramatic as a storm-tide beneath scowling clouds. There's a palpably antique presence across the entire vista. Not only do the Gwent Levels retain one of the largest surviving tracts of grazing marsh and ditch system in all of Britain, but they're also profoundly old in character and shape. Reclaimed from tidal salt marsh in Roman times, this ancient landscape was once the preserve of the sea, either inundated by tides or entirely submerged during epochs when sea levels were higher than they are today. Legionnaires first enclosed the Gwent Levels with a sea wall some 2,000 years ago to harness its fertility for grazing. But when the Romans abandoned Britain in the fifth century their sea walls fell into disrepair and were eventually breached, allowing the sea to sweep in once again, completely burying the land beneath alluvium. In the late eleventh century a renewed effort to reclaim the levels began in earnest, as the lure of those lush stretches grew stronger. As a result, there is little in the painstaking arrangement of land and water that doesn't owe its existence to human hands, the whole patchwork of fields, pastures, waterways and marsh gained from the sea by the strain of flesh, muscle and bone. Like a palimpsest laid over that earlier Roman landscape, another sculpted stratum in the long relationship between coastal people and the sea was laid down.

Magor Marsh had been my first port of call. 'This is the last remaining piece of fenland in south-east Wales,' said Sorrel. 'It was the nature reserve that prompted the formation of the Gwent Wildlife Trust in 1963, to stop it from being sold and developed.' It hadn't taken long for me to understand its significance – the place thrummed and buzzed with summer life. Common blue damselflies glittered in the meadow grasses and swallows curled through the dry, simmering air. An electric-green musk beetle roved the gnarled bark of an old willow. That practice of looking attentively and up close at things that Sorrel suggested had already established the extraordinary ecological diversity and vitality of the Gwent Levels in general, home to a remarkable range of charismatic species that includes rare invertebrates and aquatic plants, one-fifth of Wales's Cetti's warblers, uncommon bees and other insects, plentiful otters and avocets, and the rootless duckweed, the world's smallest flowering plant and one that's found nowhere else in Wales – so tiny that you could hold thousands of them in your cupped hands. It's a place that comes into dazzling focus as you near.

*

I'd walked the sea wall westward, lines of linnets leading me on until I found the bend of shore near the village of Goldcliff. The swirling waters were the colour of weak tea, a milky brown wash on the turning tide, all the silt and sediment of the estuary stirred up and scattered with stunning light.

In 1188 Baldwin of Forde, the Archbishop of Canterbury, journeyed throughout Wales while recruiting for the Third Crusade. Travelling with him that year was Giraldus Cambrensis, the Archdeacon of Brecon. Cambrensis, or Gerald of Wales as his name translates from Latin, was an avid chronicler of place as well as a respected scholar. By the time he was chosen as the archbishop's companion, he'd already documented his journey to Ireland in *Topographia Hibernica* and would go on to describe their time together in Wales in two volumes invaluable for their historical particularities: *Itineranium Cambriae* and *Descripto Cambriae*. While navigating the southern coast, Gerald described Goldcliff – or Gouldclyffe as it was spelled back then – as 'glittering with a wonderful brightness'. That luminous effect was the result of the sun's rays reflecting off a vast bed of gold mica at the base of twenty-metre limestone cliffs, a phenomenon magnified by the water when seen from a ship in the estuary. The cliffs that Gerald had noted – 'a rocky eminence, impending over the Severn' – are no longer to be found, nor is Goldcliff an island as it was at the time he described it, but that glittering brightness remains. The sun glints off the rising rush of water, the moon-pulled sea that heaves into the Bristol Channel with transfiguring speed. And beneath that great weight of water is something far older than even Gerald's chronicle of remembered light. Something his boat may well have passed over nearly eight centuries ago, unknowingly afloat above a seabed of ancient relics.

At the mercy of tides, storms, sea-surges and time, a series of remarkably unspoiled Mesolithic footprints have held sway against the elements, made safe by enclosing layers of sediment on the foreshore. Embedded some 8,000 years ago, when sea levels were considerably lower and the habitat was salt marsh, those protective wrappings of clay and silt have only in the last few decades eroded sufficiently to make visible the astonishing traces of another world at low tide. The human footprints belong to men, women and numerous children, a tribal community who would have hunted together along those watery margins. Each indentation seals a single moment of existence, a preserved second of impress on this Earth that was then hardened and cured by the sun until a large spring or autumn tide entombed it inside sediment for the following eight millennia.

I was led to the footprints by Rick Turner, a retired inspector of ancient monuments for the Welsh government. 'It's extraordinary that these prints are preserved in such a fluid landscape,' he said when we spoke about his experiences. 'The estuary has this magician's touch about it. It's an incredibly hostile environment in which you can find, for a time, these remarkable things. And then a veil is drawn over them.' Rick had been responsible for carrying out archaeological and historical projects across the whole of south Wales in his career, but one landscape stood out for him. 'The Gwent Levels is the most magical of the places that I've worked in or known.' He spoke about the 'ancient sense' that surrounded the prints, not only of the human marks left behind all those millennia ago, but also of the animals and birds that existed alongside them. While some of those creatures remain features of contemporary Britain, such as deer and gulls, there are prints that act as memorials to things long vanished: the steps of wolves and aurochs are preserved amidst acres of shining silt, as are the splayed incisions of the common crane, a magnificent bird that once bugled over vast tracts of marshlands and moors, but which was relentlessly hunted to extinction by 1600. All the echoes of that interwoven past are still down there, submerged beneath the quickening pulse of the sea, a glittering brightness spun across the estuary.

*

Losses in this expansive landscape aren't confined to the distant past, however: for a period of nine years at the beginning of the twentieth century not a single water vole had been seen in the Gwent Levels. The animal occupies an unenviable position in modern Britain as the nation's fastest-declining wild mammal, its population having nose-dived by as much as 90 per cent in the last forty years, the combined result of habitat loss and predation from non-native mink originally introduced for fur farming. An enchanting, semi-aquatic rodent, and the inspiration behind the character of Ratty in Kenneth Grahame's *The Wind in the Willows*, the water vole cleaves closely to fresh water, burrowing in the earthen banks of rivers, lakes, canals and ponds while feeding exclusively on waterside vegetation. But it was a creature that had joined those cranes and wolves of the estuary, disappearing from the local faunal record until a successful reintroduction scheme returned the diminutive mammal to the levels in 2012. Since then the water vole has spread over three miles from Magor Marsh on its own, its population journeying outwards like the ripples from a stone dropped into still water, recolonizing its former habitat reen by reen.

Reen, from the Welsh *rhewyn*, is the local word for the watery ditches that crisscross the landscape like arteries, the primary feature of a complex hydrological system that was dug over many centuries, and which includes a variety of components, from parallel field depressions known as ridge and furrow to shallow surface grooves called grips. On a map of the region the reens and these other ditches appear in bewildering blue numbers, 900 miles of them laid out like a dense grid of city streets, slowly carrying water from the uplands out to sea. And it's these earthen-banked waterways, beautifully fringed by reed sweet-grass, water horsetail and purple loosestrife, which set the Gwent Levels apart, making the landscape unique both culturally and ecologically.

'We have 144 Red Data Book aquatic invertebrate species across the levels,' said Sorrel when she'd handed me a net, encouraging me to go pond-dipping for the first time since I was a child. 'That's the diversity and rarity that you're looking at here, because each reen is subtly different. You get fast ones, slow ones, shaded ones, not-so-shaded ones – so you have this massive variety of reens which suits a massive variety of invertebrates.' Once I got started I found it hard to stop, twirling my net through the clear amber water in a figure of eight as Sorrel had suggested, then tipping it into a tub of water and peering at the treasure I'd hauled up, all the saucer bugs, water boatmen and pond skaters swirling and skittering around a floating mat of duckweed. Looking closely, every single one of those myriad blue lines on the map is wholly distinctive, supporting a singular cast of aquatic wildlife according to the reen's physical characteristics, as if each waterway were a stage for a different play.

Most of the present-day reens are medieval in origin, some of them the handiwork of monks who lived and worshipped on the levels. Laying willow mats across an especially wet field to reach their grange farm near Magor Marsh, monks attached to Tintern Abbey inadvertently seeded an evocative line of majestic old sallow trees still standing today. Such is the uniqueness of this historic, human-shaped landscape that the Gwent Levels have been designated as a Landscape of Outstanding Historic Interest. This register of cultural monuments was established with the intention of raising the profile of inimitable places in Wales, while providing guidance for any development proposals within them. And like those woven wands of willow that have sprouted into trees, culture and nature are deeply entwined across this celebrated landscape, giving rise to the wild diversity of the reens.

*

In recognition of the irreplaceable ecological richness of those reens, the Gwent Levels are listed as a suite of eight adjoining SSSIs, the term inadequately expressing the beauty of that ancient place, but at least meant to safeguard it from damage. From above you'd see how that nearly seamless stretch of protected land on both sides of the River Usk reaches all the way to the estuary, a shimmering green sweep threaded by living waterways and studded with church spires. And from up there you'd have a clear view of what fourteen miles of motorway might look like, disfiguring its secluded heart.

Despite the protective measures, the Welsh Labour government, with little support from other parliamentary parties, intends to lay six lanes of concrete and asphalt over the Gwent Levels, building a new section of the M4 to ease rush-hour bottlenecks where the current motorway is pinched from three lanes to two in the Brynglass Tunnels north of Newport. Their chosen route – aptly named the Black Route in proposals – would carve open four of those SSSIs and the Special Protection Area of the River Usk, as well as fragmenting the Landscape of Outstanding Historic Interest and ruining four ancient woodlands, at a minimum cost to the taxpayer, including VAT, of over £1.7 billion, or roughly £550 for every man, woman and child in Wales.

'This should be sacrosanct,' said James Byrne as we walked a wildflower meadow at the sunlit end of an afternoon, the whole field sparkling with beautiful translucency. 'There are so few of these special places left.' Originally from County Down in Northern Ireland, James worked for Wildlife Trusts Wales. Fluent in the contemporary language of conservation, he struck me as a good example of the new face of the environmental movement, as at ease in the outdoors as he is discussing policy at governmental meetings on climate change or talking to people on their doorsteps about local wildlife issues. He was attentive to their questions and his dry, Ulster humour made him immediately approachable.

Inevitably we found ourselves talking about places designated as SSSIs as we walked the levels, stopping now and then to watch reed warblers clinging to the tasselled tips of tawny summer stems. 'They were only ever supposed to be a representative sample as a protected habitat within an area,' said James. 'Let's say there were five ancient woodlands within a search area, and that could be a county or whatever, then it would protect one, because it's a representative sample. But instead of being the representative sample, they've over the years become *the* sample, because everything else is being eroded away or developed or chopped down.'

The motorway would spell the end of the Gwent Levels as an intact repository of cultural and natural wealth, something that even the great flood of the Bristol Channel in 1607 couldn't manage, despite the terrible tally of death and destruction that those rising waters wrought. As the study for the characterization of the place as a historic landscape makes clear, 'the sum of the whole is greater than the sum of each part'. Along with the direct loss of habitat beneath the concrete footprint of the motorway, one of the largest single losses of protected land anywhere in the UK, the M4 bypass would also rupture the vital cohesion of the place, acting as an impermeable barrier to all flightless wildlife and isolating wild animal populations on either side of the divide.

'It seems ironic,' said Kathy Barclay, an environmental officer at Magor Marsh, 'that we're reintroducing water voles and re-establishing a population that's going to be cut in half. Nothing's going to go beyond the motorway.' And not only will little wild-life travel beyond the looming barrier, but it's also likely that the damaging effects of the motorway will be widely felt, as each of the unique reens is coupled to another, linking up in a vast, inter-connected system. Any pollution from the motorway that enters one of the reens – whether from noxious fumes or a toxic spill – would be carried along like disease in a bloodstream, fouling each of those singular, underwater worlds that the extraordinarily sen-sitive invertebrates are entirely dependent upon.

The ramifications of the motorway are greater still because the RSPB and Wildlife Trust Wales chose the Gwent Levels as one of the sites for their Living Landscapes programme; a project that seeks to expand on Charles Rothschild's idea of protecting par-ticular places, it moves beyond the boundaries of a nature reserve like Magor Marsh in order to connect land, habitat and other ref-uges throughout a larger area with the critical help of local farmers, communities and landowners. At its heart is a vision of restoring natural permeability across a wider, often degraded landscape by enticing the spread of biodiversity via wildlife-friendly corridors, bridges and land buffers. For a species like the shrill carder bee, which favours wildflower-rich meadows and traditional pastures, the vision of a living landscape is essential to its survival. Once common throughout most of England and Wales, it is now possibly the loneliest of Britain's bees, hanging on in only a handful of spots, largely because of habitat loss and the fragmentation of its territories. But instead of expanded habitat, where connectivity could initiate local flourishing of the insect, the M4 would further fracture the hopes of its recov-ery, pushing this rare and beautiful creature ever closer to extinction.

'In interviews,' said James, 'people sometimes ask me, *Why are you stopping progress?* And my reply is, *It depends on what you call progress. Is a 1960s solution to transport appropriate for the twenty-first century?* I think progress is looking at innovative ways of what is effectively moving people around at predictable times of the day, and should not be, *You know what, we'll just take Point A and Point B and shove concrete in between.*' James is acutely aware of the snowball effect the proposed Black Route would set in motion, splintering habitats and communities, unstitching the interconnected qualities that lend the levels their particular substance and worth. And so, alongside championing greater investment in innovative public transport and sustainability schemes in the south Wales corridor that the M4 serves, he and the Gwent Wildlife Trust have taken the unusual decision to support, if absolutely necessary, an alternative road option to the one the Welsh government is proposing.

Environmentalists are frequently typecast as being implacable in their opposition to infrastructure development, and while this may at times be true, the stereotype also intentionally masks the more pragmatic face of the movement, silencing those who seek to find solutions on issues of development for the sake of larger environmental concerns. Knowing that the Black Route would inflict by far the most catastrophic damage on the suite of thriving ecosystems, the Gwent Wildlife Trust lent its assistance and expertise to Stuart Cole, Emeritus Professor of Transport at the University of South Wales, and his alternative proposal for a Blue Route to offset congestion on the M4. Taking into account the draft plan's inflated traffic forecasts and the Welsh government's plan to create an integrated metro rail and bus system for south-east Wales – a project they inexplicably failed to factor into their submission regarding projected future demand on the M4 – Professor Cole designed a far cheaper and less damaging alternative largely utilizing existing roads. His route is by no means ideal; it would still appropriate land in one of the SSSIs and violate the premise of protected places, but it should also be seen as an important step in seeking common ground in the pursuit of differing objectives.

Deep down I knew that James would prefer to be advocating for the preservation of this living landscape solely on its intrinsic value – for the inalienable right of those rare invertebrates to continue inhabiting those safeguarded reens and for the historic value of the levels to be sufficient in its own right to deserve our protection – but his honesty of approach in examining alternatives reflects his determination to salvage what he can from the wreckage. To put the place and its nature above his convictions when further conflict might risk an even greater loss. The government, however, saw it differently, categorically dismissing the alternative proposal in favour of their Black Route, an option that Professor Cole described as 'inconsistent with the Welsh Government's sustainable development duty, climate change commitments and aspirations to halt the loss of biodiversity'.

*

'It's hard to believe what these fields once were, and what they still are. When the tide comes in you get a real sense of their history.' I'd stopped one afternoon at a café near the village of Goldcliff after seeing Wayne Mumford, the owner, standing on a picnic table while trying to photograph baby starlings in the eaves. 'When I think that the Romans and the monks built this area where there's so much history, and all the life that lives in the reens, I can't understand why anyone would want to build a motorway through the levels.' Wayne had shaken his head in the same dismayed way that Lisa Morgan had inside Donnie's Coffee Shop in the village of Magor the day before, though her voice was sharpened with anger and frustration. 'I have to drive into Newport about five times a week and does the current motorway bother me? No. If I have to wait a little longer does it bother me? No.' She went back to wiping the counter-top before continuing. 'The sad thing is that politicians think they can ride roughshod over people. And if they take a little bit, generally they'll take a little bit more.'

The government's own website admits that during its consultation process it received more comments against the motorway proposal than for it, but dismisses them without a trace of irony as possibly being 'the result of interest groups' initiatives' while simultaneously championing the support they've received from corporate business. But even the Federation of Small Businesses in Wales has come out against the road, arguing that there are far better ways of spending such a colossal sum of money to sustainably develop the economy of south-east Wales. And despite the so-called need for it, no one I spoke to was actually in favour of a motorway across the levels. Not bikers, birdwatchers, lorry drivers, soldiers or publicans. Regardless of whether the people I met lived there or elsewhere in Wales – and the vast majority of them were regular users of the M4 tunnels and knew their congestion issues first-hand – they all articulated the same point of view: a deep concern about the project's gargantuan cost at a time when local services were being cut and a passionate belief that the place should be preserved as it is.

One afternoon I took a taxi from Magor to the village of Red-wick. Smoothing the flow of traffic on the M4 is one of the government's stated aims and I was curious to know what my driver thought about the proposed bypass. He should have been the ideal supporter, particularly as he'd only just started his business and was critically reliant on dependable journey times for it to grow. A choked road and stuttering traffic could mean the loss of a fare and negative reviews but, as we travelled deeper into the heart of the Gwent Levels, reens flashing and flickering in sunlight to either side of the road, he made his thoughts perfectly clear. 'No, I don't want the motorway at all and I'll tell you the two reasons why. Firstly, it would ruin the environment and the wildlife. Secondly, it would cut off my town of Newport,' he said. 'There are so many Roman ruins, and there are ancient footprints out by the river here as well. I'm not against progress, but I don't think ruining the environment or isolating a city, an already struggling city, is progress.'

What was particularly affecting about my conversations across the Gwent Levels was that I hadn't specifically sought them out. Just a casual mention of the bypass and the stories flowed like water from a burst pipe. We're repeatedly told that the natural world matters little to most people; that it's so low down on the list of political priorities that it doesn't even warrant a mention in most election campaigns. But over the course of these journeys to threatened places I began to understand how untrue this assertion is. Whether it was a desire to raise children in a clean environment, the regular enjoyment of local wildflowers and birds, deep concerns about the potential fallout from fracking, or committed personal responses to the twin threats of climate change and bio-diversity loss, I became aware just how important nature, in its widest possible sense, is to many citizens and communities. As elsewhere, though, people in the Gwent Levels felt their voices didn't matter; that theirs were of little relevance to the agendas of those who rule, disdainfully dismissed as just the 'result of interest groups' initiatives'.

'I take my five-year-old boy onto the levels all the time,' said Lisa back in the coffee shop. Charlie, her son, had autism, and Lisa found the levels to be one of the few places where he seemed calmer and more at ease with himself and the world. 'He's catching tadpoles in the reens, walking through a field of cows. That's what children should be doing. I've been very strident about the motorway, because once the place is gone, we can never have it back again.'

*

Thirty years after first arriving in south Wales, Kathy Barclay is as committed as ever to the region she calls home, sharing her considerable knowledge of the landscape and ecology of the Gwent Levels by teaching environmental education at Magor Marsh. Sitting in the reserve's office, I watched as she pulled a skull from a plastic bag.

'Do you know what animal this is?'

'No,' I said.

'It's a baby badger skull, but it's an awful story.'

As with so many of the found natural objects that had been discovered on the reserve, or had made their way there from somewhere else, I knew the badger skull would soon have the company of other relics – nests, feathers and broken eggshells; dried butterflies, beetles and an assortment of leaves – that graced a long table in the classroom. Whatever the circumstances of its demise, the badger would go on to play an important role in a lesson someday.

'A farmer phoned me last night,' said Kathy, placing the skull in a steel basin. 'He wanted me to look at something by a badger sett on his land.' I took my mug of tea and we steered towards her work station, sitting squeezed between computer desks, bookshelves and cabinets piled high with papers. 'I went over and together we had a look at the sett,' she continued. 'There was this skull at the entrance that he'd wanted me to see, which seemed to both of us a strange place to find it.'

'What happened?' I asked.

'Badger baiting,' she said. 'They smashed in its front teeth with a large stick. They do it so that the badger can't hurt their dogs. Then they release them to play with it at first, and finally the dogs just tear it to shreds. The farmer was so upset.'

Year Five arrived with electric pandemonium. Children rushed through the main door, chattering and laughing as they gathered around tables, swapping seats with each other to be closer to friends. The kids were all nine- and ten-year-olds, students at the Magor Church in Wales Primary School and regular visitors to the reserve. To remind them of the significance of Magor Marsh, Kathy began by asking the class what a nature reserve was. Arms rifled up from each table until a girl near the front was chosen. 'A nature reserve is a place for wildlife,' she said. 'You have to trust them and they'll do their own thing there.'

'And what is habitat?' Kathy asked. She chose one of the raised hands.

'It's a home for wildlife,' said a boy near the back.

I was fascinated by the children's replies to Kathy's questions, but however much I tried I couldn't keep the image of the young badger at a distance. It kept heaving into view, like a figure seen through moving mist, sharpening the distinction between the children's empathic response to the natural world and the site of the killing. From where I sat I knew that I could stand unnoticed and walk through the open door to the next room, where the badger's skull sat in a basin ready to be cleaned, an intricate dome of bones to house a complex, sentient brain, forever singled out by the brand of a smashed hollow where its teeth should have been. As the kids threw their hands enthusiastically into the air, answering questions about animals and the natural world – sometimes with admirable authority, sometimes with wild inaccuracy – I was torn between their keen vivacity and the scene of the badger's last stand, its desperate, tormented minutes beside the shelter of its sett. I could hear the shrill yipping of the dogs as they enacted their savage training, faithful to all they'd been taught to do in the secrecy of remote fields and unfrequented edgelands. I could hear the eager taunts and encouragement of the men, the toothless badger raging in helpless defence as it was shredded without mercy. And I could see the frail and frightened light of its eyes, clouding to dark and empty space at its end.

'Now give me some examples of habitat,' said Kathy. The answers came fast: *Reens! The water! The trees! Grass! Underneath the ground! The mud! Tree trunks! Meadows! Dead leaves!*

'That's excellent. I can think of one more. Does anyone know it? I'll give you a clue.'

Before she'd had the chance to reveal her hint, a girl's voice from the front of class broke through. 'The sky!'

These classroom discussions were leading us somewhere, along a path to the point where theory meets practice: we were going pond-dipping. When we reached our spot alongside a reen further into the reserve, the class divided into groups, each issued with a net, a deep plastic tray, spoons for separating reclusive creatures from their sheltering duckweed, and jars for any especially prized specimens to examine further when back in the classroom. I watched as the kids scooped water, weeds and a wealth of aquatic creatures from the reen with enormous delight, scrutinizing with rapt fascination the tubs where they'd tipped the contents of their nets. They pored over delicate ramshorn snails, tiny, flickering bloodworms and the startlingly large beasts that are dragonfly nymphs, racing back and forth with their sopping nets, hollering to each other about a particular discovery, or laughing when someone returned with an arm wreathed in weeds. That small reen of their fascination and focus had their undivided attention. As Richard Louv once wrote about such compressed concentration, they were lost in one of those 'small galaxies we adopted as children'.

While the microscope of Sorrel's adage is a tool for enlargement, children continually remind me that magnification can also be perceptual. It's not only scientists and archaeologists who get up close to things, for it's the native and intuitive approach that kids take to the natural world. When it comes to wonder, children are the true specialists: they are particularly open to that state of astonishment that we associate with awe. Through a blend of intense perception and heightened imagination, they are capable of discovering an entire world in a small fragment of nature when given the opportunity, something which is increasingly at risk these days. For some of the classes that Kathy teaches, Magor Marsh is the children's first experience of a nature reserve. '*Where are we?* they'll ask, wondering if it's a zoo. And then they'll say, *So do you feed the animals?*' And for some coming from inner-city areas of Newport a trip to the marsh reveals animals to them for the very first time. 'I've been asked more than once if horses are giraffes,' she said. 'But it doesn't take long before that awe and wonder shines through.'

In *Last Child in the Woods*, his seminal work on children and 'nature-deficit disorder', Louv examines the implications for children spending less time in contact with the natural world. He highlights the threatened range of benefits that engagement with nature from an early age can bring, including increased self-confidence, mental focus, essential development of the senses and creativity, reduced levels of anxiety and stress, and improved physical and emotional wellbeing. 'A widening circle of researchers believes,' writes Louv, 'that the loss of natural habitat, or the disconnection from nature even when it is available, has enormous implications for human health and child development. They say the quality of exposure to nature affects our health at an almost cellular level.'

Adults have a critical role to play in facilitating this positive engagement – and for also making sure it's available for disadvantaged children with little potential access to nature – embracing the innate interest and fascination that children have for the natural world and nurturing it as they grow, making sure there is time for unstructured outdoor play and the possibility of contact and connection with nature whenever possible. To encourage ecological literacy alongside the kind of caring concern and compassion for wildlife that might prevent brutalized badger skulls from turning up at Kathy's office in the future.

And this learning curve can be reciprocal. Children's enormous capacity for connection stems, at least in part, from practising an equality of interest. They make little distinction between what adults might describe as major or minor finds, responding to creatures, sensations and places of all shapes and sizes with an equal degree of absorption, so that the feather of an egret can be as wondrous to them as the bird it came from. As adults, however, we tend to lose that ability to identify intensely with the smallest of things around us, what the writer Jim Harrison calls 'the luminosity of what is always there'. Instead we typically favour the bigger picture, the large-scale landscapes and the more noticeable of their wild animals, if we take an interest at all. But paying attention to the multiple ways in which children engage so richly and unselfconsciously with the natural world, like those schoolkids excitedly riffling through pond weed in their tubs of water, can be a restorative act of noticing. It can return to us some of our old curiosity and keenness. As George Orwell wrote in his essay 'Some Thoughts on the Common Toad', 'I think that by retaining one's childhood love of such things as trees, fishes, butterflies and – to return to my first instance – toads, one makes a peaceful and decent future a little more probable.'

*

Near that golden curve of coast written about by Gerald of Wales some eight centuries ago, I saw three lagoons adjacent to a needle of water on my map of the Gwent Levels. I slipped through a kissing gate at the far end of a field. An embankment unrolled on either side of me, topped with a series of wooden hides, like sentry posts along a border. I rose up the ramp of one of them, entering the pine-scented darkness within. Laying down my pack, I hitched myself onto a high bench, letting my eyes grow used to the dimness before leaning forward to unlatch and then lift the heavy shutter.

It was all sea-glow and glister through my small window, a

summer breeze stirring the surface of the lagoons. Dozens of avocets, their feathers as white as new snow, waded gracefully through the shallows, or took curling, peeping flights over their island nests. Skylarks hung in the pale blue sky, their spangled songs falling like leaves through the air.

Over the far sparkle of water a buzzard knifed through the air. Crows rose to meet it, harrying the raptor at every jink and turn, clasped to its form as though shadows. Redshanks and lapwings volleyed towards the intruder as a second line of defence, then avocets angled upwards, a row of white and black dominoes falling headlong into the air. I watched the buzzard steer southward and away from them, but as I did, something glimmered at the thin and uncertain edge of my vision, that small corner of each eye that conjures phantoms as often as it reveals anything real. What I'd seen – or believed that I'd seen – were two birds arriving over the estuary, glimpsed, for the briefest of moments, solely as darkened silhouettes against the sun, lowering on vast open wings as if descending by parachute, and vanishing upon landing as mysteriously as they'd materialized.

A quivering thrill raced through me. I had an inkling of the birds' identity, but it didn't make any sense to me. At least not in south Wales. I glassed the marsh at the far side of the lagoon, but nothing was visible beyond the tall palisade of reeds and rushes that had cloaked the birds as soon as they'd touched down. I stepped outside, following the raised embankment towards the sea wall, and entered the final hide. This time the air inside was dense with expectancy. I slowly unfastened the shutter and there they were, framed by a window of summer-grasses and bathed in sharp coastal light, the glint of a scarlet crown on each of their graceful heads. I stared in amazement at a pair of cranes.

Common cranes were once sufficiently abundant in Britain to

be served in bewilderingly large numbers at royal banquets, but eventually became another in the long list of extinctions that shames these islands. It wasn't until a pair began breeding in Norfolk in the 1970s that 400 years of absence was brought to an end. Following their slow and gradual reproductive success, along with the natural arrival of other cranes from the continent, the idea of reintroducing them to various parts of Britain grew in strength. Between 2010 and 2015, the Great Crane Project released ninety-three cranes on the Somerset moors and levels, just over the Severn Estuary from where I stood. The process of restoration is arduous, a labour of love and commitment as much as of scientific finesse. The eggs of wild German cranes are first taken early enough in spring, under the guidance and monitoring of a local crane organization, to ensure that the pair has enough time to lay a second clutch. The harvested eggs are then transported to Slimbridge Wetland Centre in Gloucestershire, where they are artificially incubated. Once hatched, the chicks require a formidable degree of attention, all provided by staff that need to dress in baggy grey suits and head coverings that loosely resemble the clothing of beekeepers in order to avoid the young cranes misidentifying with them as distinct individuals. All of their needs are provided for by these human carers. At between ten and sixteen weeks of age the young cranes are transported from Slimbridge to a release pen covering two hectares of the Somerset Levels, where they spend the following three weeks acclimatizing to their new environment in the care of their surrogate parents, learning how to react to predators through the use of crane alarm calls and how to avoid humans and vehicles. Only then are they ready for the wild, and released into the open skies of the West Country.

Given the correct habitat, and a human willingness to work

towards co-existence, there is no reason why previously common animals can't undergo a renaissance in numbers. While it's impossible for specialist species such as cranes to return to historic population sizes – the vast majority of the wetlands they once relied upon having been drained or built over since the industrial revolution – it remains entirely feasible for them to regain a presence in what remains of their lost habitats. All of which makes the preservation of places like the Gwent Levels of paramount importance.

Damon Bridge, director of the Great Crane Project, believes the UK today could support 100–150 pairs of breeding cranes. 'The preservation of wetland habitats is absolutely critical to the crane's survival,' he told me. 'They roost every night in wetland habitats – and without the wetlands there will be no cranes.' The fragmenting and whittling away of suitable and protected places not only reduces the size and biological carrying capacity of the space itself but also makes what remains all that much harder to preserve. With the precedence of prior development having already been set, the continued unstitching of a place's essence is made manifestly easier, any arguments about its inalienable status rendered weaker, until a place is gone in all but name.

The cranes began to move, leaving the marsh to circle the lagoon across the cracked mud of an evaporated scrape. In a world that's increasingly obsessed with speed and efficiency, being in the company of cranes restores some sense of equilibrium. There is no hurry when it comes to these birds: standing as tall as 1.3 metres, their movements are delicately measured and supremely poised, each lifted leg a meditation, each pause a holding of the breath. You feel both suspended and buoyed by their presence. Although I was amazed to find them there, my surprise said more about the overall rarity of such birds than it did about the topography of the encounter. Because it's to habitats like the Gwent Levels that the cranes ultimately belong, these rich, watery plains so resplendent on the rim of the estuary. And they suit them completely, giving lift to the horizon like venerable lone trees or the spires of medieval churches, living parts of the complex, breathing whole.

Two people waved madly at me as I eventually walked back along the path.

'Have you seen the cranes?' they burst out when I joined them.

Grant and Carole were Welsh bikers as well as birders, dressed in black leathers for a day of riding the roads in fulsome sunshine. 'This has to be so rare in Wales,' said Grant. 'What a beautiful bird to have on the Gwent Levels.'

Something so surprising, magical and unlikely, the cranes had infused our respective days with a shared joy. They'd heightened our response to the very world itself. And as cranes spread to other wetlands, reclaiming past territories like those water voles expanding reen by reen, the possibility for wonder and connection that they bring with them becomes more common and accessible to us all. It could even become a regular part of our lives again.

I would later learn that for the past year this same pair of cranes had been regularly crossing the Severn Estuary from the reintroduction programme on the Somerset Levels. And in the summer of 2016, a year after my encounter with them, they nested on the Gwent Levels and raised the first Welsh-born crane chick in four centuries. This family of three, including the young bird – named Garan, the Welsh word for crane, by members of the reintroduction team – have reinhabited a place long known to their ancestors, restoring the tie of antiquity between their species and the local landscape that's memorialized by those ancient footsteps beneath the tide, each new impress a signature of restored presence.

'What the birds need now,' said Damon, 'is continued maintenance of quiet, wet, undisturbed, invertebrate-rich breeding habitat, as can be found in parts of the Gwent Levels.' When I asked him what the reintroduction project meant on a personal level, it was children who were foremost in his mind. 'I often think about what it will be like, when I have retired, to be able to wander down on the moors in the spring and hear cranes bugling away. And that my children, who are now eight and ten, will also be able to come down onto the moors when they are both retired and hear the cranes bugling. I think that is really something quite special.'

*

The impact of roads on the evolution of human societies has been profound. In the fifth century BC, the Persian king Darius the Great constructed the Royal Road, consolidating his entire empire through the improved system of communications it brought to bear across an enormous span of territory. Since then roads have facilitated commerce, infrastructure and movement, opened up markets for the exchange of goods and services, made communities less isolated, and provided the essential conduits for the cross-pollination of ethnicities, unrelated societies and differing cultures. They've expanded the circumference of our geographical experience, simultaneously making the world far larger and yet strangely intimate, affording many citizens opportunities to explore beyond the parish of the familiar in ways that would have been largely unthinkable in earlier eras.

But as the proliferation of roads has increased exponentially in response to a rising global population and the understandable desire for ease of movement, the enormous social, health and environmental costs of their transformative powers are becoming starkly clear. Numerous studies have shown that increasing road capacity, whether through building new ones or improving those already existing, results in an overall rise in traffic levels rather than the easing of congestion on the network, a phenomenon known as 'induced demand'. The concept was graphically, though questionably by today's standards, summarized in a quote commonly ascribed to the American historian and urban theoretician Lewis Mumford, paraphrased from an article he wrote for the *New Yorker* in 1955: 'Building more roads to prevent congestion is like a fat man loosening his belt to prevent obesity.' While the Welsh government states in its draft plan that one of the aims of the new motorway is 'reduced greenhouse emissions per vehicle and/or per person kilometre', it is the *total* emissions that matter when it comes to the greenhouse gases fuelling climate chaos. And the increased emissions resulting from induced demand also contribute to the soaring air pollution levels that blight many urban centres, resulting in spikes of associated pulmonary diseases and other illnesses.

Under EU law, hourly levels of nitrogen dioxide mustn't exceed 200 micrograms per cubic metre more than eighteen times in a calendar year, but by 5 January 2017 – just *five* days into the year – Brixton Road, in the London borough of Lambeth, had already surpassed its annual allowance. Primarily produced by the engines of diesel vehicles, toxic nitrogen dioxide pollution is believed to be responsible for 5,900 early deaths each year in London alone due to long-term exposure to the invisible gas, as well as the drastic decline of house sparrow populations in urban areas. And Brixton is, sadly, not unusual; many other streets in the city will exceed legally permitted levels barely days or weeks into the year. Putney High Street, in the borough of Wandsworth, exceeded the legally permissible level of nitrogen dioxide in the atmosphere over 1,200 times in 2016. Across the UK as a whole, air pollution from road traffic is responsible for over 50,000 early deaths per year according to a government consultation paper – 23,500 as a result of nitrogen dioxide and 29,000 from the inhalation of the particulate matter produced by all petrol engines, the residue of oily unburnt soot. The situation is described by Penny Woods, chief executive of the British Lung Foundation, as a 'public health crisis'. And children bear much of the long-term risk. Due to heightened rates of physical activity, they tend to inhale larger amounts of air than relatively sedentary adults. As their lungs are still growing, such early exposure to air pollution can lead to increased incidences of asthma, bronchitis, pneumonia and respiratory infections, as well as poor mental development. In the words of a recent editorial in the medical journal *The Lancet*: 'Children are destined to lead their early lives at the mercy of adult decisions.'

And yet, despite the devastating and proven impacts that road traffic brings to bear on human health, the construction of new roads – that 1960s solution for a twenty-first-century issue, as James Byrne had described it – is still considered by many to be politically expedient for the economic growth of a nation, as though those early deaths were a price worth paying for a greater goal. While he was the British prime minister, David Cameron, in advocating for a bypass road, described the Brynglass Tunnels of the M4 as a 'real foot on the windpipe of Wales', neglecting to mention that, in health terms, the motorway's proposed successor would be a literal foot on the windpipes of local people. For all that we've gained over the ages from the building of roads and the subsequent forms of movement they've enabled, we've become blinded by the benefits we've reaped, unable to see beyond them to the implications of an expanding network and the greater use of vehicles that their presence encourages. As Britain's overpriced and often unreliable privatized railway system pushes more and more people onto the roads in private cars, we expose ourselves to ever-increasing health and environmental risks. We are stuck in a debilitating mental space just as confining as any traffic jam.

Roads, of course, are just the mediums for many of the negative impacts associated with them rather than the explicit cause. While the actual footprint of a road can destroy a significant amount of underlying land, it is largely the related consequences of such infrastructure that compromise the wider environment and fabric of human life. These can include, to name but a few: noise disturbance, chemical pollution and collisions with wildlife. It also includes what has been called 'contagious development', a process whereby the construction of thoroughfares provides greater access to other areas, thus opening them up for more roads, more land-use changes, further associated resource extraction such as logging, and further human-caused disturbance of biodiversity. As the government's own map of the proposed Black Route reveals, areas of protected land on the Gwent Levels to the north of the proposed bypass have already been selected for use at some indeterminate time, squared off and crosshatched in pale pink lines, a note in the legend describing them as land now allocated for future development.

Utilizing open-access digital maps to detail the prevalence of roadless areas across the planet, the authors of a study in *Science* in 2016 noted that the intensity and variety of negative effects is greatest along a one-kilometre ribbon parallel to either side of a road, consequently defining a roadless area as land existing only beyond this buffer zone. While roadless areas covered 80 per cent of the Earth's surface, these were fragmented into nearly 600,000 pieces. More than half of the patches were less than a square kilometre in size, 80 per cent were less than five square kilometres in total, and only 7 per cent were greater than one hundred square kilometres. When the authors extended the buffer to five kilometres, a distance more realistic in terms of the many contagious developments affecting surrounding landscapes and ecosystems, the size of the planet's roadless areas was substantially reduced, covering only 57 per cent of the world's surface and broken into just 50,000 patches as a result.

It is clear that continued road building further fragments an already piecemeal landscape, particularly in such regions as the eastern United States and western Europe, where land is so densely layered with roads that the study's colour-coded maps quickly reveal that very little of it could be considered roadless by the authors' definition. In 2015 a further study by Nick Haddad, published in *Science Advances*, on fragmentation and its impact on ecosystems revealed the degrading effect of chipping away and bisecting habitats such as the Gwent Levels:

A synthesis of fragmentation experiments spanning multiple biomes and scales, five continents, and thirty-five years demonstrates that habitat fragmentation reduces biodiversity by thirteen to 75 per cent and impairs key ecosystem functions . . . These findings indicate an urgent need for conservation and restoration measures to improve landscape connectivity, which will reduce extinction rates and help maintain ecosystem services.

Considering that by 2050 the total length of the world's roads is expected to increase by 60 per cent, this need will only grow more pressing, as will the importance of investing in more sustainable forms of public transport and reducing movements whenever possible. As the science writer Michelle Nijhuis remarked in response to both studies, 'no matter the ecosystem – forest, prairie, patch of moss – the effects of habitat fragmentation are ruinous'.

*

What's at stake with the Welsh government's plan is not solely the exceptional environment of the Gwent Levels, but the kind of future we wish to leave as our legacy. Do we honour protective measures for the purpose they were intended, leaving intact those places of unique natural and cultural significance, safeguarding them with moral authority as much as legal creeds? Or do we dismiss them as irrelevant, narrowing our focus until it excludes all but a relentless fixation on economic development as the only measure of progress and wellbeing, corroding the wider duty of care we've been entrusted with? In 2015, when the Welsh government passed the admirable Well-being of Future Generations Act, an enlightened piece of legislation that made frequent use of the word 'sustainable', it noted that sustainable development was the key to 'improving the social, economic, environmental and cultural well-being of Wales'. But that the Gwent Levels can be sacrificed for the sake of such development reveals just how empty of meaning the concept of sustainability can be. 'We need to think of different solutions,' said Kathy as we talked at Magor Marsh – an acre of which, rich in otters, water voles, reens and aquatic invertebrates, had already been listed in a compulsory purchase order sent by the government to the Gwent Wildlife Trust. 'The history of this place, and the cultural aspects of it, are irreplaceable, so once you've wrecked it, it's gone. It's absolutely gone.'

The Future Generations Act obliges public bodies in Wales 'to make sure that when making their decisions they take into account the impact they could have on people living their lives in Wales in the future'. After the schoolkids had finished reen-dipping, I'd walked back through Magor Marsh towards the classroom with them as they carried a small selection of creatures in glass jars to look at under the microscope, to bring that captivating world beneath the surface of the water into even greater focus. As swifts clipped the corners of the sky and dragonflies zinged across our path, I talked to a number of the children, asking them what it was they enjoyed about coming to the Gwent Levels.

'I really like the wildlife,' said Rico, a British Asian boy who was both shy and small for his age, 'but also the peace and quiet.'

Yves had been a bundle of tense energy during the reen-dipping, a pretty and athletic girl who'd unwound considerably by the time we walked back, saying, 'It's nice to be quiet here.'

Jim was handsome, self-confident and sharp, the kind of boy it's easy to believe has everything going for him in life. 'When it's noisy at home,' he said, 'I find peace here.'

Each and every child, spoken to individually, gave the same two reasons, as if drawing on a communal well of common sense. Firstly, they adored the wildlife, the very things that accord the levels their technical designations, and which underscore the attachment that so many have for this celebrated area. But secondly, and of far greater surprise to me, they all said they loved the calming peace of the place. What the children articulated was that they still urgently require nothing more simple and restorative than silence in nature – a fact easily overlooked in our busy digital world.

At a time when children spend increasingly less time outdoors, Richard Louv is acutely aware that the obstacles to engagement with the natural world are many and complex. But when children *do* find a place they feel an attachment for, he's absolutely clear about the consequences of its loss. 'If a geographic place rapidly changes in a way that demeans its natural integrity, then children's early attachment to land is at risk. If children do not attach to the land, they will not reap the psychological and spiritual benefits they can glean from nature, nor will they feel a long-term commitment to the environment.'

That future generation – the citizens that the Well-Being Act was intended for – had already forged an important bond with this place, a set of emotional and imaginative connections that immeasurably enriched their lives while helping to sustain their critical development. And they were also the ones who will be left to live with our decisions, growing up in a world increasingly impoverished by the loss of unique places and wild species and gravely threatened by a heating climate. 'If we hope to improve the quality of life for our children, and for generations to come,' wrote Louv, 'we need a larger vision.'

As we crossed the final bridge by the nature-reserve offices the children stopped talking and watched the water instead. A sudden hush of wonder descended over them when a water vole swam across the reen, stilling them for several minutes. The fragmentation of wonder is as ruinous as the fracturing of habitats, for it steals at an early age the possibility for intimate connection with the natural world, making a future for water voles, cranes and badgers all the more difficult to ensure. And, at a fundamental level, it curtails a child's inner potential while lessening their full experience of the world, not through any decision or desire of their own, but because we've chosen to send them down that poorer path.

9

Between Earth and Sky

There were a thousand worlds within this one world of grass.
~ John Madson, *Where the Sky Began*

We were to gather as strangers in the darkness, drawn together for a few April hours to witness an ancient grassland rite. I'd risen at four, stuffing extra layers of clothing into my rucksack to keep out the cold. When headlights speared the night through the window, I stepped outside and closed the door to the cottage I was staying in, and then struggled inside an enormous pick-up truck, the top of the vehicle's wheels touching my hips. 'You know how some guys reach middle age and go out and buy a sports car?' said the driver when I'd finally clambered inside. 'Well, this is my middle age.'

Chod Hedinger had an easy, old-timer affability about him, a laid-back casualness that seemed to suit the country-music station presets on his radio. In the dim glow of the dashboard I could see that he wore a grizzled beard and baseball cap. He spoke with a warm drawl as we drove the night roads, talking about his four years in the US Air Force, when he was stationed in Texas and Japan. Returning to civilian life, he'd worked in a grocery store before becoming a supermarket manager, eventually winding down his working years as a salesman seeking out new markets for gourmet foods throughout the Midwest. For the last sixteen years, though, whether employed or retired, he'd volunteered as a guide on the Konza Prairie. 'Sometimes when I'm at home my wife will say, *I think the Konza is calling*, which is my signal to get out of the house for a while.'

Chod cut the lights after we'd pulled into a lay-by. I knew from an aerial photograph in the cottage that I stood on the eastern edge of the Konza in the Flint Hills of central Kansas, one of the last large remnants of tallgrass prairie to be found anywhere in the United States. I stepped into silence while we waited for the others, the night air freighted with the sweet scent of grass. Headlights stroked the road as a few cars pulled up alongside us. As soon as Chod had ticked off a list of names on a scrap of paper, we car-pooled through darkness. An upland sandpiper startled in the spectral beam of our lights, stiletto-billed and strikingly ghost-like; it flared to one side and vanished as though it had simply wrapped the skin of night around itself. It was nearly 5.30 a.m. when we came to a stop, setting off on foot in a procession across the prairie. Dawn was still illegible on the horizon and so we walked in the glow of Chod's torch.

Chod finally stopped and raked the beam of light over a low wooden hide – our prairie shelter for the coming hours. We all hunched small and shuffled forward to take a seat on a wooden pew, pressed as close as the leaves of a book. While we waited we got to know those beside us, their faces glimpsed in the stark glare of mobile phones. Zane was an oil-well engineer and wildlife photographer from Montana, who'd trudged a tripod and back-pack of gear inside with him. Beside Zane sat Emily, a biology student at Kansas State University. She was showing him an app on her phone that traced migratory bird flocks through thermal imaging, a glowing mass that moved eerily across the screen, when suddenly she said, 'The other day I realized that I've been in love with birds for nine years now, and I thought, *That's half my life – amazing.*'

At the far end of the hide, where he was squeezed beside a married couple from Kansas City, Chod cleared his throat and began to speak, asking us to lower the shutters. 'They're not bothered by our voices,' he then said, 'because they have only one thing on their minds at this time of year.' He paused for the low ripple of laughter before closing with his punchline: 'Sex'.

It was still dark when we heard it – a deep and otherworldly pulsation of sound. More expansive and ethereal than a bittern's boom, it was as though it had been caused by successive winds pouring over the lip of an open bottle. It was trancelike in its longevity, a constant, mesmeric murmur, the drone of a bass note on a perpetual and intensifying loop. When wings skimmed the roof of the hide a second boom soon followed, the first now punctuated by a layered track of laughing and cackling trills, a rising tide of whoops and hollers and hoots. Still wrapped in darkness, we sank into the spellbinding songs, utterly blind to their source until a faint smear of light gathered on the horizon and began to pool across the prairie.

Bordered by the rolling hills of tallgrass, prairie chickens strutted in wild splendour on a sward of shorter grasses. Magnificent in their breeding plumage, they wore a lustre that the sun couldn't compete with on that overcast morning. A pair of coffee-brown crests, called pinnae, tapered upwards like the shoots of spring crocuses at the side of their heads. From their necks dangled yellow pendants of skin that inflated whenever a bird volleyed another boom over those assembled for the ceremony, and a curling lemon sliver hung like a crescent moon above each eye. At the tip of the air sacs bloomed a purple patch of skin when prairie air was pushed through the valves, inflating the empty membranes like balloons at a fiesta. And with each exhalation a trembling new note supplemented the swirling songs, delivered on the winds and deepening the intensity of the lavish grassland routine.

These congregations of prairie chickens are known as leks, and the communal grounds for the display are remembered by them and returned to over successive years, the grassland equivalent to the human dance floor. Lowering their heads so that their bodies presented lines as level as a horizon, eight males fanned and tilted their tails, angling their wings outwards at a sharp, broken pitch so that the brown and white barring on them was vertically aligned. They then charged like miniature bulls across the grasses, hooting and cackling against the insistent, spectral sound of the drone notes. They stamped their feet in rapid-fire rhythm, jumping into the air like they'd stepped on a bed of hot coals, each choreographed move designed to impress nearby females. They leapt, clucked and sang together until a northern harrier ghosted into view, sufficiently near that they suddenly slinked as one into the long, obscuring grasses, suspending the ceremony until the raptor had slipped away into the grey distance. They then returned – resuming a ritual that has been theirs since the beginning of their kind, its beauty unfurling in the pale prairie air.

After two hours of watching from the hide, Chod motioned to us that it was time to leave. We wriggled from the blind to the clapped wings of scattering birds, emerging into a charged and luminous world. The flaxen sweep of tallgrass prairie spread in all directions. For all our unfamiliarity with our fellow companions, we'd shared something unforgettable that bonded us that

day; it was immediately noticeable in the way our band of disper-
sing strangers hugged one another and laughed together aloud. 'A
lot of this is hard to put into words,' Chod told me later. 'A lot of
it just comes from the heart.'

*

One image recurs more than any other in the chronicles of those
European colonists who made their way west out of the dense
deciduous forests of what is now the eastern United States. As
trees gradually thinned to reveal immense open skies and limitless
horizons, these homesteaders and settlers repeatedly related the
experience of encountering an 'ocean' or a 'sea' ahead of them –
as though they'd mistakenly veered off course and touched the
shores of the Great Lakes. Of course, it wasn't oceans of water
that they wrote about with a blend of incomprehension and awe,
but rather vast realms of grass: treeless prairie expanses that rolled
in undulating waves to the far edge of their vision. And the only
apt and adequate metaphor that came to many of their minds
when faced with a landscape so alien to their experience was the
seemingly endless body of water they'd crossed to reach the continent in the first place.

That inland ocean was composed of three distinct but adjoining
habitat types, seamlessly woven together as a contiguous tapestry
of grass. From the eastern forests where those colonists first
encountered the grasslands, the tallgrass prairie, and its spectacular stands of big bluestem, spread onwards, like the settlers
themselves, into eastern Kansas and Oklahoma, and north to
Manitoba, covering much of Iowa and Illinois and large swathes
of Minnesota and Missouri. West of the tallgrass, a world of

mixed-grass prairie held sway, a transition zone graced primarily by the elegant sprays of little bluestem, occupying the central corridor of the Great Plains, reaching as far north as Saskatchewan and spearing south into Texas and New Mexico, while carpeting much of the Dakotas, Nebraska, western Kansas and Oklahoma. At which point the shortgrass prairie took over, running to the foothills of the Rocky Mountains, a home of blue grama and buffalo grass that wrapped the western edge of the Great Plains. Together, these various prairies composed 40 per cent of the surface of the United States when Europeans first landed on its shores, a sea of grass that was the largest single biome in a continent of exceedingly rich biological diversity.

Stemming from the French word for meadow, and bestowed upon the grasslands by early Gallic explorers, who had discovered in their colourful assembly of flowers a resemblance to the fields of home, prairie owes its existence to a great trinity of elemental forces: rain, wind and fire. In the historic and ongoing struggle for dominance between the kingdom of grasses and the empire of trees, prairie ascendancy is maintained only when these three factors help defend against large-scale woodland incursions. A relative lack of precipitation is the initial key to the establishment and longevity of prairie. As water-laden clouds build into towering columns along the continent's west coast, they are spun eastwards by prevailing winds until eventually jettisoning their cargo over the Rocky Mountains, leaving the Great Plains to their east in the rain shadow of the range. The dry circumstances of the plain are ideal for the short grasses that coat the western prairies, but make life profoundly difficult for most trees. Moving further east across the plains, precipitation gradually increases as warm winds from the south funnel moisture northwards, falling to enough of an extent as to allow mixed-grass prairie to grow more lushly, while still being defended against forests by the relative scarcity of rain. By the time you reach the tallgrass prairie, however, where big bluestem can hide a horse in stands reaching more than three metres high, there is sufficient rainfall for these towering plants to flourish, but also for gallery forests to establish themselves and line the gullies and clefts of the prairies. And it is here that the grassland community requires the helpful efforts of those other two elements to aid in its supremacy.

The winds of the Midwest are legendary – pummelling bouts of air that can turn a mild winter's day into a punishing test of seemingly polar endurance. These are winds that hum, whine, scream and sigh throughout the seasons, menacing the earth by stripping moisture from the soil as quickly as it's replenished by rain. So efficient are they at drawing water off the land that these winds are just as accountable for evaporation as the blazing heat of summer, meaning that trees are unable to gain a foothold beyond the hollows where water lingers. The prairie's grasses, though, some of which are able to drill down to a depth of over ten metres in dense, interlacing networks of roots and fine rootlets, are able to locate nourishment in the most trying of climates and weathers.

Together with wind and aridity, grasses also owe loyalty to fire. Unlike trees, whose growth extends from the aerial tips of their branches and the expansion of the trunk through the division of cells in the layer of cambium beneath the bark, grass grows from the earth upwards, its essential living systems of replenishment and renewal secluded beneath the soil, so that they're safely tucked away from flames when wildfire races through its domain. Regenerating swiftly from the blaze, grass sends new shoots through the fertilizing duff of cinders and ash from its protected crown and underground rhizomes, while the growing parts of any tree saplings that had found a tentative purchase on the prairie would have been incinerated, making rejuvenation unlikely. Two things were primarily responsible for the fires so essential to the continuation of prairie. Lightning was the first of them, a common natural feature of the Midwest's violent summer storm systems. Historically it ignited roaring infernos that would feed on the litter of dry grasses, raging across immense tracts of neighbouring grassland. These roiling conflagrations were quenched only by the arrival of rains, the exhaustion of fuel, a shift in the direction of wind, or encountering the uncrossable barrier of a river. The second cause of fire was cultural, however. It was a tool utilized by prairie Indians to make root digging possible and encourage the growth of fruit-bearing shrubs, as well as to force bison* in a predetermined direction during a hunt, or to lure them to places of fresh forage where they could be more profitably stalked. After the fires had smouldered out, the prairie would be renewed in the wake of their visitations, the smoking, charred vista turned swiftly luminous with succulent green grasses.

In the end, though, it was the plough rather than trees that undid the dominion of prairie. As European settlers spread west across the grasslands in the 1800s, they recognized opportunity in the offering. The dark, loamy earth they saw beneath their wagon wheels and boots, the result of untold years of vegetable decomposition, the prairie recycling the nutrients of its grasses and flowers back into its densely matted soil, was some of the richest and most productive land to be found anywhere in the world.

* The terms 'bison' and 'buffalo' have both been commonly used to describe the largest land animal in the Americas still in existence, *Bison bison*. For the sake of continuity I have chosen to use 'bison' throughout, but any mention of 'buffalo' in quoted material refers to the same animal.

With the invention, in 1873, of John Deere's steel-mouldboard plough, designed specifically to contend with compacted prairie sod and the tendency of its soils to cling to the blades of its cast-iron predecessors, the work of obliteration was swift, economical and thorough. Driving the highly polished steel through the intertwined network of roots, settlers could actually hear tough prairie natives like leadplant snapping as loudly as guitar strings. Not even the densest of sod and most resilient of roots could resist the harrowing blades, farmers making short work of the continent's most expansive living ecosystem. The 'garden that had bloomed and fruited for millions of years, waiting for man, lay torn and ravaged,' wrote the author Hamlin Garland in 1917, reflecting on his farmland childhood in the Midwest in the 1860s and 70s. 'The tender plants, the sweet flowers, the fragrant fruits, the busy insects, all the swarming lives which had been native here for untold centuries were utterly destroyed.'

By the beginning of the twentieth century the tallgrass prairies were utterly unrecognizable. The 'thousand worlds within this one world of grass' that John Madson so eloquently described were almost entirely gone, replaced by a blanket of agricultural crops. Today, former tallgrass prairie states such as Iowa and Illinois hold less than 0.1 per cent of their original native grasslands. As a result, prairie is now more globally rare as an ecosystem than tropical rainforest, and it is the most threatened biome in all of North America. What remains of it are mere fragments, as though the tide had fallen away from that ancient sea of grass, leaving just ponds and puddles across an enormous expanse of sands.

*

One such fragment is the Konza Prairie. Spread across the Flint Hills of eastern Kansas, the Konza has kept its native flora tall, diverse and wild, its 8,000 acres too stony for ploughing and now protected through a purchase by the Nature Conservancy. While an area of the prairie is open to the public, much of its space is preserved as a site of ongoing scientific study under the auspices of Kansas State University, a place where, for example, specific watersheds are burned at different rates – every one, two, five or ten years – to determine the role of fire in maintaining the integrity of a prairie ecosystem, experiments whose results have profound implications for the conservation of those remaining grassland patches.

Few landscapes have fascinated me imaginatively as much as open grassland – all the space, silence and light that I sensed must gather at their edges and spill inwards, as if being poured like water into a bowl. But when such otherwise attentive observers of place as Charles Dickens describe tallgrass prairie, which he visited in Illinois in 1842, as 'oppressive in its barren monotony', it begs the question of how we should best attune ourselves to landscapes that lack the visual immediacy of striking variations in form. The first thing I discovered was that grasslands are premised on a profoundly sensuous, if subtle, presence. The prairie dominates the landscape in a languorously suggestive manner, as if only hinting at the things it holds within. Instead of the easily impressive features of other landscapes, whether vast stands of towering trees, the uplifting spires of snow-capped mountains, or canyons and lakes of improbable depths, it's the quieter aspects of the prairie that encourage intimacy, drawing one in beyond the oceanic swell of grasses into a more confiding rapport with an interconnected world of stalks, flowers, roots and seeds. It's an ecosystem that asks you to see, or perhaps feel, a place with regard for its reclusive character, allowing its essential light and winds to play their ineffable roles in defining an environment that requires your proximity for it to turn revelatory. 'From a distance it doesn't look like there's much going on. It looks like a lot of emptiness, like an ocean,' said Carol Davit, executive director of the Missouri Prairie Foundation, in a TEDx talk about why prairie matters in the modern world. 'But think of all the life in an ocean. It's the same with prairie, you have to stop and look closely and then you'll see immense detail and diversity.'

My walks on the Konza led me into a realm of beckoning beauty. There was the electric teal sheen of eastern bluebirds and the robotic blips of brown-headed cowbirds. Little bluestem took on a glowing red hue in rain, as though lit by the embers of remembered flames. Coyotes yippered madly at dusk. And there was the stirring ascendancy of light, the way it flickered through pale clouds like an old cinema reel. While wind, fire and aridity are responsible for the prairie's presence, at heart this is a country made by light. There is nothing vertical to impede its fall, nothing other than clouds to deflect its descent, and so it drops from the sky with clear fidelity to its origins, the luminous energy and extravagance of our nearest star. The effect it has upon the land is mesmeric, as though the sun were a sovereign and the prairie its glorious realm. The magnificent sweep of light is orchestral, scrolling in seconds across the bevelling hills between pillows of cumulus cloud, all the hay-coloured grasses turned harvest gold in the contrapuntal interplay between sunburst and shadow.

As I was returning to the cottage one afternoon, a pick-up truck slowed on the dirt road I was walking along, sending up a cloud of dust. Although the calendar read early spring, Kansas had been rainless for weeks, and the earth already wore the parched and cracked visage of late summer about it. I recognized the face at the open window from the university hall where I'd spoken the previous evening, talking about the possibility of being at home in more than one place through the cultivation of awareness and attention. 'I'm not big on reading books,' said Joe Gelroth, friendly but firm through the open window, making clear that he didn't waste words when there was work to be done, 'but I enjoyed what you said about home. And this is home for me.'

Joe ran the Friends of Konza Prairie, a non-profit body that worked to support the grassland through volunteer teams and outreach, organizing wildflower walks, educational programmes and the training of guides. While just a fraction of its earlier immensity, this patch of old tallgrass was not only a crucial refuge for prairie-specific species of wild plants and animals, but also a haven for humans, its importance dwarfing its relative size in the landscape.

I met Ashley Thackrah in the old stone farmhouse that now sheltered the Konza's educational, scientific and administrative staff. A young woman with an infectious enthusiasm for her educational work with children, she talked to me about how the guides tried to reach out to the kids by encouraging them to use all of their senses. 'We really try to focus on getting out, on seeing how the prairie feels. And sometimes it's the kids that are most grossed out and freaked out by the bugs that are the ones catching the most of them by the end of the day.' As sunlight broke through her office window, I asked Ashley what long-term effect this engagement with the prairie might have. 'One of the teachers emailed me to say that some of her students had blossomed after visiting the prairie – *She just opened up and blossomed*, she said – and that's incredible.'

Midway through my conversation with Ashley, Jill Haukos arrived at the office. Jill was the Director of Education at the Konza, and she brought a tangible and motivating presence into the room with her.

'Why is it important to preserve the prairie, to protect the remnants that are left?' I asked her.

'This is their place,' she said, talking of local people. 'I'd like them to have pride in their sense of place. To see the incredible beauty of it. The prairie is a different world and you have to be shown it, and then you can care about it. And once you care about it you can begin to protect it. The other day I passed a truck that had a sign on it that said *Tree huggers suck*. What happened to this person that they think this way now? I certainly don't think that truckers suck. So I'm trying to reach that driver as a child.'

*

Photographs can haunt us. They have the power to make heard the silenced voices of the past; they have a way of returning things to us that we've tried to forget, or illuminating histories we've never known. Taken in North America in the 1870s, there's a black and white image that troubles me as much for its casual perfection and graceful geometric lines as its terrible subject. To stare at it for any length of time unsettles my sense of perspective. So brutal is the honesty of the image that it projects a strange yet appalling beauty – deeply disturbing precisely because it seems too unreal to be true.

Other than a glaring sky and narrow band of grassed-over earth in the foreground, the entire frame of the image is consumed by a hill of bison skulls. They are stacked as neatly as pieces of split oak in a woodpile. Bleached blindingly white by sunlight, each pair of horns has been conscientiously manoeuvred in such a way as to best slot together with the neighbouring skull. Dwarfed by the towering mound of bone, two men appear in the photograph as well, one at the base, the other at the summit. They are wearing top hats and black jackets, each posed with a leg propped up on a skull, as if it were a footstool in a saloon. They seem proud to be associated with such devastation. It's impossible for me to gauge how many individual skulls might make up the swollen slopes of bone, but others have tried. Unable to determine precisely how far back the hill stretches, they've conservatively extrapolated from its visible dimensions in relation to the approximate height of the men that 180,000 bison skulls compose this towering prominence alone.

The nineteenth century was a graveyard for the American bison. At its beginning, an estimated 30 to 60 million of the animals roamed their territory on the continent, though native American tribes such as the Comanche had already begun hunting them to the very limit of their regional sustainability, as increasingly powerful firearms and horses enabled them to supply a growing market for bison meat and hides. But whatever toll indigenous hunters were taking on bison at the time, it paled in comparison to that exacted by white Europeans. Recent immigrants to the continent, many settlers indiscriminately massacred bison to reduce grazing competition for cattle, the carcasses of the dead animals, according to J. M. Baltimore in 1889, left to 'fester and rot, their bleached skeletons to strew the deserts and lonely plains'. Bison were also killed so that their hides could be exported to Europe, while whole herds were decimated solely for their bones. Shipped to an assembly point, such as the one depicted in the photograph, the skulls and skeletons were ground down into cheap agricultural fertilizer, all those countless, complex prairie lives turned to dust. The railroad industry was complicit in the carnage, eliminating enormous numbers of animals to prevent them wandering onto the tracks and delaying or cancelling services. Hired marksmen shot bison from moving trains, a practice that became a popular recreational pastime, sportsmen booking passage on cross-country services to stand at carriage windows and slaughter whatever animals passed them by.

However beautiful and sustaining its surviving remnants continue to be, the wider prairie landscape records a litany of grievous wrongs. It's a chronicle of violence and loss that unfolds across the country, the damage worked into the very roots and remembering earth of the grasslands themselves, those great traumas and lasting indignities that sit at the very heart of American history. And these are wrongs that haven't yet been righted, as the violent response in 2016 to the unarmed water protectors of the Sioux Nation viscerally revealed. Peacefully protesting against the passage of an oil pipeline at Standing Rock Reservation in the Dakotas, the water protectors were regularly attacked with security dogs, water cannon, tear gas and rubber bullets as the National Guard was brought in to assist local law enforcement and state troopers with its tanks and armoured vehicles, deliberate actions that caused a number of serious injuries. This physically forceful response was radically different from the way in which law enforcement had responded earlier that year with a laid-back, hands-off approach to the armed occupation of public land by right-wing and white-skinned militia members at the Malheur Wildlife Refuge in Oregon.

I was travelling south from the Konza Prairie through the Flint

Hills with Dave Rintoul, an ornithologist and Professor of Biology at Kansas State University, when he opened my eyes to the landscape in the altering light of its history. Barn swallows sculled northwards with a new season in tow as we passed a stone church in the valley bottom. 'For a short time this area was a reservation for the Kaw people,' said Dave as we left the church behind us, 'before they were forcibly moved on to Council Grove and eventually Oklahoma.'

And yet there was almost nothing in the vastness of the former grasslands to commemorate the dismal losses endured by this native people. The history of the prairies and plains pivots on an overwhelming absence, a frontier narrative given momentum through exodus and forced clearances, its pioneering promise to leave an empty slate upon which a new story of belonging could be inscribed.

At the height of the mid-nineteenth-century slaughter of bison the US Army began intentionally targeting the animal for a more insidious purpose. They killed it in order to starve the Plains Indians into accepting white authority, to break their ancestral, nomadic hold on the land by severing their ties to its mobile form of sustenance. In his book *The Buffalo Harvest*, US Army colonel and bison hunter Frank Mayer reported a high-ranking officer once saying to him that 'there's no two ways about it, either the buffalo or the Indian must go. Only when the Indian becomes absolutely dependent on us for his every need will we be able to handle him. It seems a more humane thing to kill the buffalo than the Indian, so the buffalo must go.' A scorched-earth policy was enacted. As the great bison herds of America were winnowed down to a thin sliver of their once formidable numbers, native peoples were violently displaced from their familial grounds and forced by necessity onto reservations, with the explicit intent of making them dependent on government handouts. In the process, the word 'Indian' became, without irony, synonymous with 'savage'. In 1874 General Philip Sheridan, the officer primarily tasked with clearing the prairies of Indians, pleaded with the Texas Legislature not to pass a bill that would have outlawed the killing of bison by buffalo-hunters, saying: 'for a lasting peace, let them kill, skin and sell until the buffaloes are exterminated. Then your prairies can be covered with speckled cattle.'

While a journal entry made by one of Cabeza de Vaca's captains during the Spanish expeditions of the 1530s noted that bison were so abundant that his group had to wait a full four days for a herd to finish crossing a river in the Texas and New Mexico region, a railway engineer in 1873 said it was possible to walk a hundred miles along the Santa Fe railroad without touching the earth, by stepping instead from one bison carcass to another.

*

In *My Ántonia*, the final novel of her celebrated prairie trilogy, the American novelist Willa Cather described an enthralling and elemental phenomenon: the way in which wind animates the prairie, transforming it into a beguiling and shifting presence, seemingly autonomous, as though volitional in its desires and unrestrained by the mere biological codes of its inheritance: 'As I looked about me,' she wrote, 'I felt that the grass was the country . . . And there was so much motion in it; the whole country seemed, somehow, to be running.'

Wherever I wandered on the Konza, dipping down into the sheltered gullies or climbing over the rounded grey backs of the limestone hills, I could feel that enlivening spirit alongside me, in the hushed rustling voices of bluestem, cordgrass and Indian grass. Even on the stillest of days a barely perceptible draught would set the grassland momentarily swaying, all the dry stalks of last summer's splendour arching and waving as one.

Cather was born in 1873, and much of her inspiration and intimate knowledge of the prairie stemmed from an absorbing period of time that began a decade later, when her family moved from Virginia to rural Nebraska. She developed a foundational fascination for what remained of the prairie, relishing its weather, horizons and wildlife, one that she cherished for the remainder of her life, even after leaving the grasslands behind and resettling out east again. But it was a prairie, by then, that lacked its iconic animal spirit.

On my desk sit two tokens of the tallgrass. Despite radically different properties, together with an unknown span of time and a state line that separate their sources, the items in all probability share a genetic provenance. The fragment of bone is the size of a school eraser, the same colour and curve as a worn Mediterranean roof tile in miniature. It could be stone the way it feels against my fingers, smoothed over time to a glossy finish. It was fished from the gravelly edge of a prairie creek in Iowa by Camille Meyers, a writer and graduate assistant at Iowa State University. Together with Laura Hitts, a fellow author from the university's Writing and Environment programme, we'd travelled to a parcel of land owned by the institution, where the three of us had been searching for migrating birds in the still-leafless trees. Clear water rippled around a bend when we reached a creek, leaving an exposed gravel bed. Camille scoured the pebbles and riverine debris, talking us through a process for finding fossils. Where water rubs away the sedimentary seams along a river, it exposes fragments and flakes of an older, more abundant, world. Wiping grit from a piece of bone she believed belonged to a bison, its darkness a sign of its antiquity, Camille handed it to me as a gift to take home.

The other memento of the prairie is as yielding to my touch as the bone is inflexible. It's a thatch of bison hair I found snagged on one of the wire fences that keep the animals from straying beyond the boundaries of the Konza Prairie. Resembling a brown scouring pad, it carries a distinctive, outdoors odour – something as earthy and enduring as a forest floor. Such tough, wiry hair helps the bison bear winter so well, adapted to the long periods of ice, blizzards and winds that it faces on the Great Plains, an emblem of its evolutionary resilience and steadfastness in its habitat. But holding these two things in my hands evokes something beyond the physical attributes of the bison's existence; in the span of time that separates them, they remind me that it's possible to replenish the present, to restore a link from the past to the broken and fragmented landscapes of today. To build a bridge where loss has been a chasm.

While figures vary from source to source, the number of bison that remained alive in the United States by 1885 was certainly less than a thousand, and possibly fewer than five hundred, nearly all of them found on private ranches. Of the tens of millions of animals that had roamed the prairies and plains in all their totemic grandeur in 1800, almost none still tracked across the open landscape, the immense thunder of their prodigious herds swiftly turned to a barely audible whisper. A pitiful few survived the slaughter in the wild, including twenty-three that had sheltered in a remote corner of Yellowstone National Park, the only place in the nation to have retained a continuous population of wild bison. Though the

animal's future looked bleak, the passionate efforts of a few committed individuals, as is so often the case, made a remarkable
difference. People like James 'Scotty' Philip, a South Dakotan
rancher and senator known as 'the man who saved the buffalo',
whose letters home to Scotland from the Great Sioux Indian Reservation, where he lived with his Native American wife, Sarah
Larribee, detailed his outrage at the government's treatment of
indigenous people, as he intimately understood the Sioux's reliance
on the bison and the cultural ramifications of its demise. Purchasing
a small herd of bison from a man who'd rescued five calves during
the last major hunt along the Grand River, Philip drove them in
1901 to a pasture he'd prepared in South Dakota with the intention
of preserving the species from extinction. By the time he died suddenly in 1911, Philip's herd had grown to number a thousand, more
than had existed in the entire nation at the nadir of the bison's
plight. Or people like Mary 'Molly' Goodnight, who pleaded with
her rancher husband to save the very last of the prodigious southern bison herd on their Texas Panhandle property. While Charles
Goodnight has received most of the public accolades and historical
acclaim for building a 250-strong herd of bison from the ten to
twenty that had remained, it is his wife Molly who deserves the
greater praise, determinedly rescuing calves orphaned by hunters,
then bottle-feeding and personally attending to them until they'd
reached adulthood. Those herds – the Philips' and the Good-
nights' – went on to play a crucial role in the resurgence of the
bison, being two of the foundation herds that were used to reintro-
duce the land's epic native ungulate to national and state parks.

Since the founding of the American Bison Society by William
Hornaday and President Theodore Roosevelt in 1905, aimed at
the protection and future spread of bison, reintroductions have taken

place across the country and into Canada. The first involved shipping fifteen animals by rail and wagon from the Bronx Zoo to the Wichita Mountains Wildlife Refuge in Oklahoma in 1907, and since then the animal's numbers in the United States have risen to around 500,000, though only 30,000 belong to conservation herds rather than commercial stocks. Seeking a greater expansion of the bison's range and numbers on Indian land, with the concurrent aim of promoting ecosystem restoration alongside cultural and spiritual solidarity, the Inter Tribal Bison Co-operative (now the Inter Tribal Buffalo Council) was formed in 1990, bringing together fifty-six tribes in nineteen different states, representing a collective herd of 15,000 bison. Its former president, Fred DuBray, articulated the co-operative's aims in a PBS documentary called *American Buffalo: Spirit of a Nation*: 'We recognize the bison as a symbol of strength in unity. We believe that reintroduction of the buffalo to tribal lands will help heal the spirit of both the Indian people and the buffalo. To re-establish healthy buffalo populations is to re-establish hope for Indian people.' The bison's modern status remains precarious, compromised by insufficient diversity in its genetic pool, its susceptibility to brucellosis, a disease that was introduced via livestock in the early twentieth century and which causes spontaneous abortions in pregnant females, and its confinement, for the most part, to strictly demarcated properties. But it remains feasible that bison, as with so many animals of all shapes and sizes, could regain even more of their lost place in the world, spreading, with the goodwill of those who now own and manage the land, to terrain they once knew, gradually revivifying a depleted planet.

On one of my last evenings on the Konza I left the cottage as the sun began to slide behind the hills, sending a spray of light upwards into the air. Across the rolling swells of grass, bison could be distinguished by their dark, perambulating forms, an image rendered more poignantly beautiful by their near extinction. Their reintroduction to the Konza Prairie began in 1987, when thirty animals were donated by the Fort Riley Military Reservation, a fitting acknowledgement, I'd like to hope, of the army's complicity in the murderous years of the nineteenth century in Kansas. Together with other donations, purchases and natural reproduction, the Konza herd now totals around 300 bison grazing 2,400 acres of fenced tallgrass.

I climbed a track in their direction, the light draining from the sky. The herd rose diagonally up the slope, both it and I slowly converging on our routes that evening. There were some forty to fifty bison in the herd, the largest congregation I'd been witness to at such close quarters all week. If it wasn't for the fence that separated us I wouldn't have come that near, as bison are amongst the most powerful and unpredictable animals on the planet. Males can weigh up to a thousand kilograms and are capable of reaching speeds of sixty-four kilometres an hour, while also being surprisingly adept at jumping, able to leap to a height of 1.8 metres. Secluded within the coffee-coloured fur are colossal stores of energy that sustain it through winter. And bison move across the land with sure-footed equanimity, anchored to a grassland world that once spread for thousands of miles in all directions. Despite an entire century having elapsed since bison had last inhabited the Konza, the reintroduced animals returned to the buffalo wallows their ancestors had worn smooth, those resonant depressions in the earth that had turned to shallow, grassed-over bowls in their absence.

The nearest bison was now only metres from me. Its dark liquid eyes moved in my direction, and for a few moments the evening stilled before the animal whirled swiftly and kicked uphill as the rest of the herd joined in, a muscular brown torrent heaving across the darkening prairie, the sound of their hooves a thunderous, multitudinous drumming. I actually *felt* the bison as much as saw or heard them, and the whole country seemed, once more, to be running.

*

I woke to heavy rain, banks of low cloud concealing the glass towers and soaring stone edifices of downtown Chicago. I caught a bus that shuttled me past Wrigley Field baseball stadium and through a dense grid of streets and neighbourhoods on the city's North Side. After reaching my stop I walked westward, the rain having eased to a cold drizzle, until I found an elegantly commanding building of dark brickwork, punctuated by high rectangular windows and a shallow portico of pale stone. Originally built as a Masonic lodge in the 1920s, the building has been home to the American Indian Center since 1966, an organization founded in the 1950s to assist native people who'd arrived in Chicago in the wake of the Indian Relocation Act.

The law had been aimed at assimilating American Indians into the wider population by cutting ties to their historic land bases, encouraging them to leave reservations by offering moving expenses, work-clothing grants and vocational training in cities selected specifically by the government. The act triggered a rapid increase in urbanization amongst American Indians, and the Chicago centre was critically situated to forge a pan-Indian sense of community in the midst of the widespread isolation that soon followed as tribal support systems were severed by the exodus. Affordable housing proved to be persistently insecure as it was predominantly located in those urban areas most likely to be slated for demolition and redevelopment by the city, and a chronic lack of meaningful and well-paid employment at the end of the training programmes took its toll on those who had migrated to the cities, sometimes resulting in homelessness and addiction issues. The centre acted as both a haven and a safety net for those who were undone by the Relocation Act, a place where native rights and roles could be reasserted through communal bonds, where dignity could be renewed from within.

I knew a little of this history when I arrived, but I was particularly interested in how the building's external space had proved as invaluable as its interior at forging connections and community in recent years. Slotted between the pedestrian pavement and the building is a sliver of land, little more than three metres wide and around forty in length. In North America, frontage space of this kind is predominantly maintained as neat but lifeless lawn, but that narrow ribbon of earth edging the American Indian Center is radically and joyously different.

A sidewalk prairie garden, it is home to 172 species of plants, grasses, sedges, shrubs and trees native to pre-settlement Illinois, meaning native to prairie, that biologically rich grassland that lends Illinois its colloquial nickname of the 'Prairie State', despite the fact that less than 0.1 per cent of it still exists there. The garden first took root when a group of women in the community seeking medicinal plants seeded the empty space in front of the building. Thus was sown a vision: a restored prairie garden to coincide with the centre's urban ecology programme. And it became a way of rekindling connections between city children and the landscapes of their ancestors if they were descended from prairie tribes, and also a means to encourage understanding of the role of edible, medicinal and ceremonial plants in the lives of all native peoples, many of whom would have little experience of them in their urban upbringings. It was a pathway to restoring lost relationships.

The prairie garden was entering its spring ritual of rise and renewal. I knelt to photograph the white globes of bloodroot on the cusp of opening. It was still cold and damp, but the first purple coneflowers speared the ground and the unfurling white petals of foxglove penstemon resembled the snow that still fell in Chicago in April. But it wouldn't be long before black-eyed Susans raised their yellow heads and the new shoots of little bluestem lanced sunwards to sway in the wind off Lake Michigan. It wouldn't be long before bee balm, sunchoke and goldenrod thrummed with the summer hymns of insects in the city, before thatches of sweet grass and sage could be harvested again, knotted in tight bundles and burned for those ceremonies of old. And it wouldn't be long before goldfinches, fox sparrows and red-crested kinglets took up residence in this unexpected patch of prairie, animating the space with the rhythms of their flight.

With a theatre stage and large halls floored with wood, the centre's interior was an impressive space, hung with tribal flags and banners in an array of colours, symbols and designs. I got talking to Lisa Bernal, a long-term volunteer at the centre and a member of the Sisseton Wahpeton tribe. She spoke with considered wisdom. 'In school they teach you how to write, they teach you how to add, they teach you how to multiply, and they teach you about time. Here we're teaching them why – why we do this, how it will benefit you, what it's done for the animals, what it's done for the Earth, and about respect and the relationships that we have with the Earth.'

It came as no surprise to learn from Lisa that prairie chicken dances were important ritual features of American Indian tribal ceremonies wherever the bird was once found. They had danced its dance because they had shared its world, a kinship of place and ties, where, according to Mojave poet Natalie Diaz, there's little distinction between the land and the body. The narrow garden of the centre seemed emblematic of such alignment. In an essay about his restoration work on it, Dr Eli Suzukovich of the Little Shell Band of Chippewa Cree describes how native youth made 'important connections to land and place through their interactions with the plants and other organisms and their continual return to the garden. By the end of the summer, many youth became protective of the garden and truly claimed it as their space educationally, culturally, and spiritually.' The community had harnessed hope through the act of restoration. Lisa needed to get going. 'I have a friend coming in soon who's bringing in a bunch of seeds, so we'll be spreading some love somewhere!'

I was shown up a flight of stairs to a bare, loft-like space with two desks secluded at one end, where I was greeted by David Bender and Emily Loerzel. In his forties, David identified as Standing Rock Sioux and Big River Chippewa. Having long been involved with native rights issues, he saw the garden as part of his complex identity. 'I do a lot of different things, and gardening is one of those things. There is a spiritual aspect to it, too – we use those medicines, we use that tobacco that we grow, we use that sage that we grow.'

'The garden is another way of trying to preserve and bring back little things that we know in an urban context,' said Emily from the adjacent desk. In her early thirties, Emily identified as White Earth Ojibwe. A former opera singer, she now worked in community liaison at the centre.

'Our people have experienced a great loss of culture and

identity, along with our traditional relationships we have with each other and with land,' said David. 'Loss of language, loss of knowledge. And we're talking about loss from even my parents' generation. My father grew up in an era where he was taught that being Indian was the worst thing you could be. He thought of being Indian as something really ugly and dirty, and he wanted to be anything but Indian. Now with my generation I'm the exact opposite – I feel like being Indian is one of the most important things about who I am, as an identity, and being a father, a parent of two kids. Now I'm up to the point where I feel it's my duty to learn as much as I can about these plants and to pass that on to other kids and to my kids as well.'

'It's our responsibility and our right to bring back our history and our culture and the way that we once were,' added Emily. 'And that's important because, with such devastating loss and inter-generational trauma that occurred throughout the centuries, post-colonization, this is just a very small way that we can . . .' She paused for a few moments, the timbre of her voice suddenly changing when she picked up the thread of her thinking. 'I mean it's gardening and seems so simple, but in reality it's very powerful. This isn't just a way of us maintaining and preserving; this is a way of wellness. That's not to discredit modern medicine, because of course it's very powerful, but it's keeping our plants and our vegetation. And our garden is a beautiful way to supplement and to promote health. How health is and was.'

'And it's more than just a token of what we used to be,' continued David. 'I look at it as who we are, and what made us into the people that we are today. The plants and the kinds of food that our people ate. If you think about it scientifically and evolutionarily, then we are literally the earth that we come from. And then you look at the kinds of health problems that our people have today with diabetes, heart disease, different types of cancers, addictions – so if you look at all those things then you'll be able to understand that the answer is not in a clinic, the answer is out there in the prairie, with those plants and those animals that made our ancestors who they were, because we are our ancestors.'

*

Significant meaning can be invested in place names. Our physical landscapes are partially defined by them, given human credence and imaginative accessibility through the act of description. Cultures throughout the world have employed place names of varying degrees of exactitude and poetry to parse their surroundings for the sake of greater acquaintance – a practical, and sometimes existential, response to the challenges of living in a particular environment. Old English toponyms were typically devoted to the local, to such specifics of the parish where most people lived out their lives as where a river could be forded, or the meeting point of roads. The historically nomadic native peoples of the Arctic, however, required names for a more expansive relationship with the land, one that was primarily dictated by hunting. The Baffin Island Inuit, according to Barry Lopez in *Arctic Dreams*, call Ellesmere Island Oomingman-nuna, meaning the place where 'the muskoxen have their country', illuminating a vastly different scale of geographic consciousness and necessary spatial awareness. Place names have also been used as weapons, as tools of cultural domination and colonial expansion, the linguistic servants of empire, extending dominion through external designations alongside the obliteration of local languages. Occasionally, however, place names have been chosen with solicitous care, to reflect upon what's gone before, or to atone in some small measure for the past. Essential acts in the reshaping of relationships.

Before the Midewin National Tallgrass Prairie was established some forty miles south-west of Chicago in 1996, its lands were known as the Joliet Army Ammunition Dump. Prior to that it had been called the Elwood Ordnance Plant and the Kankakee Ordnance Works. But go back a little further, to the days when Illinois was still a prairie, and those same lands were not only inhabited by the Potawatomi Indians, along with smaller numbers of Ottawa and Ojibway peoples, but were also described by a different set of languages and relationships of use. So when the Joliet Arsenal – as it had colloquially become known – underwent a radical transformation, a new name was needed to recognize its renewal. The US Forest Service – the agency that took charge of the prairie reserve after it was handed over by the military – wished to use a Potawatomi word in honour of the tribe's historic tenancy and rightful claim of spiritual and physical belonging to the landscapes of old Illinois. After contacting the nearest tribes with ancestral, if now scattered, connections to the region – the Citizen Band Potawatomi Indians of Oklahoma and the Prairie Band Potawatomi Tribal Council in Kansas – the Forest Service chose to name the tallgrass prairie Midewin.

Midewin, pronounced Mih-*day*-win, is the name for the Grand Medicine Society of the Anishinaabeg peoples, which include the Potawatomi. Descending from the Potawatomi word *mide*, meaning mystically powerful, it refers to the community of healers who keep Anishinaabeg society in balance, safeguarding the wellbeing of its constituent tribes. As the US Forest Service states in relation to the prairie at Midewin:

These indigenous values are reflected in the current use of the name and represent healing the natural world . . . The US Forest Service recognizes the significance of this Potawatomi name and is committed to its respectful use. We are conscientious in explaining its meaning and acknowledging its importance. We believe that the restoration of the prairie is in keeping with the purpose of the Potawatomi Midewin Society, and our intention is to honor that purpose.

Healing is a potent word. It has the power to rescue hopefulness from hurt, to seal the worst of our wounds and bridge some of the simmering divisions of this world. It evokes a way forward, if not entirely beyond the reach of pain, then at least towards a place where it might be tended to and accommodated. It clears a space for atonement and reconciliation.

Arthur Pearson met me off the train in South Chicago. In his mid-fifties, Arthur was once a prominent actor. His work on the stage, which saw him performing in theatres across the country for the best part of fifteen years, had been primarily Shakespearean, something that finally led to a change in professional direction for him. 'It was a great honour and privilege to inhabit Shakespeare's remarkable and beautiful language for so long,' Arthur said as we drove out of Chicago on our way to Midewin, flurries of snow buffeting the windscreen, 'but I began to feel like there wasn't much more for me to say with his words that he hadn't already said.' This led Arthur to devote more time to his other passions: conservation and restoration.

While restoration frequently carries a domestic or cultural connotation – think of restoring old houses to their original features, or picture restorers working to bring back the intended gleam to a painting or frame – in recent decades it has also come to signify an ecological rehabilitation of damaged lands, a long-term undertaking that enables ecosystems to function again after suffering significant harm and neglect. It's a process of environ-mental healing, a Midewin for many places. Great sprays of little bluestem seeped away to the horizon on either side of the earthen path, its winter tints of red and auburn lending a seasonal light to the prairie. Stalks of big bluestem laddered into the grey sky, rocking in the wind and crackling like summer fire when they collided. Through Arthur's keen and intimate knowledge the land slowly began to reveal its aspects, contours and customs to me. Working for the Gaylord and Dorothy Donnelley Foundation, an organization that aims to support, celebrate and encourage con-servation and the arts, believing that 'natural lands – preserved and restored on a landscape scale – are critical to the wellbeing of wildlife, plant life, and human communities', he was an engaging guide to place. Discussing the historic loss of tallgrass prairie, Arthur employed a metaphor that remains to this day the most effective and striking I've yet heard for conjuring a visible under-standing of the scale of the grasslands' lessening.

'If you take a 25,000-square-foot house that was once all prairie, all you now have left of it is a four-inch by four-inch tile in the kitchen. But to be truly accurate,' he said, 'you'd have to take that tile and smash it into little pieces which you threw to the winds.'

What's left of the tallgrass has turned up in unlikely spots, found in fragments along railway embankments where a grassland verge was left clear in a previous century, or discovered in scattered pion-eer cemeteries, where the men, women and children who'd once moved westward were lowered into the earth in the shadow of native flowers and grasses before the encircling prairies were all gone. It's lingered on in small, neglected pockets and forgotten corners of the land, all those places that, through foresight, coincidence or circumstance, were pardoned from the plough. These relicts are all the more essential for their rarity, living examples of one of the richest ecosystems ever to grace the planet.

But at Midewin a plan was in process to regain some of what has been lost; to enlarge, through both vision and land, what prairie might mean today. Ecological restoration is a complex issue, eloquently synthesized and explored in Paddy Woodworth's *Our Once and Future Planet*, which succinctly details the benefits, optimism and problems of the task, including the absolutely essential need to communicate and find common ground with the communities that use and live in or around the places proposed for restoration, especially when local people value the non-native species or cultural facets embedded in the contemporary landscape. Rarely are our great attachments to place founded on ecological purity, but are instead fostered through a love of the way a place exists in people's everyday experience. Considerable care is needed to chart a sensitive course, or run the risk of alienating local communities and undermining their essential support.

At Midewin, the plan was to restore the ecological systems and processes of its 20,000 acres to a historical point prior to its utilization for agriculture and armaments. While many of its hundreds of munitions bunkers still remain, some to be retained after the restoration as a reminder of its other historic legacy, it's hard to imagine what the Joliet Arsenal felt like in its heyday. Unlike Lodge Hill in Kent, the military activities on this site left ruined ground in their wake. During the Second World War alone, according to journalist Erin Gallagher after interviewing Midewin archaeologist Joe Wheeler, the 'ammunition plant produced a billion pounds of high explosives, 26 million 105-mm artillery shells, 43.7 million T N T demolition blocks, 6.5 million anti-tank mines and 1.2 million bombs ranging in size from 250 to 4,000 pounds each'. A period of closure ensued at the end of the conflict, before the ammunition dump was reopened during the wars in both Korea and Vietnam. The prairie has filled in those spaces now, leaving a few ghostly presences of the work carried out there. Instead of a landscape of railcars being loaded with ordnance to be shipped out or stored in bunkers, and 10,000 workers bending to their tasks, Arthur and I walked a space of wetlands and prairie, a half-dozen Wilson's snipe exploding from the clear skin of a marsh, crackling like live wires as they hurtled into the distance, their fleeting forms eclipsed by sudden snow. In their wake burbled the beautiful songs of chorus frogs, a watery score that could be heard across the grasslands long after we'd left their pools behind. As with other restorationists I've spoken to, Arthur viewed ecology as extending beyond the land itself. 'It will have brought out the best in us,' he said when describing the act of remaking Midewin. 'In some fundamental sense we restore land and something in us is restored.'

But that act of restoring is pinned to a process, a journey that asks you to witness the land looking far worse than it once did before it eventually improves. 'Like any restoration,' said Arthur, 'whether it's my house or this prairie, it's gonna look ugly before it gets better.' I could already sense the names and colours to come: smooth blue aster, prairie ironweed and goldenrod; black-eyed Susan, wild indigo and prairie blazing star. Their summer sway of mauves and bruised blues amidst the leaning spires of grass, the flashes of carmine, lemon and rose, all taking hold of the prairie again. But this lush appearance will have been preceded by a plain of raw buckled earth, when the underlying drainage tiles of the agricultural fields and arsenal were removed in their thousands, and backhoes and bulldozers scoured away a layer of contaminated earth. And it occurred to me then, seeing this radically altered landscape, that restoration, in its broadest sense, is another form of resistance, a literal digging in, as the allotment holders at Farm Terrace had shown me, on behalf of the worth and possibilities – both present and hopefully to come – of a place that matters. It's a further formulation of defiance against loss, an act of solidarity beyond a purely human dimension, but deeply communal, too. Alongside soil scientists and restoration ecologists, projects of this nature are critically reliant on volunteers, those who devote their spare time to getting their hands dirty, doing the necessary and back-breaking labour that healing the land demands, the unsung work of seeding, weeding and hauling invasive brush away, investing their free hours in actions that may not see fruition until a time well beyond their own. Tracing the possibility of a place through the collective belief in its value, Arthur said that it represented the 'hopefulness and creativity and imagination of people'. He continued as we began walking again. 'We've destroyed so much, but can heal some of it as well.'

Arthur and I followed a meadowlark at a distance as it swung between shivering stalks of big bluestem, the bird's native pedestals for its season of song. In sporadic but bitter snow, the meadowlark was the bearer of sun that day, the yellow purse of light on its breast gleaming through the gloomy hours as it sang. The whole place seemed to move with the spirit of new beginnings.

'One of the challenges for such large restorations is seed,' said Arthur as he showed me some of the plots where plants were raised and painstakingly harvested by hand. 'But in a way there's nothing more gratifying than coming along like an old-time farmer and stripping seed from the stalks.' All those remnant prairies, fragments like the Konza scattered far and wide across that former sea of grass, were suddenly magnified in their significance – the need for their preservation as critical for the endurance of other places as the value and worth of their own. They were the source of those new beginnings, the essential link between past and present. Restorations throughout the Midwest have used their seed, particularly when found in close geographical proximity, in order to maintain local and genetic character, sowing the prospects of future places into the greater tapestry of the land.

Restoration doesn't negate the ethic of preservation, however. It should be seen primarily as making good on old debts. Irreplaceable native grasslands were the unique result of intimate interactions between plant communities, soils, climate, native peoples, bison, wind and fire over the course of 12,000 years. Nothing in our lifetimes could ever come close to the intricate layers of prairie richness and meaning that only time and the right conditions can achieve. Instead, restoration is a way of healing what's already been harmed, a way of reclaiming lost habitats and enabling wildlife to thrive for its own sake rather than ours. And it is a way, according to Arthur, 'to preserve, protect, honour and respect our ecological heritage. We've pushed this landscape to the limit,' he continued, 'and to have this vision that it could heal is to see the full circle that it has travelled.' Already there was talk of reintroducing prairie chickens to Midewin at some point in the future as well, allowing that ancestral dance of theirs to unfold in this place once more.

I'd seen a small world in the process of returning, all those prairie roots going down again, drilling deep into the dark Illinois earth as people remake the tallgrass that was taken. Before leaving we stood on a knoll in the chill winds to watch bison that had been released onto the land. To see them foraging in a sunken dip of grassland just outside of Chicago, an image of majestic and inimitable presence, was to witness the possibility of restitution. It was proof that the actions of individuals and organizations can alter the balance of shared value, expanding it to include lands and animals as part of our fragile yet irreplaceable inheritance, the sustaining foundation to the greater meaning of the name Midewin.

10

The Nest Protectors

And though hope can be an act of defiance, defiance isn't enough reason to hope.

~ Rebecca Solnit, *Hope in the Dark*

The Pakke River was slung low in its bed, a wide cradle of stones that would rock with wild winds and water during the monsoon season beginning in June. But in early March, at the tail end of the Indian winter, the river needled like a kingfisher through the hills, its narrow blue flow marking the border between the Pakke Tiger Reserve to its west and the Papum Reserve Forest to the east. Rising in emerald tiers from the river plain, the reserve forest is the homeland of a Nyishi community, a tightly bound tribal people who inhabit the jungle in small scattered settlements. In 1977, when the western flank of the waterway was designated as a game sanctuary, eventually becoming a tiger reserve in 2002, a number of Nyishi villages were relocated by the government from inside the newly marked exclusion zone, transferred to the far side of the dividing line and their inhabitants given in recompense incongruous concrete homes that had little in common with the inventive and adaptable qualities of the Nyishi's vernacular bamboo architecture. But like so much of what I was to learn during time spent with the Nyishi, these borders of separation, whether between landscapes of designated use or the lives and needs of both human and non-human animals, are considerably less definitive and enforceable in the living world. More often than not they are porous, fluid and blurred.

To reach Pakke, you rise off the hazy Assamese plains into a world of poured water and sharply defined hills, the stirred verdancy of Arunachal Pradesh's rippling ranges. Set in the wider geographical region of the Himalayan flood plain, which includes two internationally recognized biodiversity hotspots, supporting nearly 8,000 flowering plants, over 600 bird species and some 150 mammals, including such totemic megafauna as Bengal tigers, elephants and leopards, the most northerly tropical rainforests on the planet are threaded by cascading waters into a tapestry of fertile and diverse beauty. Pressed tight against the borders of Bhutan, Tibet, China and Myanmar, the state is also a land of ancient trackways, human communities having travelled there from those surrounding regions long ago. Home to twenty-four main tribes and 110 subtribes, Arunachal Pradesh is a tableau of ethnic diversity, though many of the tribes share attributes of identity, from commonalities found in their languages to cultural practices and spiritual principles, crossovers that are the result of historically pooled lines of descent and broadly animist beliefs.

Many stories are caught up in the flow of the Pakke River. For all of its slender tendencies at this time of year, its plains are a more accurate measure of its oscillatory moods. Spread out beneath the forested hills, and percolated with the accumulated fertility of minerals and rich topsoil rinsed downwards by monsoon rains, they are a tangible record of recent livelihood. The raised earthen borders of hundreds of agricultural plots and rice paddies clearly marked their surface, but instead of being able to identify millet, mustard, turmeric, ginger, maize, tobacco or coriander, all I could see were clumps of bird-rich scrub and tangled thickets of trees, as the plots slowly but irrevocably eroded into wild riverside again. Arriving on the heel of several inundations, which had grown increasingly violent and common in the valley, a flash flood in 2004 swept away a year's worth of sustenance in mere hours. Those devastating flood waters, however, were just the final notes in the demise of agricultural subsistence for the Nyishi, the coda of their river-plain cultivations. The community had reluctantly already begun to relinquish the land to elephants.

While the nine tigers of the reserve – a significant number for the 872 square kilometres of the park's territory – are the emblematic animals of the forested hill country, elephants are easily the wider region's most dominant, non-human mammal. Their dung turns up on forest paths near the Nyishi villages as regularly as sheep droppings in the Yorkshire Dales, and from the moment I arrived I was warned to be careful while out walking. 'You have one of two choices if you meet an elephant,' said an elderly Nyishi man. 'Climbing a tree or running. Neither of which is very good.' These forest creatures aren't as habituated to human presence as some Indian elephant populations, so they can be particularly aggressive when feeling threatened or unexpectedly confronted in their home territories. Stories of death by elephant in Pakke, of both villagers and park rangers, were especially poignant because of the prodigious local respect shown to these wild and sensitive behemoths. But while the Nyishi have long lived together with the elephant, a period of regular crop raids, when the animals even began consuming a root crop that until then they had always left untouched, coupled with the mounting destruction from floods, finally forced the community into retreat from their rice paddies and plots. No amount of staying up all night on rickety bamboo platforms, riskily confronting intruding pachyderms by firing rifle blanks into the darkness to scare them away, was worth what they received in return from the earth. The Nyishi are a people who live at the very crossroads of human and wild-animal trajectories, conjoined in a place where co-existence isn't merely a theory or philosophy, but a daily and often difficult part of being there.

*

Chukhu Loma had an idea of potentially transformative power. As with so many daring thoughts and suggestions that necessitate a decisive break with tradition, asking us to rethink patterns that feel true because they're so deeply ingrained in all that we do, he was nervously uncertain about the reaction it would trigger from fellow members of his tribe. But as a forest officer for the Pakke Tiger Reserve, Chukhu had been witness to an unfolding ecological and cultural tragedy. From his unique vantage point – Nyishi in ethnicity but also a government official responsible for the conservation of forests and their wildlife – he clearly saw how the continued hunting of hornbills outside the protected confines of the reserve was placing unsustainable pressure on the four species found in the region. The core of the park, he'd come to concede, could no longer replenish its peripheries. Unless a radical change in hunting practices could be encouraged amongst his people, the long-term survival of Arunachal Pradesh's official state bird couldn't be guaranteed.

The hornbill has considerable cultural resonance for the Nyishi. They associate it, especially the great hornbill, with qualities bordering on the spiritual; a wild species that is essential to their tribal identity, customs and beliefs. The incomparable aspect of its anatomy that distinguishes most hornbill species from other birds on the planet, the beautiful and often brilliantly tinted appendage called a casque that rides atop its upper bill, confers ceremonial significance through its use in traditional head-dresses worn by male members of the tribe. Through the Nyishi the casque moves from the crown of one creature to that of another, a passage of substantial ritualized meaning for the community, but one that has increasingly come to compromise the existence of the revered birds themselves.

Known as a *bopia*, the Nyishi head-dress is an upturned bowl of densely woven cane that fits snugly against the skull, displaying a prominent tuft of bear fur at its front. There was some disagreement amongst those Nyishi I spoke with as to whether the *bopia* had historically been worn only by those of high status in the community, such as village elders, or whether it was common for all men to don one, but in the days when tribal males wore long hair, this tuft was instead fashioned from a knot of their forward-combed locks. The fur piece, called the *podum*, is bound with thick coils of turquoise, lemon or verdigris thread and held in place by a long silver needle. Behind the *podum*, and tilted backwards on the wearer's head, angles the orange and yellow casque and upper bill of a hornbill. Unlike the commonly seen Nyishi machete, kept in a scabbard typically adorned with the fur of Asiatic black bear or the capped langur monkey, the head-dress is predominantly reserved for ceremonial or celebratory events these days. But these two items – the machete, which is carried daily into the jungle for practical purposes, and the *bopia*, ritually signifying membership of the tribe – are inseparable elements of Nyishi identity.

The Nyishi employed several methods to procure hornbills from the forest, including bow and arrow, guns, and a resin daubed on regularly frequented tree branches, which gummed up a hornbill's feathers to the point that it was unable to fly. And it was this killing of hornbills to harvest the casque, alongside the degradation of primary forest in the region, that was having a crippling effect on the bird's population. But Chukhu Loma had a vision for retaining the tribe's unique customs, while simultaneously preserving the hornbill that was so meaningful to the community, by fashioning a facsimile of the casque to adorn the head-dress. Not unsurprisingly, his suggestion was met with both anger and ridicule from many of his people. He was accused of betrayal, but Chukhu persisted nonetheless, unwilling to abandon his idea just because it proved unpopular at first. He explained his reasoning and appealed to his fellow tribespeople's historic sense of respect for the environment until, following a slow and steady accretion of assent, the tribal elders agreed to his proposal.

So popular has his vision become that a variety of replica bills have now been constructed from fibreglass, wood and clay. Working together with the Wildlife Trust of India (WTI), Chukhu and the Forestry Department implemented a conservation model that works on the premise of exchange, handing out a replica hornbill casque to anyone who turned in an original head-dress. As the originals were prone to rapid deterioration, swiftly losing their glossy colour in the absence of the fatty secretion which is regularly applied by the living hornbill, there was the added incentive of durability to the trade.

Rinku Gohain, an elephant veterinarian working out of Pakke Tiger Reserve for the WTI, invited me to see some of the originals, alongside their facsimiles. He handed me a casque made of clay that his organization was experimenting with. It was too heavy and fragile in comparison to the fibreglass version to be ultimately successful, he reckoned, but it revealed just how beautiful these duplicates could be when made with the right material. The finish was exquisite, a sunset smear of orange worked into the lemony yellow curve. Rinku then opened a cardboard box and decorated the veranda steps of his office with some of the recently exchanged casques once belonging to the hornbills of these forests. In the afternoon sunlight he lined them up beside handed-in strips of Asiatic black bear and capped langur monkey fur from the scabbards of machetes. There was a sad beauty to the assembly, the dry dusty patina of the past alongside the odd elegance of the evolutionary shape not completely undone by death and deterioration. Amidst the crumbling casque helmets persisted a faded splendour, deepened by the gleaming clay replicas beside them. Seen together, they were a pairing of paths, a reflection of the choices being made by members of the Nyishi, inner transformations turned tangible and real. In each of the tribal homes I would visit in Pakke I saw one of the artificial *bopias*; against the odds, they had become as resonant and real as the originals.

*

The great hornbill collapses its wings like the folds of an accordion being squeezed free of air. Its close presence is revelatory – and overwhelmingly beautiful. Hidden behind a rough hide of bamboo and cut leaves, I'm at eye-height with the enormous bird, secluded on a level plane because its nesting tree is rooted well down the slope to my side. With its metre-and-a-half span of wings now folded away, the long fan of its white tail, wrapped by a single black band at its lower end, helps balance its great heft. A buttery blush spreads over its head, as though it had flown upwards through a summer haze of pollen and anointed its feathers with grains of gold. Its eyes shine darkly red, like a pair of garnets. And its bill, the bird's most unique and flamboyant feature, has a great scything extravagance to it, a sweeping blend of tangerine and lemon on the upper curve contrasted by a creamy white on the lower, capped with that desirable, kingly casque.

Hornbills nest in remarkable fashion. After choosing a suitable tree cavity, the female enters and proceeds to entomb herself within, applying a seal that she's mixed together from a recipe of mud, dung and spit that will bake hard in the jungle heat and last the duration of the breeding season. And there, inside the cavity, for the four months that raising her young demands on average, and during which time she'll moult into an entirely new set of feathers, she'll lay eggs, incubate, feed and tend to her chicks until they're ready to fly free, finally breaking the seal to enable their escape. All that remains of her connection to the outside world is a single narrow slit, allowing a creak of sunlight to enter the chamber as in a prehistoric barrow.

Aparajita Datta has studied these birds in Pakke since beginning her PhD in the mid-1990s. 'Arunachal Pradesh is really the last haven for hornbills for the five species that occur in north-east India,' she said as we sat together in one of the Nyishi villages. 'We've done surveys across many of the other states in the north-east and the situation is really bad. They survive in little pockets, little islands, which are very small protected areas.' Now working for the Nature Conservation Foundation (NCF), an Indian environmental organization committed to developing partnerships with local communities where species are threatened, Aparajita had watched the process of large-scale change unfold from day to day, including the rapid levelling of forests on the Assamese side of the border when the Bodo tribe laid claim to a huge expanse of land during their armed insurgency. 'Basically, I saw that forest go while I was doing my PhD research around Pakke,' she said.

The great hornbill swings its head towards the cavity of the tree. The female, clearly hungry and alert to his presence, dips the tip of her bill through the gap. Having spent the previous hour or two searching the jungle canopy for ripe fruit, the male begins to feed his mate through that thin connecting window. Hornbills have a long-term investment in the way they forage and feed. Combing a diet of fruit from the forest, they're reliant on the fecundity, density and diversity of its arboreal life forms. Fruit makes up anywhere from 75–100 per cent of an Asian hornbill's diet and, depending on the hornbill species, can consist of between thirty and forty different types within a single year. Such variety is partly the result of the birds' need to maintain nutritional balance, and partly because the seasonal availability of fruit necessitates foraging from a wide range of tree species. The birds' presence is inextricably linked to the productivity and timing of local flora, and without a healthy, diverse forest, they'll struggle to survive.

Over time, hornbills increase their species' chances of survival by acting as seed dispersers within the landscape. Known to both ecologists and local people as 'gardeners of the forest', they are directly involved in the maintenance and rejuvenation of the jungle. Swallowing fruit whole, the birds digest the edible outer layer, called the aril, leaving the seed itself undamaged. And while small seeds, such as those of the myriad fig species found in tropical forests, pass through the digestive system to be later defecated, these larger seeds, which can reach sizes of four centimetres or more in length, are rinsed clean by stomach acids, regurgitated and then spat out, often some considerable time later and a great distance from the parent tree. Aparajita had recorded eighty-five species of tree fruit in the collective diet of Pakke's different hornbills during her work. 'They disperse around 30 per cent of the tree species that are known here,' she added. Some of those fruit seeds, journeying in the bellies of the hornbills as they glide through the forest canopy, will eventually break ground as saplings. And of those young shoots, a few will go on to replenish the forest as mature fruit trees, providing further forage for the extended lineage of the hornbills that seeded them, while simultaneously creating important resources for nearby human communities.

The male hornbill tilts his head away from the nest and then snaps it swiftly forward, as though releasing the taut rubber band of a slingshot, catapulting a single fruit upwards from his stored hoard. It rolls down the runnel of his lower bill until he snares the moving fruit at the inflexible tip of his beak, holding it there with balletic dexterity. As the female nudges towards the light, the hornbill swings his head towards the slender gap in the nest seal, placing that single piece of fruit – foraged, swallowed, ferried, regurgitated and gifted – into her waiting bill. Having fed her the first one, he retracts his head as if rearming the slingshot, coughing up another jewel of a fruit from his forest stash and rolling it to the tip of his bill. Piece after piece he gently feeds to his mate – ranging from a tiny scarlet berry to a striking black fruit the size of a date – making this unusual method of nesting possible for the species.

Such striking delicacy is a reminder of the importance of relationships. It is believed that hornbills are monogamous throughout their long lives, and the interaction between the two echoes the essential connection between these birds and the fruitfulness of forests. Everything in the jungle is connected with everything else, something David George Haskell describes in his beautiful book *The Songs of Trees*, exploring the interactions and reciprocity of ties, remarking that 'human lives and tree lives are made, always, from relationship'. Without a close affiliation with other things, we will always be less than what we could possibly be.

*

Great hornbill, *paga*. Wreathed hornbill, *pou*. Oriental pied hornbill, *gare*. Rufous-necked hornbill, *puyo*. I asked Suresh Pait to explain the meaning of the Nyishi words that Takum Nabum and Papi Tayem spoke aloud for each of the hornbill species found in Pakke. It's hard to imagine a more generous spirit than Suresh's. A teacher in one of the village schools, his great shining smile and frequent deep laughter were equalled in appeal only by his sincere and tireless commitment to this place and its wildlife and people.

At the outdoor dinner table that night, lit by two of the solar-powered lamps that were an essential feature of all households owing to the chronic and long-lasting power cuts in the region, Suresh, Takum and Papi began laughing while sifting through possible meanings of the word *paga*. They broke into rapid Nyishi and then Hindi, which Suresh attempted to translate in between bouts of giggles. Finally, he whispered, 'We think it might mean *on top of*.' Takum concurred with a quick nod, his paan-stained lips widening to a red smile, adding 'we think' to reinforce the uncertainty of the definition. Papi slapped her hands against her legs with delight. What followed was a tumultuous convergence of voices, all loudly debating whether 'on top of' might relate to the great hornbill's pinnacle position amongst the birds for the tribe, or whether it could be connected to the placement of the casque on top of one's head when donning the ceremonial head-dress. 'Maybe,' said Suresh, barely able to speak through the tears of his hysteria. 'Maybe,' chimed Takum, again mimicking Suresh's English. Their laughter was clearly in response to another interpretation, but whatever it might have been they didn't share it.

Of course, the Nyishi could be deadly serious as well, an essential capacity when inhabiting a landscape that requires as much caution and care as theirs. Rarely armed with anything more deadly than a machete, they're reliant on a sensory understanding of the forest and its innumerable sounds and felt atmospheres to keep them clear of animal confrontations, carrying a complex mental map with them, three-dimensional in form and filled in with the shared cultural memory of the tribe's interactions with the other-than-human world. They understand the patterns of wild pathways, where and when a particular creature commonly moves, and how its behaviour might be predicted at different times of the day, season or year, recalling timings and tendencies, personalities and predilections. A comprehensive relationship with their surroundings has been imperative to the Nyishi for as long as they've existed; their original animism, the precursor to the Christianity that the tribe has largely converted to in recent times, would have flourished from such ecological correspondences. When I asked Suresh what the foundational beliefs of the Nyishi would have been prior to conversion, he raised his hands to the sky and smiled his usual, beaming grin. 'Nature, of course.'

Nature, and its conservation, was at the heart of another local initiative: the foundation of the Ghora-Aabhe Society. Roughly translating as 'council of village elders', the Ghora-Aabhe Society was formed in 2006 with the encouragement of Tana Tapi, the Pakke Tiger Reserve's chief forest official, who has been instrumental in forging ties between the park and its near communities, to the benefit of both, bringing together the *gaonburahs*, or village heads, from each settlement in a formal arrangement that has enabled them to advocate for conservation in the region as a respected group of elders. Takum was the chairperson of the society. 'The Ghora-Aabhe Society is a model that is based on the customary laws of the Nyishi,' he said when I asked him to describe the purpose of the council. 'Unlike NGOs, which depend on a specific species, or which depend on the funding you have relative to that project, this is something that we have started voluntarily, irrespective of funding.'

Along with enforcing laws on illegal timber felling and poaching, the Ghora-Aabhe Society raises awareness about environmental issues throughout the region, and ties them to a social welfare fund critical to these remote settlements. Money raised through their eco-tourism initiatives goes towards such basic educational needs as pencils and blackboards, as well as workshops for women in the community to explore self-help initiatives and possibilities for livelihood.

Under Indian law, these villages, some of which were relocated by the government from the tiger reserve in the first place, shouldn't even exist. The state's Forest Act makes it clear that no one should be living in the buffer zone forests, and yet, 'For the people here,' said Suresh, 'this is their land.' An issue still unresolved by the government, this indeterminate status has resulted in an enormous amount of uncertainty in the lives of the Nyishi, which makes the Ghora-Aabhe Society's efforts all the more remarkable given the reasoning behind its founding. 'When we were moved here,' said Takum, 'we thought, *OK, we've given to conservation but we've not had any community welfare*. We thought that Pakke Park should be saved, but for conservation to happen there and in the surrounding forests you also have to take the community along. If we didn't continue conservation, then what was the point of giving up our land?'

*

As we'd climbed through the jungle to reach the great hornbill nest, passing towering cauliflorous figs, whose green fruit erupted from their trunks and stout branches like Brussel sprouts on a stem, Pahi Tachang would occasionally flash a tender smile in my direction before his face resolved once again into a mask of enigmatic blankness. So detached did he at times appear that Pahi could have been elsewhere, but after a while in his company I understood that this was just his way of channelling a sensitive attention to the world around him. I watched how he navigated the forest with an active openness to its edible and medicinal properties, relating stories of important leaves, roots and stems through the intimate prism of Nyishi needs. He showed me a tree he called *doona*, whose bark is stripped away so that a resin begins to exude from its flesh. Once collected, the sap is allowed to harden, after which it's burned to keep mosquitoes, carriers of malaria in the region, at bay. The jungle was a composite place for him – home to the wildlife he clearly cared about, as well as a larder, pharmacy and timber store for his people.

Around fifty years old, Pahi has been instrumental in the work of hornbill conservation around Pakke. He is *gaonburah* of Mobuso 2, a remote settlement of just four houses reached by a juddering drive up the rocky riverbed. Back in 2010, Pahi and a fellow *gaonburah*, Tajek Wage, decided to invite themselves to a gathering of Indian and foreign visitors who were meeting to discuss the tiger reserve and associated environmental issues. The two Nyishi men, after a lifetime within the forests – which for Pahi included being relocated outside the park boundaries when he was young – understood that while the park was relatively well protected, the reserve forest continued to suffer terribly from hornbill hunting and habitat degradation. And so that day they sought ways of co-ordinating with the Forestry Department in the stewardship of the jungles outside the remit of the tiger reserve. Until that time there had been little work carried out on the status of hornbills outside the park, though they all knew the birds were seamlessly using both spaces, crossing the boundary waters of the Pakke River, something I experienced one evening when the birds emptied the green canopy of the tiger reserve, journeying east as darkened silhouettes, the great dipping sun drenching the abandoned floodplain in burnt orange light as they set off to roost near the Nyishi villages. 'It's a continuum for them,' said Aparajita.

'Compared to when I was a young boy,' said Pahi, 'people don't see great hornbills. Either they've disappeared or declined in number. In Pakke Kasang, a more northern area, in my youth, my father's generation basically, I used to see many more great hornbills.' The shifting baseline of biodiversity isn't confined to the industrialized and intensively farmed countries of the West, but is found wherever ecological pressures exist, which covers just about everywhere these days. 'Slowly we've decimated the population. Future generations will not see them like we did. So that's why we need to protect them.'

An idea was seeded that day when Pahi and Tajek spoke with the assembled visitors; one that has grown to compelling proportions. At its simplest, it's about hunters becoming protectors, turning away from a traditional practice in order to guard against further depletions and the diminishment of the shared jungle. But like any decision of such magnitude, it concerns so much more than a definition: it's about altering one's way in the world. Agreeing to work without a salary for a year, the three original nest protectors – Pahi, Tajek and Budhiram Tai – combed the reserve forests in search of hornbill nests, each find worth 1,000 rupees (about £11) that Aparajita, on behalf of NCF, would pay them as an honorarium. Awareness drives were simultaneously launched by the Ghora-Aabhe Society, which travelled to all the

Nyishi villages in the valleys and hills of western Arunachal Pradesh, raising support for the project as well as warning against the threat of the local extinction of hornbills and illegal poaching and logging in general.

The original notion of locating and documenting nests in the reserve forest was just the first step in a transformative vision that eventually grew into a fully fledged and ongoing project run by the NCF called the Hornbill Nest Adoption Programme. It is premised on the concept of shared parenting, whereby donors, from individuals to institutions, can adopt and sponsor a hornbill nest for a small sum of money, the proceeds helping to pay for the salaries and equipment of the nest protectors and the project's administration. A total of sixteen nest protectors now monitor their own specific tracts of the reserve forest, locating nests and recording data about the sites and breeding status of the birds, while also guarding against the illegal logging of the nesting trees and the poaching of wild animals. The project is critically hinged to local concerns, and it works because its conservationists are those who know the forests intimately.

At the weekly meeting of the nest protectors, conducted on a bamboo platform looking down over the Pakke River and its broad plain under a sky of pale turquoise, I watched the gathered guardians – ranging in age from their early twenties to seventy – submit their data from the previous week. Respectfully removing sandals at the foot of the bamboo steps, each nest protector had travelled from his or her village to meet Devathi Parashuram, the NCF's local co-ordinator, who inputted the data she was given. She also downloaded still images and video clips taken by the nest protectors, each of them having been given a camera to help record hornbill activity, which had already led to footage of rarely recorded behaviour in the wild.

Long discussions about illegal logging unfolded as the data were being gathered. While small-scale harvesting of forest resources is an elemental aspect of the Nyishi way of life, large-scale commercial extraction was made illegal in 1996. But on one of my walks through the jungle the sound of chainsaws followed me like a lost dog all morning. Organized by a few local people, who transport labourers over the border from Assam to carry out the physical work, such commercial felling places the nest protectors in a precarious position. Not only are they from the same tribal community, but they could be relatives of those ordering the felling. When I asked them about those responsible, the nest protectors said that it was only people on civil service contracts for the local government who were able to afford logging equipment and hire labour – meaning, in their opinion, that it was the people least in need of supplemental income in their community who broke the customary laws upheld by the Ghora-Aabhe Society. It's simply about 'greed and not need', said one of the men during the meeting, acknowledging the tensions when he described a recent confrontation during which loggers vowed to cut down hornbill nesting trees if the nest protectors continued to prevent them from carrying out their tasks.

Once the work of the meeting was completed, Devathi offered to translate my questions. In her late twenties, Devathi was a calm presence on the bamboo platform; she wore a flower-printed yellow shirt that seemed to reflect the tranquillity with which she dealt with the simultaneous queries and submissions from the circle of gathered protectors. Originally from Bangalore, she now lived in a Nyishi village for most of the year, and clearly had the group's respect. She was not only immediately likeable but also disarmingly honest and self-effacing about her role, both in conservation in general and in her specific work with local people. 'My parents have just arrived from Bangalore and I'm terrified,' she said with a bubble of laughter. 'They really are city people, and for them it's all been very abstract.

They just think I walk around in a forest all day. I think they're starting to understand what I do. When we go nest monitoring I bring bread and butter and we end up using the machete to spread the butter. I never imagined I would ever be doing that!'

Asking the nest protectors about the relationship between their people and the hornbill, I learned that while hornbills were traditionally hunted for their casques and for food it was also considered taboo to kill a male during the breeding season, especially if the female was sealed inside the tree cavity. Even amongst the more circumspect young, a strong belief existed that bad luck, or even death, would be the consequence of such a crime.

The jungle is a multitudinous world. 'Even today,' said Devathi, 'when I was recording someone's data, I said, *Oh, why have you only gone twice this week?* And he said, *The other day when we went there were elephants, and there were baby elephants as well, so they were very aggressive.* And so they had to run from them.' Only a few days later we would be silently stalked and chased by an adult elephant in the tiger reserve, and the mind-emptying sound of the park's Nyishi guard cocking his ancient rifle and yelling *Run, run, run!* will stay with me for ever. The composite quality of the jungle demands a necessary attentiveness from the tribe that closely resembles grace, a refinement of body, mind, spirit and senses born of the intimacy of having known its spaces since birth. 'I went to the forest with Tajek Wage recently, who is now seventy years old,' continued Devathi, 'and I have all my trekking gear on and hiking boots. And he comes barefoot, moving so fast and knowledgeably in the forest. And some of these nests are really hard to get to, going down steep slopes and scaling heights. I'm on all fours, like no dignity whatsoever. And Tajek's just walking up – he finds the perfect footholds and gets down so easily while I'm sliding on my butt!' This ease in the jungle is part of the reason the nest protection project has been so fruitful. Between 2012 and 2017, 40 nests were protected in the reserve forest, helping 103 hornbill chicks to fledge, a particularly notable figure considering that not all the nests are active every year and that great hornbills and wreathed hornbills typically raise only a single offspring in a breeding season. These gains might eventually result in the long-term growth of hornbill populations outside of the park, and the stabilization of those within its confines. And, in time, through the respectful deepening of the relationships between humans, hornbills and jungle, it could mean the renewal and preservation of a forest home for all.

*

We rolled through Nyishi country along dirt roads. Boys and girls walked dry riverbeds and earthen paths on their way to school. An elderly woman wore a great latticed basket in the shape of a tortoise shell on her back, crammed full of firewood to use for cooking and cold nights. Leaving the motorcycles outside the bamboo home of Taring Tachang, we descended into a world of running waters, the backcountry of the raised villages.

Takum had told me that the primary incentive and motivation for the Ghora-Aabhe Society's involvement in conservation was the community's youth, and so I had set out with Taring and Tajek Tachang – both in their mid-twenties – to learn about their work as nest protectors. We walked through countless creeks and streams that morning, stepping across a great fan of tributary waters broken by hilly spurs and ridges. From each sliver of shining water we'd rise through jungle before dropping down again to another silver bend in the bottoms, where minnows flashed away like sunlight off the windows of a passing train. As the morning steamed with tropical heat, Taring led us through this braided world with ease, knowing this place of his with the sureness of a language learned since birth.

Tajek and Taring were a study in opposites. Where Tajek was cerebral, fascinated by the minutiae of the hornbills' lives and behaviour, Taring was physical, relying on bodily strength and craftwork in his connection to the land. Tajek, who tapped the white swoosh on the side of his baseball cap when I asked him about the traditional *bopia*, saying he much preferred Nike to Nyishi when it came to headwear, was the only male member of the tribe I met who didn't carry a machete; Taring, on the other hand, used his extensively, slashing and carving clear our route where stray vines and saplings had encroached on the path. While Tajek was buoyant, joyful and companionable, Taring carried a burden alongside his fluency with land, a weight that he bore silently through the jungle.

In the morning heat, butterflies glimmered over the streams as if pulled from a kiln in tones unique to each firing, tangling together in a deep well of light. Eventually we reached a vast *behlu* tree (*Tetrameles nudiflora*), distinguished by a long vertical cavity some two-thirds of the way up the trunk. The *behlu* stood sentinel in that patch of hillside forest. Seeing it like that, rising clear above a patchwork of largely low-growing scrub and a few mid-sized trees, brought home how degraded the jungle was in places. Aparajita had told me that while tree densities in the protected tiger reserve were around 400 per hectare, they ranged from only 100–200 per hectare in the reserve forest where we stood. This loss of jungle, essential not only for the hornbills but for the Nyishi themselves, had led the Nest Adoption Programme down an additional path: rainforest restoration. From a nursery in one of the villages, thousands of native saplings were heaved up slick slopes to aid natural regeneration and the cumulative efforts of the hornbill gardeners in particularly ravaged areas. The trees included those, such as *behlu*, that are favoured by hornbills as nesting sites, together with fruiting varieties for feeding purposes. But there were species suitable for human needs too, to be eventually made use of as firewood, food and building materials, enabling the local community to share in the long-term benefits of the forest's rejuvenation. 'They're for hornbills and our children,' said Tajek, turning his proud grin my way.

We had a clear view of the tree cavity. Two years previously, this hole had been occupied by an oriental pied hornbill, but the nest had been usurped the following year by a pair of wreathed hornbills. According to Aparajita, these unusual takeovers were due to an increased scarcity of nesting trees. Hoping to see a wreathed hornbill put in an appearance preparatory to breeding, we didn't have to wait long to hear the breathing of wings overhead, deep, murmuring and near. Each hornbill species has a signature flight sound, as Tajek would reveal to me a few minutes later when he mimicked with wide eyes the *see-see-see* of the wreathed hornbill and the deeper *ooh-ooh-ooh* of the great hornbill. He would have already known the incoming species from its wing sound alone, but it took me a final tilt of my neck to see that it wasn't a wreathed hornbill, as expected, but a great hornbill clamped to the trunk. It arched its neck and head forward to scrutinize the cavity, conducting a property viewing. It then hopped from branch to branch, stopping to engage the great orange arc of its casque to preen its wing feathers, which were spread into a fantastic fan against the silvery beige bark. A huge, white-furred foot, as shaggy as the trousers of a lynx, rose to scratch at its bulbous bill. With a great exhalation of wings the hornbill then flew off over what remained of the forest, the young men beaming as the deep *ooh-ooh-ooh* could be heard long after the bird had vanished from sight.

On our way back, I noticed how Taring's mood had changed since seeing the great hornbill at the nest he was in charge of monitoring. Some of the weight he carried had been lifted, a burden that was the aftermath of tragically crossed paths. Beneath a moonless sky on the flood plain, where that river of stories and borders winds, his identical twin brother, Takeng, had been killed during a crop raid. Stationed on the family's bamboo platform keeping watch over their paddy crops, he'd cracked off a few blanks from his rifle to scare off an approaching elephant. Assuming it was solitary, a lead animal that would then signal to the rest of its herd that it was unsafe to proceed, Takeng had descended from the platform, only to encounter another in the darkness, unsettled and angry. 'He ran and ran and ran,' Suresh had told me, 'until he was too tired to run any more and was trampled to death.' The boy had been one of his students at the time. 'Even we at the school couldn't tell the two brothers apart.'

It had been hard for Taring to return to the jungle, he'd said, where signs of elephants were not only prominent but pervasive. But working on the hornbill project had helped restore in him a sense of purpose amidst the awful grief of loss. For its aims were not only to protect hornbills and restore the ecological quality of the reserve forest, but to empower people, too. To give young men like these an opportunity to work in a place that offered little in the way of livelihood since crop raids had put an end to farming. To embolden women like Mesum Tachang to become Pakke's first female nest protector after discovering an active hornbill nest in the forest. When told that it would be monitored by one of the men, her desire to be a part of this nascent collective effort only deepened her resolve to be involved: 'Why should I give it up when I found it?' she'd said to her husband. 'I want to do this.'

Conservation isn't only about wildlife and habitats, for it can also revitalize local economies and strengthen the bonds of a community. In the case of Pakke, social and educational improvements have been tied directly to environmental ones, while retaining important patterns of life for the tribe. Rather than take leave of this place as he'd thought about doing, Taring has chosen to stay and monitor hornbills despite the near presence of elephants, sharing with them the falling green light of the jungle canopy above him.

*

What the Nyishi exemplify as a community is the ability to question and challenge our deepest and most enduring traditions – the customs and repeated rites that shape and aid in the definition of one's personal and group identity. Traditions are of immense value and worth, helping to ground us within recognizable patterns passed down through the generations. They can lend coherence to what sometimes feels like the arbitrary seasons of a life; they can be burnished with beauty, meaning and purpose, solidifying bonds between past and present, between people and place. But for traditions to retain their vivifying power and continued relevance, particularly when our natural environments and their wildlife are suffering unparalleled, catastrophic harm, it's essential that those customs reliant on the natural world as their source material are questioned – honestly, deeply and resolutely – as to whether they still have a place in a shifting, more fragile world, or whether we cling to them solely because repetition has glazed them with the sheen of the eternal. Resistance to loss and the larger degradation of the natural world isn't concerned solely with external forces, but can also signify a rethinking of the way we do things that emerges from deep within our cultural and personal identities.

In the autumn of 2016, according to a report by Birdlife Cyprus and the RSPB, as many as 2.3 million songbirds were killed on the Mediterranean island of Cyprus, either snared in mist nets strung between acacia trees or stuck to limesticks, purposely placed perching branches that appeal to birds after long migratory journeys across the sea, but which they discover upon landing are sleeved with thick, inescapable glue. As many as 150 different species of birds were affected, and the vast majority – including hoopoes, golden orioles, bee-eaters and rollers – were simply cast aside as collateral damage, killed and then discarded as the injuries they'd sustained were too serious for the birds to be able to fly again. These species aren't required for the hunters' particular needs, because they're seeking far smaller quarry, specifically blackcaps, robins, buntings and warblers, all of which are served whole – either boiled, fried or pickled – in a traditional dish called *ambelopoulia.*

Migrating birds once provided an ideal opportunity to supplement a meagre diet. But, while not minimizing the unforgivable fact that poverty, often extreme, still exists in many parts of Europe, protein is far more widely available and affordable in Cyprus today than it was when the custom of eating songbirds originated. Even according to those who catch, cook or eat the birds, *ambelopoulia* is served solely because it is an island tradition, particularly relished by those who can afford its steep cost. The exhausted birds, drained of energy after sea-crossings that can be rife with raking winds and storms, land on any scrap of earth they can find, making them particularly susceptible to capture. And for those small life forms that are the trappers' target, mystifyingly tangled up in the shrubs of the island that would have appeared as a saving grace after such long journeys, each one of them is killed with a needle puncture to the throat. They are then served by the dozen on a plate – sad, feeble and scrawny without feathers, their legs and neck crooked and curled inwards as if deformed – and eaten whole for a cost of €40–50 per dish. Currently illegal in Cyprus, the traditional delicacy is profitably traded all the same. And the problem with tradition, particularly when Europe lost 421 million birds between 1980 and 2009, the majority of them belonging to once-common species of song-birds, is that 2016 wasn't an isolated aberration. Instead it was just another turn in the repeated calendar of ritual, so that 2017 and 2018, and all the years that preceded them, were only less or more deadly in relative terms for migrating birds. If 2.3 million trapped birds seem like a lot, it's worth noting that in the late 1990s, before a government crackdown on illegal poaching lowered levels sub-stantially, it's estimated that as many as 10 million songbirds used to meet their deaths in the mist nets and glue of Cyprus each year. And those numbers may well be decreasing, in part, only because there are simply far fewer birds left in the world still to catch.

What would it mean for the birds of Europe and their potential plenitude if *ambelopoulia* was challenged by its adherents in a way similar to that of the Nyishi in their relationship to the hornbill? What would it mean to the birds of Malta, many of them illegally gunned down during spring and autumn migration on the basis of tradition? And what would it mean for the exceedingly rare hen harrier and other avian and mammal predators that have traditionally been killed on British grouse-shooting moors in order to maximize the profitability of bagged game in the name of rural customs?

As detailed in Mark Avery's *Inglorious*, the Glengarry Estate in Scotland is perhaps most famous for its litany of kills, when, between 1837 and 1840, the following animals were culled as per gamekeeper's policy with regard to predator control: stoat and weasel 301, pine marten 246, wildcat 198, polecat 106, badger 67, otter 48, kestrel 462, buzzard 285, red kite 275, goshawk 63, hen harrier 63, white-tailed sea eagle 27, osprey 18 and golden eagle 15. Perhaps the most startling aspect of this inventory is that there is no conceivable way that such numbers of killed creatures could be accrued in a four-year period today, even on an estate such as Glengarry, with 6,500 acres of land to its name. As with dwindling populations of songbirds for *ambelopoulia*, rapid declines of other wildlife have made this impossible. But while many of these species are now protected in Britain, furtive traditions of culling continue on many, though by no means all, grouse moors. While proponents of driven grouse-shooting highlight the conservation benefits resulting from intense moorland management and control of predators, including increased numbers of such ground-nesting species as lapwing, curlew and golden plover, this framing of an ecological argument through select and popular species misses a critical point (something opponents of driven grouse-shooting can also be guilty of by focusing solely on the hen harrier to the exclusion of all else): that for an ecosystem – such as that of Pakke's jungles, where the restoration of the forest is ultimately of more value than simply the presence of hornbills – to be considered rich, vital and functioning, a claim made by many supporters of grouse-shooting about the moorlands they clearly care for, it must absolutely be varied, complex, interconnected and inclusive, even if that ultimately means that fewer of those beloved ground-nesting birds exist there.

Mutual acrimony and absolutism make progress all but impossible on the issue of driven grouse-shooting, but a more complete and vibrant landscape could begin to take shape if both sides could agree to find creative ways of absorbing increased predation of grouse in an overall more diverse habitat, preserving some form of shooting tradition alongside a different approach to moorland management. It would by no means be easy to accomplish, especially in light of the considerable vested interests and finances involved in shooting, but the decisions undertaken by the Nyishi in their relationship to hornbills reveal that deeply felt customs can be altered without necessarily compromising their underlying essence, taking into account a changed world where there is simply less of everything that we once imagined was boundless. It requires purpose, vision, courage and, most significantly, compromise, but is undeniably achievable. Otherwise we need to ask whether there's a place in a diminished world for such traditions.

Of course, the Nyishi aren't alone in their initiative. There are many other compelling stories out there of people altering the collective course of rites and customs when it comes to the natural world, ones no less valuable for having received little media attention, our preoccupations with the 'newsworthy' being largely tone-deaf to the quiet and local, the unobtrusive but transformative. And there's no point in singling out *ambelopoulia*, spring hunting in Malta or grouse-moor management in Britain without considering traditions from another essential angle. While cultural customs are the most readily identified when discussing the nature of tradition, we all conduct ourselves in ways that imbue our lives with discernible patterns, acts repeated to the point of ritual within our cultures of consumption. Things that so many of us do without thinking – buying a plastic water bottle or a takeaway coffee in a disposable cup – but which, cumulatively, can have a profound and damaging effect on the health and viability of natural communities throughout the world. Even the habit of convenience can become a kind of tradition.

We're often led to understand that green consumer decisions and lifestyle choices are worthy but ultimately pointless endeavours within a system so definitively geared towards the maintenance of power and profit, but this fails to recognize the true potential of action. Within an expanded context of reflective responsibility, each personal decision, each declaration of intent to follow a path that is more questioning in scope and consideration, has the potential to ripple outwards, because that idea of *furtherance* isn't solely concerned with negative effects but also the positive. For it's never simply a choice between a plastic water bottle and refilling a flask; it's a choice between sticking with tradition as we know it in a consumer sense and finding ways of responding differently through the kind of lives we choose to live, decisions which could potentially manifest themselves in all manner of ways over time, from community organizing and environmental engagement to political activism, as when volunteers, spurred on solely by the hopeful actions of one man in Mumbai, spent three years helping clear the city's Versova Beach of 5,000 tons of mostly plastic waste, making it possible for olive ridley turtles to hatch there in 2018 for the first time in twenty years.

While such personal choices aren't nearly sufficient on their own to remedy the systemic problem of plastics or deforestation, individual change can be a galvanizing, cathartic force, beginning small but capable of rapidly transforming into a groundswell of catalytic public opinion, as seen in a global context with the stirring, student-led marches and strikes demanding political action on climate change. When the personal becomes the political, it has the power to reconfigure realities, by putting the necessary pressure on governments to legislate against the fossil-fuel companies and powerful corporations responsible for the overwhelming majority of the planet's environmental damage, as seen in Taiwan in 2018 with the announcement, partly in response to a concerted campaign from local environmental groups, of a total ban on all single-use plastics to be phased in from the following year. Sometimes it takes just the first step towards questioning the way things are for the radical possibility of people acting in cohesion to take shape, for the aspirational to turn active; to create the indispensable space where hope can become courage can become change.

*

Papi spoke almost no English at all, but on one occasion her words were not only completely accurate but instantaneous as well. Over dinner that evening, a plosive, gruff barking grated the firefly quiet like the cough of a tubercular patient. *'Barking deer!'* said Papi, her eyes alight in the dim shadows cast by candles on the table, a storm having severed the electricity supply again. She stood beside me as we peered into the dark night, the harsh wheezing just beyond the edge of the camp. 'What is it?' said Papi, as if querying the deer itself. 'Do you see something?' I asked her. 'No,' she replied. Only after retiring to bed and reading a pamphlet on Indian mammals by torchlight did I finally understand what she'd meant. Barking deer elicit their hoarse bellow in response to nearby predators. Papi *was* speaking to the deer after all; she was saying, 'What are you barking at?' I switched off the torch and sank into darkness as I went through Pakke's possible predators: leopard, bear, elephant, wild dog and tiger.

Those nights revealed to me almost as much as the light of day. I would often be woken by a stirring of sound outside the wattled bamboo walls, brought to acute consciousness by Pakke's wild animals. I would hear the near roaring of elephants or the faint strains of a herd down by the edge of the river; I'd hear a pack of wild dogs, all howling and hollering in elliptical turns, a shivering sense of their nocturnal passage from the way the sound shifted over time. And those nights taught me something vital about the tenor of the place and its wildness as I listened; while it was both remote and fraught with perils, a human community, alongside the dedicated efforts of ecologists, was working to sustain not only itself but the integrity and intactness of a place, expanding the nature of home to include the other-than-human, to bring the forest within range of the heart.

'I love watching the hornbills,' said Nikje Tayem, an older nest protector whom I accompanied into the jungle several times, 'especially when the male is feeding the female.' We were sat beneath a great hornbill nest when the former hunter, who'd spent years killing hornbills for their casques, added, 'And now I will only protect them.'

What is taking shape in Pakke is a process that has the rich potential to realign the paths we have so often taken in our interactions with the natural world: to expand the notion of relationship so that it radiates beyond the human sphere, including wildlife within its scope in a way that foregrounds co-existence rather than difference as its defining principle. For the Nyishi, Pakke is home to owls, barking deer, leopards and civets. It is home to goldenbacks and barbets, forktails and tanagers. And it is home to people, tigers, hornbills and elephants. The stories that flow on that river between ideas, dividing lands intended for nature and those for humans, contain elements of each, for it is towards the wholeness of their home that the Nyishi strive, crossing that border between species, people and places, bound together upon the ancient, spinning Earth.

As with all human stories, though, that purpose is strewn with pitfalls and problems. There are rumours, unsubstantiated but troubling all the same, that a nest protector is illegally logging wood for sale. There are times when one of the senior ecologists is too strictly focused on biodiversity aims, strongly recommending commercial tree crops for local livelihoods because they benefit hornbills, despite local people longing to find ways to restore their rice paddies and protect them from elephants. Stark poverty and hopelessness can be seen in one of the villages, its dire situation written on the terse and unwelcoming faces of itinerant labourers from elsewhere in the state. And empty bottles of Indian Forty Rifles whisky, the signature drink for those with alcoholic problems in the tribe, litter illegal timber camps.

But it is precisely these difficulties, not concealed or sanitized during the time I was there, which lend the work being attempted its very heart. For Pakke is no perfect or idealized society. It is authentic, frank and vulnerable, and prone to the everyday differences and dilemmas that all communities must navigate in the broadest sense of their relationships with the world. The efforts to rethink traditions, protect hornbills and restore forests aren't being carried out in some magical vacuum where disagreements, rancour and seemingly unsolvable problems don't exist, but rather in the midst of a candid landscape of often contested complexities, confirming that change and transformation are possible wherever they are instigated. It was this honesty that made the place seem so hopeful. The kind of hope that is active, engaging, energizing and real.

11

Radical Amazement

Our goal should be to live life in radical amazement.
~ Rabbi Abraham Joshua Heschel, *God in Search of Man*

We were deep into a strange September. Overnight the English autumn had been swapped for a Mediterranean summer. Heat rose off the fen country in a haze. Beneath a tremulous blue sky, where faint wisps of cloud scrolled past, the horizon was replicated in glassy waves, rippling and glimmering like the edge of the sea. Their wings lacquered with light, brown hawker dragonflies inscribed countless precise shapes above the lode as they cut through the air with ease. Flowering water lilies cupped the sun until they glowed, and the saw-sedges, tawny and tangled beneath the dry weight of a second summer, rasped as we passed. The fen had been stripped back to the raw kernel of its origins: earth and water beneath a vast, untouchable sky.

The Great Fen Basin, where layers of dark, spongy peat had been laid down over millennia when rising water levels drowned low-lying inland forests, once pooled over a substantial portion of eastern England. Its primal meld of decaying vegetation, sedge, bog, reeds and marsh had spread from Cambridge north to the Lincolnshire Wolds, and as far west as Peterborough and up to the dry Brecklands in the east. It was a waterlogged realm some 4,000 square kilometres in extent, where an abundance of otters, eels, cranes, beavers, waders and wildfowl thrived in the propitious terrain, and drier islands of human habitation perched on clay escarpments and the silty upliftings that rimmed the wetlands. There the fenlanders lived in close contact and interaction with water, fashioning intricate local solutions to grapple with the challenging fluidity of conditions. They employed stilts to stand clear of the sopping bogs and bone skates to skim the winter ice. They wove willow hives and gleaves to snare slippery eels and harvested osiers for basketry. They cut peat for fuel, dug clay for bricks, and scythed reeds and sedge for thatching. Sculpting lives to the wild fit of the fens, they were at home with the seep and spill of dark water.

Though the Romans were the first to try taming the basin's waters, it wasn't until the 1600s, when the fourth Earl of Bedford began the widespread process of drainage, that the fen country would be irreversibly altered in complexion. Land speculators, known as 'merchant adventurers', funded the colossal scheme in exchange for parcels of profitable agricultural terrain once it was drained. The earl assigned Dutch engineers such as Cornelius Vermuyden the task of designing, implementing and overseeing the technical details of the transformation. But as the land dried out, its waters now channelled to the sea through a complex system of rivers, canals, dykes and ditches, it steadily began to contract. What hadn't been considered in the calculations of conversion was how the land itself, so accustomed to the inundations of water, might respond to the loss of its sustaining element. When it was siphoned from the surface of the ancient mantle of peat it leaked from its sponge-like interior as well. Thousands of years' worth of partially decayed and absorbent plant material began to shrivel. And as it dried, collapsing in on itself without its inherent liquid tension, the land sank, and sank, and sank. In 1851, over 200 years after drainage of the basin had begun, and with a drop in the level of the land already so pronounced that windmills had to be installed to pump water *upwards* to the drainage canals instead of downwards through gravity as had been intended, a column was driven into the earth near the village of Holme. That year its tip was flush with the surface of the fen, but as the peat continued to give way around it, the column was soon exposed. Today it stands a full four metres clear of the earth.

Within that sunken sea of agricultural fields, Wicken Fen rises like an island. One of only a few, minuscule fragments to have escaped the drainage of the fen country, its elevated position is the result of water still being locked up in layers of peat the colour of dark chocolate. At its heart swells the great sedge fen, an extensive tract of dense, billowing grasses; growing as much as 2.5 metres high, sedge is the archetypal plant of old fenland, its saw-toothed leaves and brown clusters of spikelet flowers waving and rattling in the prominent winds off the flatlands. Until the end of the nineteenth century, the sedge fen had been traditionally harvested by fenland communities for a period of 500 years, its grasses scythed, dried and bundled for the thatching of roofs. Now at the core of the National Trust's oldest nature reserve, established in 1899, the sedge fen's edges were tinted by devil's bit scabious, its tight balls of pinkish-purple petals held aloft on slender stems, like balloons tethered to lengths of string. A grass snake whisked into the litter of dry leaves and a Cetti's warbler rang in the second coming of the summer with its bright, metallic song. At the end of the breeding season, a nest sagged empty between stems.

To part the swaying sedges of the fen with your arms is to send myriad spiders and insects into sudden motion; to step forward is to enter a living world largely invisible from outside. Some 9,000 wild species have been recorded at Wicken Fen, making it one of the most concentrated hotspots of wildlife in all of Britain, including over 1,000 beetles, 1,000 moths, 2,000 dipteran flies, 212 spiders and 300 vascular plants. The fen also shelters wildlife that is elsewhere either extinct or rare, such as the water shrew, crucifix beetle, bittern and fen violet. This ability to nourish a spectrum of wild animals and plants that struggle to exist elsewhere makes the place a unique repository of life, an irreplaceable refuge in the sea of drained fields.

*

In *Rothschild's Reserves: Time and Fragile Nature*, Miriam Rothschild – the daughter of Charles Rothschild – and Peter Marren consider the influential role that the naturalist played in nature conservation in Britain. Noting that many of the places he believed worthy of safeguarding in his list of 284 sites have since rightly been recognized as either nature reserves or SSSIs, the authors go on to add a timely warning: 'You will also find many forgotten names, some of which are now no more than names, for they have been completely destroyed. Who has heard of Freshney Bog or Harlestone Heath or Redlodge Warren? Yet, in 1915, they were among the wonders of wild England.'

I think of Wicken Fen when reading these names: the way its spaces are glazed with honeyed light and are sung into spring by cuckoos carrying the sun and sands of the Sahara in their feathers. Animated by walkers, dragonflies, birders, reed warblers, children, greater bladderwort, boaters, cyclists and reed leopard moths, it's a place that's able to sustain all those who use and need it today solely because of earlier efforts to retain it. Amidst its tumbling light and upwelling of wild creatures, we are the beneficiaries of past resolution. Almost four centuries ago, when an army of labourers in the 1630s were converting the ancient sodden earth of the fen country to arable productivity, the people of Wicken resisted the loss of their landscape. Like the coral reefs and mangroves are to the residents of Bangka Island in Indonesia, the great sedge fen and its encircling marshlands were an integral part of the fenlanders' social, economic and cultural fabric to such a degree that it was entirely indispensable to them. In the plans to drain it they saw the loss of their whole world, knowing that the livelihoods they proudly and inventively depended upon would vanish with its disappearance, traded away with nothing in return for them. Unwilling to allow wealthy outsiders to profit from the land they'd lived with and adapted to over centuries – another form of the enclosures that have ravaged the relationship between people and common land across Britain – the Fen Tigers, as they were to become known, defied the coming losses by tearing down recently built dykes and ditches, while setting fire to the sedges and reeds in a desperate attempt to prevent work from being carried out. Riots in the village of Wicken itself halted drainage on the sedge fen in 1637. Returning to their traditional way of life in the wetlands, and granted ownership of long strips of land in a pattern that resembled the open field system of the medieval period, the fenlanders would go on to scythe the sedge of the fen until the beginning of the twentieth century.

By then the market for sedge and peat was disappearing. As roof tiles became more popular than thatch, and turf was replaced by coal for heating, local owners – descendants and inheritors of the Fen Tigers' victory for the commons – still remained hopeful for some kind of return on the land now that their traditions were no longer financially viable. These fragments of old fens, remnant examples of what was even then an almost entirely vanished system, had already caught the eye of Victorian naturalists for their vibrant tonalities of life. And so, as one century made way for another, the land passed from the fen communities into the care of conservationists. Those medieval-style strips of land were bought up in piecemeal fashion as they became available on the market, and in 1901 Charles Rothschild donated the sliver of fenland he'd purchased to the National Trust for safekeeping. But if either of those things hadn't occurred – the resistance of the Fen Tigers or the earmarking of the land for conservation – or if, in the intervening centuries, the seasonal fenland practices that kept this place alive and thriving had been abandoned by local people, then Wicken Fen wouldn't be with us today. And in time, it would have vanished from popular memory as surely as those forgotten names listed in *Rothschild's Reserves*.

It can be hard to comprehend what it means to pass on the places and natural habitats we love to future generations. Amidst the pressures of the present, a future beyond our own can feel distant and daunting to consider. But perhaps the easiest and most clarifying way of contemplating it is simply to think of today. It is to walk beneath a stunning East Anglian sky through Wicken Fen in summer, its warblers and cuckoos mingling in song as well as nest, speckled wood butterflies and hemp agrimony lighting the buckthorn carr. It's to pond-dip the medieval reens of the Gwent Levels, sea-light blending with the brimming water while common cranes parade the marshes with scarlet crowns. It's to enter the peace of the ancient woodland at Hopwas as its leaves begin their autumn turn, or to lift your eyes to the dazzling spring summits of an old redwood grove. It's to savour that piece of vital and restorative greenery still intact within a city. For *we* are also a future generation. Not a single person in Britain today was alive when Rothschild donated the strip of land that now forms a crucial part of Wicken Fen, but we are the recipients of that gift. Without the persistent efforts of countless people, often forgotten or unsung, we wouldn't have inherited anywhere near as much of the staggering beauty of the world and the elegant complexity of place as we have. We inhabit the future that those past people must have also struggled to imagine as they toiled to safeguard what they could.

But we need to do more than simply appreciate this, for otherwise what will people a century from now be able to look back on? While the global sum of land given protected status for the preservation of wildlife has doubled since 1992, a study published in *Science* in 2018 revealed that one-third of all those areas are under intense threat of destruction. By ignoring the looming devastation of human-induced climate breakdown and by encouraging through our economic, industrial and intensive agricultural practices the overall thinning of life systems across the planet, we've put our most precious places, biodiversity and wellbeing at existential risk. We are part of a shared world, where we owe acknowledgement and solidarity to other species. We must seek to ensure that different forms of beauty and cultural heritage too unique, important and exceptional to be lost are preserved from erasure. And our efforts must outlive us. We need to be caretakers for the greater good of that future we'll never know, otherwise our descendants might ask, 'Who has heard of Lodge Hill and

Smithy Wood and the Gwent Levels? Yet, in 2019, they were among the wonders of wild Britain.'

*

I stood at the edge of a misted fen. Those Indian summer days had been chased away by rain muscling in off the cold sea to the east. Clouds scudded past as if caught up in a river, and the sable manes of grazing Konik ponies bristled with wind. It seemed only fitting to experience this tract of land in such soggy conditions, for water – that nearly forgotten component of the basin's peatlands – was finally returning to Burwell Fen.

'What remains, in terms of the fabric, is fairly secure,' said Martin Lester, speaking of the fragments of undrained fen. 'It's all under protective custody, if you like. But that's not to say that it's secure in reality, because they are all postage-stamp sizes, they are all isolated pockets surrounded by seas of arable agriculture. And all of that's been drained. And as the land around you is shrinking and sinking, you find your precious little piece of fen perched up in the air.'

Now its countryside manager, Martin has worked at Wicken Fen for the past twenty years, and he speaks of it with that same mixture of easy familiarity and courteous respect that you would of a close but elderly relative. And he's honest in his appraisal of its prospects. 'Even if we can keep Wicken Fen as wet as possible, and provide all the ideal conditions, it is still entirely isolated and species will become extinct.' Despite the captivating abundance of wildlife at Wicken Fen, loss was still ever-present. Multiple types of moths, including the gypsy, reed tussock and marsh dagger, were gone. The delicate, pale-yellow fen orchid, last recorded in 1945, was gone. The common hawker dragonfly and white-clawed crayfish were gone. And, in perhaps the most resonant of the vanishings, the species being one of the primary reasons why Charles Rothschild believed Wicken Fen should be preserved for the future, the iconic swallowtail butterfly was also gone. Dependent on milk parsley as the sole food source of its caterpillar, the swallowtail had struggled because fragmentation and the lowering of the water table had made it difficult for this vital host plant to thrive.

'The only way we can counter those extinctions,' said Martin, 'is to expand the size of the reserve, to try and allow these conditions to expand into it. What we're trying to do is allow the processes that once formed the fen to become established, so that, possibly, one day, there'll be more room for this.' He swept his arm behind him in the direction of the old sedge fen.

The desire to protect such places as Wicken Fen is often described as nostalgic by those seeking to profit from their destruction. I remember how Geoff Driver was made to feel 'grubby' for his fierce commitment to Smithy Wood during the village green inquiry, belittled for his 'sentimental' desire to protect a place of value to him. These are places that are often depicted not only as impediments to 'progress', replaceable by biodiversity offsetting, but, even more dismissively, as relics of the past.

Although many of these places are significant precisely because of those pasts – their long-layered and cumulative natural and cultural ecologies – they are also radically of the *present*: vibrant, living indications of the potency of place as sustenance for both humans and wildlife. They are catalysts for contemporary cohesion and community, engines of continual wonder and delight, and spurs for deep, rejuvenating joy. They are essential for life in its widest possible sense. And while it's true that many of these places can seem like islands, snapshots of a richer world cut adrift and now fading, they are also vital anchor points for the *future*. Because from islands can be built bridges.

The Wicken Fen Vision was born in 1999, the centenary year of the nature reserve. Working on a time scale of one hundred years in order to emphasize restitution as an ongoing process (while avoiding unsettling local landowners and raising short-term expectations), the National Trust has embarked on a project to purchase agricultural land to the south of Wicken Fen when-ever it becomes available on the market. As the fen country's fields increasingly erode, their dried, crumbly peat blowing away without its binding agent of water, and as the cost of the mecha-nized drainage that keeps farming tenable becomes prohibitively high, some farmers have already been eager for the opportunity to sell. Burwell Fen Farm has now returned to being Burwell Fen, its former crops of sugar beet and cereals replaced by marshland once more, and, on the day I stood beside it in the rain, lapwings and marsh harriers sailed over the reed beds and pools that had already colonized the former fields. That old island of undrained fen is being joined to restored wetlands.

As in Pakke, where the Nyishi are extending the vitality of tropical forests beyond the border of the tiger reserve, such link-ages enable species to spread through the wider landscape and reinhabit a diversity of spaces. In Plymouth, where I'd learned about the horrid ground weaver spider and the threatened quarry where it dwelled, Andrew Whitehouse of Buglife had sketched out for me their plan to restore wildflower-rich meadows and join together already existing nature reserves through a network of what they called 'B-lines'. Described as 'insect pathways', these corridors allow invertebrates a greater freedom to roam the landscape while foraging. And in that oceanic swell at the centre of America, where native peoples and bison once traversed grasslands so extensive that they unfurled into the greatest flag that nation has ever known, the seeds of remnant tallgrass patches were enabling other prairies to rise again under a similar long-term vision and commitment. These fragments are not only of the utmost importance today, they are also critical to furnishing future landscapes with vitality.

'These are arks,' said Martin, speaking of the 0.1 per cent of undrained fens still in existence in the larger basin. 'If we can give these arks somewhere to run aground, there's a strong chance that a lot of these species will survive. Morally we can't ignore it.' To give these arks – of whatever kind and wherever they are found – somewhere to run aground means finding space in this world for things not solely human. It asks of us to rethink, honestly and openly, our expectations of the purpose of land, and the consequences of our uninhibited consumerism. It means living with the grace of restraint. It means championing the farmers and landowners who have made biodiversity an additional focus of their labours. It means making our houses and gardens more appealing to wildlife, through the addition of native plants, fence gaps for hedgehogs and bee-bricks in the walls. It means influencing politicians, whether through party membership or the ballot box, to implement legislation that is sympathetic to the natural world. It means challenging corporations, through boycotts, activism and political pressure, to amend their practices, to lessen dramatically their role in the diminution of the natural world through plastics pollution, greenhouse gas emissions and toxic spills. And it tasks us to dream boldly and to be radically alive to the world of today.

'To a lot of people rewilding is wolves, lynxes and bears,' said Martin. 'To us, rewilding is the re-establishment of those natural processes. My biggest obligation is maintaining that old part out here, but what I want to be doing is expanding it out there.' He hooked a thumb towards the re-emerging fen at Burwell. While the Native American writer N. Scott Momaday once said that 'place may be the first of all concepts; it may be the oldest of all words', place is neither a prison of the past nor an end to change. It's about how we choose to live our lives into the future. As Burwell Fen refills with water, luring in short-eared owls, rare black-winged stilts and common cranes, that wild assembly reclaims a greater place in our relationships. And perhaps, in time, milk parsley might take root as well, allowing graceful swallowtails to follow as the fen is rewilded into an expanded landscape for many. There is no single, easy remedy for the healing of the natural world, but making the Earth more livable for wildlife across its widest possible spectrum of species must be at the core of our collective efforts. In an age of loss it isn't enough to safeguard refuges, for we need to restore fluidity to the greater landscape, bridging the barriers between places and encouraging a more seamless tapestry where wild creatures and human cultures in all their complexity and richness co-exist.

Habitat restoration and the upholding of protective measures – particularly at a time when climate change is altering the base conditions of life on the planet – will only take us so far, though. Just as important is the rewilding of the human heart. To engage deeply with the luminous beauty and intrinsic significance of the living planet in a way that Rabbi Heschel may have been thinking of when he wrote that 'our goal should be to live life in radical amazement', seeing in that larger landscape of our embrace not only the inherent possibilities for life-altering wonder and enriching relationships, but also its wider implications for connection: if feelings, attachment and love can transform a place into a home, then they can also be its protector.

*

For several minutes the skies over Wicken Fen had flamed with brumal light, the sun on its low passage beneath clouds, torching the sedges, reeds and lodes to an amber glow. But the clouds soon regained their dominance when the sun fell away, sealing the world in a pallid, dimming chill. In the depths of winter I stood in the midst of crackling saw-sedges with Stephen Rutt and his father, Peter. Both are skilled birdwatchers, glancing upwards at the merest rumour of a gull or passerine and immediately decoding its kind as it inscribes the air with cryptic hints. Peter had been coming to Wicken Fen for several decades. 'I was brought here by my parents when I started watching birds and I remember being up in the tower hide in thick fog and just thought this was amazing. And then when I was twenty-five I thought I needed to get back to that place.' In turn, Stephen had been introduced to Wicken Fen by his father, the place passed down through the generations like a family Bible.

All day we'd wandered this remarkable remnant of ancient fen, the sedges and reeds shivering with winter cold. The sky above us was a carousel of clouds and light. A kingfisher blurred a blue line over the lode and a marsh harrier jigged above the reeds like a trembling lure on a fishing line. There was almost no one else around and the sedge fen stretched out ahead of us, tingling with mystery.

We waited out the cold clouding of the skies and watched the fading horizon for hen harriers. In winter, England's precious few breeding pairs are augmented by migrant birds sweeping down from Scotland and Scandinavia. Wicken Fen acts as a harbour beacon, lighting their way into a shelterbelt of sedges and reeds at the end of a day hunting the sea of fields. A female was the first to return to the roost. Her tawny wings oared her low over the whispering reeds. A few minutes later two males streaked by, circling like pale ghosts in the dusk. Others would soon follow, with an air of effortless elegance. Away to the west, the air thickening with mist feathered with pale orange light, starlings were gathering over the fen country. A murmuration was about to unfold.

At times the dark mass spun sideways to just a thin filigree of sky, like the ornamental lacework at the edge of a tablecloth. Then it ballooned into the quaking back of a whale, breaching invisible waters in a fluid arc through air. Backlit by the setting sun, it etched the sky with the calligraphy of synchronous flight. Much further away than the murmuration I'd seen off the coast at Brighton Pier, this one's presence was made visible through the sheer volume of starlings involved; far enough out over that sea of fields that it was easy to forget this weaving throng was actually composed of individual birds. All I could discern from a distance was the shape, the grace, the power and the potency of the whole. And yet that's all a murmuration ultimately is: a congregation of individual birds. At the heart of each and every assembly, at the core of that swirling spectacle in the fading fenland sky, are just single starlings. There's nothing more to a murmuration than this, until, in relationship with each other, those solitary birds forge a greater, more substantial, thing through connection.

Loss needn't be what the natural world seems increasingly to be made of, for we harbour a powerful agency ourselves, capable of harnessing those larger energies of love and attachment forged through our relationships with nature and place, transforming them to vital resistance in the active spirit of affinity. So often we shy away from speaking out because we feel our lives to be too small, insignificant and invisible in our atomized society, where power largely resides in corridors that are closed to us. We can feel impotent in the face of such hegemony, unable to effect change in the greater scheme of things. And yet, as I've seen time and time again, effective and transformative resistance to loss begins with ordinary people doing just that, speaking out. People who, simply by making themselves heard, spark others into action, galvanizing a groundswell of often already existing feelings amongst those otherwise too anxious, demoralized, withdrawn or fearful to stand up without knowing there's someone beside them. Like those starlings corkscrewing into the upper reaches of the fen country sky, change can begin with just single voices – yours, mine, hers or his. And when we raise our voices we empower others to join in, swelling to a chorus, a coalition, a murmuration.

EPILOGUE

As with place itself, the stories in this book have continued to unfold, and so I've highlighted some of the more notable recent developments below.

Despite the precedent of the Indian vulture crisis, diclofenac was approved for veterinary use by Spain and Italy in the 2010s, while an application for its use has also been submitted to the Portuguese government. Together, these three countries account for 95 per cent of the European Union's vulture populations. Anti-poison dogs now operate in Bulgaria, Spain and France, as well as Greece. In 2018, the Return of the Neophron project won the Cross-border Co-operation and Networking Award at the European Natura 2000 Awards. After four consecutive years of failed nests, the Egyptian vultures in Meteora whose chick had died when only twenty days old were the first pair in all of the Balkans to successfully raise a young vulture in the summer of 2018. Fledging that September, the young vulture began its journey to Africa, where it will spend the following few years before, hopefully, returning to Meteora to breed.

A study by the British Trust for Ornithology in 2018 revealed that nightingale numbers in Britain continued to decline while those at Lodge Hill remained stable, further confirming that remarkable but threatened place as the single most important refuge for the species in the whole of the UK. In December of that year, Homes England announced that it would no longer seek to build on designated SSSI land at Lodge Hill, a remarkable reprieve for the site, and one that followed the spirited Save Lodge Hill campaign orchestrated by the RSPB and the Kent Wildlife Trust. Although the government agency stated that it hoped to build 500 homes beyond the protected perimeter in a scaled-down plan – a development which could yet cause significant damage to the nightingale hotspot – overall it was still news that would have delighted Owen Sweeney.

Since 2014, when I travelled to Plymouth, the horrid ground weaver spider has been found in a further location in the city, making three places in total after the destruction of one of the original sites. Understanding more about the spider's ecology, biologists from Buglife have now discovered a further seventy specimens and have taken the first photographs and video footage of the live arachnid. Listed by the IUCN as critically endangered in light of its circumscribed population, the spider has also been defended from additional threats by Buglife, working closely with Plymouth City Council to reroute a cycleway that would have crossed its most important refuge.

The Ghora-Aabhe Society of Pakke received an Ecological Restoration Award in 2016 from the Balipara Foundation. Over the course of three years, 12,000 native saplings have been planted across eleven hectares of degraded jungle in Pakke, with survival rates ranging from 50 to 90 per cent, depending on the site. In 2017 two nest protectors were suspended following evidence of their involvement in illegal logging. The remaining protectors have continued their efforts and commitment alongside ecologists in spite of the setback, and the successful Hornbill Nest Adoption Programme has now been replicated at sites in eastern Assam and West Bengal.

Since the beginning of the Balkan Lynx Recovery Programme overall numbers of the rare and elusive mammal have risen slightly, while its density in Mavrovo National Park has increased, though an unexplained death of a lynx in Kosovo and the deliberate poaching of another has meant the possible extinction of the species in that country. In December 2018 a camera trap in Albania recorded a Balkan lynx in yet a further new site for the animal, raising hopes for the eventual recovery of its historic range there.

After forty-five years at Farm Terrace, Vincenzo Santarsiero took on a new plot in another part of Watford. A few of the others, including Sara Jane Trebar, joined him, naming their row of adjacent plots 'Farm Terrace' in their old place's honour. Bernard and Dorothy – Pete Baillie's memorial trees – were transplanted to a different site. By the end of 2018 the overall development plan for the area had a tagline: *Welcome to Wellbeing*. And in February 2019 Watford Council announced that Farm Terrace would become a multistorey car park, just as its plot-holders had always suspected it would.

AQUEIS – a German NGO promoting aquatic science – began a pilot project on Bangka Island in 2018 in conjunction with the university in Manado. Called the No-Trash Triangle Initiative, it involves local people, volunteers and organizations such as Suara Pulau in cleaning plastic waste from Bangka's shores. Crucially, it also investigates the origins of the debris, with the aim of creating a database of pollution sources. And along with raising awareness about the harm of plastics and ways of reducing their use throughout North Sulawesi, the project finances recycling infrastructure on the island itself. In December that year all relevant government agencies signed a joint decree stating that the supreme court decision prohibiting mining on Bangka would be upheld, hopefully bringing an end to the threat that has loomed for several years over the island and its coral reefs, mangroves and communities. But as Ulva Takke and Owen Tap said by email after the news was announced, 'as long as there is still mining equipment on the island, then we are not done with the fight'.

By early 2019, and over five years since first learning of the motorway services proposal, residents of Chapeltown were no closer to knowing whether Smithy Wood would be saved or destroyed. Sheffield Council is now awaiting a decision on a further motorway services application two junctions to the south and in the jurisdiction of Rotherham before it decides on the future of that irreplaceable ancient woodland.

In response to the committed efforts of tree protectors in Sheffield, the local council announced in February 2019 that the 120-year-old Chelsea Road elm would be spared from its tree-felling programme, thereby preserving its colony of rare white-letter hairstreak butterflies as well.

The year 2018 was the most successful for the common crane in Britain since the seventeenth century, fifty-four pairs raising a total of twenty-five chicks. National numbers have now reached 180 birds and population modelling carried out by scientists in 2018 suggested that there could be as many as 275 pairs of common cranes inhabiting Britain's wetlands in the next half century if current habitats remain intact. A public inquiry into the M4 bypass proposal was carried out in 2018. Throughout, Sophie Howe, the Future Generations Commissioner, argued vehemently against the Black Route through the Gwent levels on the grounds of the Well-Being Act, describing it as setting a 'terrible precedent' for the interpretation of the legislation, going on to say that 'Business as usual is no longer an option.' Her words, however, had little effect on government ministers supporting the plan and the verdict of the inquiry, as of early 2019, is still pending.

*

Epilogue

This book explores only a small number of threatened places. There are countless others out there in the world, whose people will be no less committed, passionate or determined to preserve them than those whose stories have been told here. While far from exhaustive, and weighted towards regions of the world where either I could read reports in a language that I spoke or had contacts who forwarded me suggestions – which means that the overwhelming majority will have passed me by – on the following pages are some of the other unique and imperilled places I became aware of while writing *Irreplaceable*.

Virunga National Park   Arun Valley, Sussex

Culloden Wood, Inverness   Oaken Wood, Kent

Panna Tiger Reserve, Madhya Pradesh

Ulcinj Lagoons and Salt Pans   Dinah's Hollow, Dorset

Giant Sequoia National Monument, California

Wood Buffalo National Park, British Columbia

Aras River Bird Paradise   Lorentz National Park, Papua

Karavastra Lagoon   Atewa Forest

Guiseley Allotments, Leeds

Clyne Woods, Swansea   South Cubbington Wood, Warwickshire

Isiboro Sécure Indigenous Territory and National Park

Mes Aynak, Logar Province

Beljarica floodplain, Belgrade

Studentčište Marsh   National Butterfly Center, Texas

Moreton Bay Wetlands, Queensland

Carrizo Plain National Monument, California

Talawe Wetlands, Mumbai   Log Wood, Vale of Glamorgan

Whitmore Wood, Staffordshire   Valbona Valley

Ancient Bostan Gardens, Istanbul

The Sacred Headwaters, British Columbia

Leuser Ecosystem   Manor Farm Allotments, London

Weaver Square Community Gardens and Allotments, Dublin

Black Swan Lake, Queensland

Northfields Allotments, London

Izembek National Wildlife Refuge, Alaska

Seamus Heaney Country, Lough Beg   Santa Cruz River

Community Reserves, Victoria   Erimitis Headland, Corfu

Askham Bog, Yorkshire

Ancient Wild Rice Beds, White Earth Nation, Minnesota

Two Mile Wood, Dorset   Frays Farm Meadows, London

Amazon Forest   Druridge Bay, Northumberland

Rampisham Down, Dorset

Cumberland Island, Georgia

Aarey Forest, Mumbai

Boracay Forest and Puka Shell Beach

Kilmacolm Meadow, Inverclyde

Otmoor, Oxfordshire

Christmas Island

Coul Links, East Sutherland

Woolsington Woods, Newcastle

McNeil River, Alaska

Kakamega Rainforest   Kresna Valley   Kemberland Wood, Kent

Cerna Valley National Park   Galiciča National Park

Chilika Lake, Odisha   Woodhall and Faskine greenbelt, Airdrie

Hambach Forest, North Rhine-Westphalia

Minesing Wetlands, Ontario

Beeliar Wetlands, Perth

Kelantan Rainforests

Merlin Park Meadow, Galway

Peace River Valley, British Columbia   Cardigan Bay

Butterfly Cave, New South Wales   Santa Ana Wildlife Refuge, Texas

University of East Anglia grasslands, Norwich

Crayford Marshes, London

Craig Major Wood, Caerphilly

The Sandlings, Suffolk

Skouries, Halkidiki   Narta Lagoon

Empress Garden, Pune

Hasankeyf, Batman Province

Sperrin Mountains, Counties Derry and Tyrone

Vjosa River

Pirin National Park

Bloors Lane Community Woodland, Kent   Makatea Atoll

Saltwells Nature Reserve, West Midlands

Coombe Allotments, Gloucestershire   Białowieża Forest

Craigentinny and Telferton Allotments, Edinburgh

AFTERWORD

By August many of the marshes on the Hoo Peninsula have cured to the colour of wheat. Pale grasses and creeks of dry reeds rattle and scratch in the humid breeze off the estuary. The flatlands are transfigured with still thistles, their spiked globes of mauve flowers drawing a rich murmur from foraging insects on the wing. I watched a kestrel as it wheeled into an updraught near the river. It hovered as if there was no tomorrow, caught in a crux of time like it was capable of stilling its days, until it slid inevitably back to earth.

At the edge of the marsh, where she'd strike out most days for a walk, a few wreaths still marked the spot where Gill had died of sudden cardiac arrest in spring 2017. For well over an hour I'd stood there with Joan, three months on from Gill's leaving, sharing stories of our friend and remembering all that she'd done for the marsh country.

'I remember being at the Labour Party conference in Bournemouth,' said Joan. 'We were handing out campaign leaflets when a government minister with some responsibility for putting the Cliffe Airport proposal forward stopped by. He approached the table and looked down at Gill, and you could see it on his face, *Oh, what a sweet little old lady*, and he said, *So what do we have here?* And Gill said, *It's a campaign against Cliffe Airport.*'

Joan dropped her voice to a mock bass. 'And she said, *But you would know all about that, wouldn't you!*' For the first time that morning we'd laughed amidst the tears.

'It was as though she'd punched him in the face,' continued Joan. 'She always seemed like a sweet old lady, but she had fire in her. Real fire.'

After saying our goodbyes, I walked out into the marsh country from the village. It's still there after all that it has faced, spread between two rivers and the sea, so atmospheric, enthralling and unique. So irreplaceable. It shimmers with warm sunlight, as if leafed in gold, and for now it remains part of the estuary's wild weave, thanks in no small part to Gill's commitment. I sat beside one of the creeks carrying water out to the river, the kestrel fanning upwards from the grasses to hover over the marshes again, and I remembered those words of hers as she'd tapped at her tender heart: *A place is inside you, a place is in here*. But it wasn't only a place that could find a home there, for Gill's passion, goodness and conviction to do better in this world would live on in the hearts and actions of all those who'd ever known her.

ACKNOWLEDGEMENTS

As human lives and their indelible connections to the natural world sit at the heart of this book, there are many people out there to whom I owe a debt of gratitude – first, for their courageous and continuing efforts to protect and raise awareness of threatened places and wild species, and, second, for entrusting their intimate stories of belonging and resistance to me. Without them, this book simply wouldn't exist.

On the Hoo Peninsula I'm forever grateful to George Crozer, Joan Darwell and the irreplaceable Gill Moore of Friends of the North Kent Marshes, for inspiring me to begin this book in the first place; to the unforgettable Owen Sweeney, for his understanding and love of Lodge Hill and its nightingales; and to Miles King, for opening the door to the MoD base during the People Need Nature project. Many thanks also to Richard Baxell, David Cox, Norman Crighton, Keith Datchler, Paul Evans, Steven Falk, Jane King, Maria Nunzia, Matthew Shaw and Marion and Catherine Shoard. I owe considerable thanks to Sue Jones, the Whitstable Biennale and the Lottery Heritage Fund for enabling me to take part in a project devoted to the oral histories and livelihoods of the peninsula, and to Colette Bailey and Shorelines Festival for the opportunity to first sketch out my thoughts above that inimitable place. Thanks also to Simon Fowler, Sam Lee, Ian Rawes and Adrian Thomas, as well as to Sarah Henshall and Neil Fuller for the enlightening perspective on the brownfield of the Thames corridor.

From various woodlands I would like to thank Charlie, Paul Brackenbury, Blanche Cameron, Geoff Driver, Liz and John Goldsmith, Daniel Greenwood, Mick Harrison, Jean Howe, Georgia and Jan Locock, Chris Perring, Iris Penny, Emma Pooley, Nicky Rivers and Ray Vanstone. Especial thanks to Melvyn Jones and Ian Rotherham, not only for sharing their insightful understanding of ancient woodlands with me but also for their invaluable written texts on the subject. Deep gratitude to my friend Jenny Walicek for introducing me to both old-growth redwoods and the wonders of elephant seals.

In the lands of the lynx I'm indebted to Nove Angelkoski, Svetlana Arsovska, Sara Gandy, Bledi Hoxha, Gjorge Ivanov, Daniela Jovanovska, Dime Melovski, Father Porfiri, Alberto Martín Rodríguez, Aleksandar Stoyanov, Aleksandër Trajçe, Metodija Velevski and Daniela Zaec. I'm also grateful to the Society for the Protection of Prespa for their inspiring environmental efforts in the transboundary region. Especial thanks to Ljupcho Melovski for sharing both his wisdom and home with me, as well as to Andrew Whitehouse for the story of a reclusive and resilient spider. I'm also grateful to Chris Tomkins and Peter Campbell at Año Nuevo State Park in California.

For the sacred reaches I would like to thank Chris Bowden, Beti Dimitrova, Vladimir Dobrev, Thanos Kastritis, Stoyan Nikolov, Victoria Saravia and Mirjan Topi. An especially large thanks to Dimitris Vavylis for sharing his work at Meteora with me. I would also like to thank Flak, Teleto, Yeto and Jermain of the Sofia-based graffiti collective 140 Ideas for their incomparable rendition of the Egyptian vulture in art.

Acknowledgements

At North Kelvin Meadow and the Children's Wood I'm grateful to Ian Black, Jayson Byles, Karen Chung, Emily Cutts, Jimmy Diver, Pete Edwards, Riikka Gonzalez, Kristin and Olive Mojsiewicz, Douglas Peacock, Alex, Jasmine and Maya Pratis, Fiona Rintoul and the welcoming group of teenagers in that joyous field. At Farm Terrace Allotments, somewhere no longer with us, my deepest gratitude to Sara Jane Trebar, who continued to keep me apprised of her close-knit allotment community even after the destruction of its foundational place. I'm also thankful to Peter Baillie, Marion Harvey, Andy Moore, Roger and Karen Newton, David Ridsdale, Vincenzo and Roseangela Santarsiero, Massimo, Luca and Emilia Trebar and Stephen Windmill.

In Indonesia I would like to thank Dean and Neal Allatt, Grace Camp, Mathilde Chavin, Markus Dahlihi, Tim Davalan, Simon and Sophie Foote, Irawan Halir, Jeanette Healey, Ed Jones, Sheila Kartika, Toni Manggangung, Alex Mitchell, Hendra Pangandaheng, Marco Reinach, Bintan Siregar, Ulva Takke and Owen Tap, Otny Thomas and the rest of the fine folks at Nomad Divers and Mimpi Indah. Together they made that world within water understandable to me.

On the Gwent Levels I'm indebted to the Gwent Wildlife Trust for sharing their considerable knowledge and expertise with me. Many thanks are owed to Kathy Barclay, Damon Bridge, James Byrne, Sarah Harris, Sorrel and Iestyn Jones, Lisa Morgan, Wayne and Wendy Mumford, Ian Rappel, Susan Richardson, Rick Turner, Grant and Carole, and the inspiring students of Magor Church in Wales Primary School. Many thanks to the editors at *EarthLines* for publishing an earlier version of 'The Sum of a Place'.

On the prairies I would like to express my heartfelt appreciation to Diane Barker, David Bender, Lisa Bernal, John Briggs,

Dru Clarke, Brenna Dixon, Joe Gelroth, Bill Glass, Jill Haukos, Chod Hedinger, Laura Hitt, Gavin van Horn, Karen Hummel, Emily Loerzel, Debra Marquart, Camille Meyers, Dave Rintoul, Ashley Thackrah, Jordan Thomas, Krista Wilgers and Paddy Woodworth. Especial thanks are owed to Arthur Pearson for the thorough introduction to Midewin Prairie, and to Elizabeth Dodd and Daniel Hoyt for the generous invitation to partake in the Long-term Ecological Reflections Program of Kansas State University on the Konza Prairie.

In India, my sincere thanks go to Rajib Baruah, Aparajita Datta, Rinku Gohain, Takum Nabum, Rohit Naniwadekar, Goutam Narayan, Rungfe Paffa (who sadly passed away shortly after I met him), Devathi Parashuram, Pranjal Pradip, Somoyita Sur, Pahi and Mesum Tachang, Tajek Tachang, Taring Tachang, Anthony Tana, Nikje Tayem, Papi Tayem and Nandini Velho. With thanks also to Narayan Sharma and his engaging class of Environmental Biology and Wildlife Science students at Cotton University in Guwahati. They opened my eyes and heart to the concerns of India's young people about the natural world. Finally, my gratitude to Jaydev Mandal and Suresh Pait, for making my time in Arunachal Pradesh and Assam not only unforgettably enriching but also the cherished foundation of new friendships.

At Wicken Fen I would like to thank Fran Barney, Martin Lester, Peter Rutt and Mike Selby.

Gratitude to the many schoolchildren and other young people around the world for continuing to make a brave, inspiring and committed collective stand against the irresponsibility of climate-change inaction.

Considerable thanks are owed to my dear friend Martin Stewart, who not only kindly offered me somewhere to stay in London on my many research journeys to the UK but also provided a perfect blend of good conversation, thoughtfulness and laughter when it was most needed.

Timely suggestions and helpful conversations with friends have influenced the shape of this book immensely, and I'd like to thank the following people for their consideration and care: Sergio Gonzaléz Asián, Pete Bell and Trudi Clamp, Juan Martín Bermúdez, Robin and Pippa Blackall, Tom Chambers, Mark Cocker and Mary Muir, Chris Dance, Murdo Eason, Sally Huband, Shaun Hurrell, Inés Jordana, Hilary Koll and Steve Mills, Helen Macdonald, Robert Macfarlane, Chris Mounsey, T. R. Shankar Raman, Stephen Rutt and Miranda Cichy, Jørgen and Kirsten Stubgaard, Yiannis Theodoropoulos and Sevi Liou, and Hamza Yassin.

I owe many thanks to Gareth Evans and Rachel Lichtenstein for generously pointing me towards Hamish Hamilton at the very moment when I was seeking a home for this book. And to my inimitable editors there, Simon Prosser and Hermione Thompson, my sincere gratitude for their enduring faith in this project and the great attention, wisdom and vision they've brought to its shaping. Many thanks also to Trevor Horwood and Craig Taylor for their deft edits and suggestions, and to Hannah Chukwu, Poppy North, Natalie Wall and the rest of the tremendous team at Hamish Hamilton for their care in making this book real. Deep gratitude to Rowena Dugdale for the elegant cover images and the beautiful murmuration on the endpapers. And to John Hamilton, who commissioned the cover – his last for Hamish Hamilton before his untimely death.

Abiding thanks to my mother and father, Pam and Ken, for their constant love and support. And to my beloved mother-in-law,

Pat Harker, who passed away as the book was nearing completion. She is, and will always be, dearly missed.

Owing to my being necessarily away from home for an extended period of time, some of the later chapters of this book were finalized in the Skipton Public Library. At a time when so many libraries are being closed because of government budget cuts and the impoverished ideology of austerity, I'm grateful that this communal space remains in existence. And it was clear from the number and diversity of people using it just how profoundly irreplaceable libraries are, essential places for the wellbeing and enrichment of both present and future generations.

And finally – to my wife, Julia. Not only for being the trusted first reader of these words and an anchor when its journeys took me far from home, but also for being the irreplaceable heart of my life.

BIBLIOGRAPHY

Agence France-Presse, 'Madrid bans half of cars from roads to fight air pollution', *The Guardian*, 29 December 2016

Airports Commission, *Inner Thames Estuary Airport: Summary and Decision Paper* (September 2014)

Aldred, Jessica, 'Scientists name world's 100 most unusual and endangered birds', *The Guardian*, 10 April 2014

Allen, Gerald R. and Erdmann, Mark V., *Reef Fishes of the East Indies* vol. 1 (Honolulu: University of Hawai'i Press, 2012)

Alongi, Daniel, 'Indonesia's blue carbon: a globally significant and vulnerable sink for seagrass and mangrove carbon', *Wetland Ecology and Management* vol. 24, no. 1 (February 2016), pp. 3–13

Avery, Mark, *Inglorious* (London: Bloomsbury, 2015)

Ballerini, Michele et al., 'Empirical investigation of starling flocks: a benchmark study in collective animal behaviour', *Animal Behaviour* vol. 76 no. 1 (July 2008), pp. 201–15, doi.org/10.1016/j.anbehav.2008.02.004

Baltimore, J. M., 'In the prime of the buffalo', *Overland Monthly and Out West Magazine* vol. 14, no. 83 (1889), pp. 515–20

Barkham, Patrick, 'Nightingales v 5,000 new homes: the battle over the woods of Lodge Hill', *The Guardian*, 25 September 2014

Barnes, Simon, *Prophet and Loss: Time and the Rothschild List* (eBook: The Wildlife Trusts, 2015)

Basso, Keith H., *Wisdom Sits in Places: Landscape and Language Among the Western Apache* (Albuquerque: University of New Mexico Press, 1996)

Bates, H. E., *Through the Woods* (Wimborne: Little Toller Books, 2011 [1936])

Beament, Emily, 'More than 800,000 songbirds illegally killed on British military base in Cyprus', *The Independent*, 16 March 2017

Benjamin, Walter, 'The work of art in the age of mechanical reproduction', in *Illuminations*, trans. H. Zohn (New York: Schocken Books, 1969 [1935])

Beston, Henry, *The Outermost House: A Year of Life on the Great Beach of Cape Cod* (New York: St Martin's Press, 1988 [1928])

Bird, Dr William, 'Natural thinking: investigating the links between the natural environment, biodiversity and mental health', report for RSPB and Natural England, 2007

Birdlife Cyprus, 'Illegal bird trapping levels remain tragically high', press release, May 2017

Birdlife International, 'The killing: a report', August 2015

Bittel, Jason, 'A single discarded fishing net can keep killing for centuries', *onEarth*, 17 May 2018

Burke, Jason, 'Indian tribe's Avatar-like battle against mining firm reaches supreme court', *The Guardian*, 8 April 2012

Burn, Chris, 'Sheffield Council's secret policy for tree-felling revealed', *Yorkshire Post*, 16 May 2018

Cambrensis, Giraldus, *The Itinerary of Archbishop Baldwin Through Wales* (London: J. M. Dent, 1912; Project Gutenberg eBook, 2015)

Carrington, Damian, 'London breaches annual air pollution limit for 2017 in just five days', *The Guardian*, 6 January 2017

———, 'What is biodiversity and why does it matter to us?', *The Guardian*, 12 March 2018

———, 'Plummeting insect numbers "threaten collapse of nature"', *The Guardian*, 10 February 2019

Carson, Rachel, *The Sea Around Us* (London: Unicorn Press, 2014 [1951])

———, *Silent Spring* (London: Penguin Books, 2000 [1962])

Cather, Willa, *My Ántonia* (London: Virago, 1980 [1918])

Cavagna, Andrea et al., 'Scale-free correlations in starling flocks', *PNAS* vol. 107 no. 26 (June 2010), pp 11865–70 doi.org/10.1073/pnas.1005766107

Ceballos, Gerardo et al., 'Accelerated modern human-induced species losses: entering the sixth mass extinction', *Science Advances* vol. 1, no. 5 (June 2015)

Chacko, Benita, 'Olive ridleys return to Versova beach after two decades', *The Indian Express* (March 2018)

Challenger, Melanie, *On Extinction: How We Became Estranged from Nature* (London: Granta Books, 2011)

Chiba, Sanae, 'Human footprint in the abyss: 30 year records of deep-sea plastic debris', *Marine Policy* (April 2018), doi.org/10.1016/j.marpol.2018.03.022

Cílek, Václav, *To Breathe With Birds: A Book of Landscapes* (Philadelphia: University of Pennsylvania Press, 2015)

Cocker, Mark and Mabey, Richard, *Birds Britannica* (London: Chatto & Windus, 2005)

Cole, Stuart, *The Blue Route: A Cost Effective Solution to Relieving M4 Congestion Around Newport* (Cardiff: Institute of Welsh Affairs, 2013)

Colston, Adrian, 'Beyond preservation: the challenge of ecological restoration', in Martin Mulligan (ed.), *Decolonizing Nature: Strategies for Conservation in a Post-Colonial Era* (Sterling: Earthscan, 2003)

Cowen, Rob, *Common Ground* (London: Hutchinson, 2015)

Crouch, David and Ward, Colin, *The Allotment: Its Landscape and Culture* (Nottingham: Five Leaves, 2003 [1988])

Dacke, Marie et al., 'Dung beetles use the Milky Way for orientation', *Current Biology* vol. 23, no. 4 (2013), pp. 298–300

Datta, Aparajita and Rawat, G. S., 'Nest-site selection and nesting success of three hornbill species in Arunachal Pradesh, north-east India: Great Hornbill *Buceros bicornis*, Wreathed Hornbill *Aceros undulatus* and Oriental Pied Hornbill *Anthracoceros albirostris*', *Bird Conservation International* (published online: 3 August 2005), doi.org/10.1017/S0959270905000213

Davit, Carol, 'Why prairie matters – new relevancies of a vanishing landscape', *TEDx Talks*, 14 April 2015

Deakin, Roger, *Notes from Walnut Tree Farm* (London: Hamish Hamilton, 2008)

Department for Environment, Food and Rural Affairs, 'Draft plans to improve air quality in the UK: UK overview document', September 2015

Derbyshire, David, 'How children lost the right to roam in four generations', *Daily Mail*, 15 June 2007

Diaz, Natalie, 'The first water is the body', *Orion*, 35th Anniversary Issue (2017), pp. 64–6

Dickens, Charles, *Great Expectations* (London: Penguin Classics, 1996 [1861])

Dodd, Elizabeth, *Prospect: Journeys and Landscapes* (Salt Lake City: University of Utah Press, 2003)

Doerr, Anthony, 'The Shell Collector', in *The Shell Collector* (London: Flamingo, 2002)

Ehrlich, Paul et al., *Birder's Handbook: A Field Guide to the Natural History of North American Birds* (New York: Simon and Schuster, 1988)

Eiseley, Loren C., 'The Flow of the River', *American Scholar* vol. 22, no. 4 (Autumn 1953), pp. 451–8

Extra Motorway MSA Group/St Pauls Developments, 'Sheffield Motorway Service Area Junction 35, M1, vol. 1: Environmental Statement', March 2014

Fisher, Catherine, *The Candle Man* (London: Red Fox, 1995)

Foster + Partners, 'Inner Thames Hub estuary: feasibility studies', May 2014

————, 'Thames Hub Airport: outline proposal to the Airports Commission', July 2013

Gabbatiss, Josh, 'One third of world's "protected" national parks and wildlife sanctuaries threatened by human activities', *The Independent*, 17 May 2018

Gallagher, Erin, 'Midewin prairie to undergo restoration', *Chicago Tribune*, 18 August 2016

Garland, Hamlin, *A Son of the Middle Border* (New York: Penguin, 1995 [1917])

Gibbens, Sarah, 'Plastic bag found at the bottom of world's deepest ocean trench', *National Geographic*, May 2018

Glynn, Steven and Anderson, Kevin, 'The potential impact of the proposed M4 relief road on greenhouse gas emissions', Wildlife Trusts Wales, January 2015

Good, Thomas P., 'Ghosts of the Salish Sea: threats to marine birds in Puget Sound and the Northwest straits from derelict fishing gear', *Marine Ornithology* vol. 37 (March 2009), pp. 67–76

Griggs, Mary Beth, 'Eight amazing architects of the animal kingdom', *Popular Mechanics*, May 2011

Gussow, Alan, *A Sense of Place: The Artist and the American Land* (Washington, DC: Island Press, 1997 [1972])

Haddad, Nick M., 'Habitat fragmentation and its lasting impact on Earth's ecosystems', *Science Advances* vol. 1, no. 2 (March 2015), doi.org/10.1126/sciadv.1500052

Hallmann, Caspar A., 'More than 75 percent decline over 27 years in total flying insect biomass in protected areas', *PLOS One*, 18 October 2017

Hansen, Margaret M. et al., 'Shinrin-yoku (forest bathing) and nature therapy: a state of the art review', *International Journal of Environmental Research and Public Health* vol. 14, no. 8 (August 2017), doi.org/ 10.3390/ijerph14080851

Harrison, Jim, 'Eat or Die', *Brick* no.81 (2008) pp. 142–8

Haskell, David George, *The Forest Unseen: A Year's Watch in Nature* (New York: Viking, 2012)

———, *The Songs of Trees: Stories from Nature's Great Connectors* (New York: Viking, 2017)

Heschel, Abraham Joshua, *God in Search of Man: A Philosophy of Judaism* (New York: Farrar, Straus and Giroux, 1955)

Holthaus, Eric, 'Soon the only coral reefs we see will be on the nature channel', *Mother Jones*, January 2018

Hopkins, Gerard Manley, 'Binsey Poplars', in *Gerard Manley Hopkins: The Major Works* (New York: Oxford University Press, 2002), pp. 142–3

Huband, Sally, 'Driftwood', *Earthlines*, July 2016, pp. 8–13

Hughes, Terry P. et al., 'Spatial and temporal patterns of mass bleaching of corals in the Anthropocene', *Science* vol. 359, no. 6371 (2018), pp. 80–83

Hunt, Elle, '38 million pieces of plastic waste found on uninhabited South Pacific island', *The Guardian*, 15 May 2017

Ibisch, Pierre L. et al., 'A global map of roadless areas and their conservation status', *Science* vol. 354, no. 6318 (December 2016), pp. 1423–7

Jabr, Ferris, 'Can prairie dogs talk?', *New York Times*, 12 May 2017

Jarvis, Brooke, 'Bearing witness: Chris Jordan on art, grief, and transformation', *yes! Magazine*, 14 April 2010

———, 'The Messengers', *Pacific Standard*, 8 September 2015

Johnston, Ian, 'UK air pollution deadlier than across half of Western Europe, reveals WHO report', *The Independent*, 17 May 2017

Jones, Kendall R., 'One-third of global protected land is under intense human pressure', *Science* vol. 360, no. 6390 (May 2018), pp. 788–91

Jones, Mel, *Sheffield's Woodland Heritage* (Sheffield: Wildtrack Publishing, 2009 [1989])

———, *Trees and Woodland in the South Yorkshire Landscape: A Natural, Economic and Social History* (Barnsley: Wharncliffe Books, 2012)

Kavanagh, Patrick, 'The Parish and the Universe', Collected Pruse [sic] (London: MacGibbon & Kee, 1967)

King, Gilbert, 'Where the buffalo no longer roamed', *Smithsonian.com*, 17 July 2012

Kolbert, Elizabeth, *The Sixth Extinction: An Unnatural History* (London: Bloomsbury, 2014)

Lamb, Joleah B. et al., 'Plastic waste associated with disease on coral reefs', *Science* vol. 359, no. 6374 (2018), pp. 460–62

Langenheim, Johnny, 'AI identifies heat-resistant coral reefs in Indonesia', *The Guardian*, 13 August 2018

Lanham, Drew J., *The Home Place: Memoirs of a Colored Man's Love Affair with Nature* (Minneapolis: Milkweed Editions, 2016)

Lavers, Jennifer and Bond, Alexander, 'Exceptional and rapid accumulation of anthropogenic debris on one of the world's most remote and pristine islands', *Proceedings of the National Academy of Sciences* vol. 114, no. 23 (2017), doi.org/10.1073/pnas.1619818114.

Laville, Sandra and Taylor, Matthew, 'A million bottles a minute: world's plastic as "dangerous as climate change"', *The Guardian*, 28 June 2017

Leigh Fermor, Patrick, *Roumeli: Travels in Northern Greece* (London: John Murray, 2004 [1966])

Lewis, Rob, 'Giving voice to the silent things', *Corvallis Gazette-Times*, 9 March 2018

Liptrot, Amy, *The Outrun* (Edinburgh: Canongate, 2016)

Lopez, Barry, *About This Life: Journeys on the Threshold of Memory* (London: The Harvill Press, 1998)

———, 'The American Geographies', in *Crossing Open Ground* (New York: Vintage, 1988)

———, *Arctic Dreams: Imagination and Desire in a Northern Landscape* (London: The Harvill Press, 1999 [1986])

Loren, B. K., *Animal, Mineral, Radical: Essays on Wildlife, Family, and Food* (Berkeley: Counterpoint, 2013)

———, 'Process or product: the inextricable beauty of nature and art', Center for Humans and Nature, 2017, www.humansandnature.org/process-or-product

Louis, Nathan, 'Multi-storey car park to be built at Watford General Hospital', *Watford Observer*, 6 February 2019

Louv, Richard, *Last Child in the Woods: Saving Our Children From Nature-Deficit Disorder* (London: Atlantic Books, 2010 [2005])

Macdonald, Helen, *H is for Hawk* (London: Jonathan Cape, 2014)

———, 'The Living Beauty of Wicken Fen', *New York Times Magazine*, 11 April 2015

Macfarlane, Robert, *The Wild Places* (London: Granta, 2007)

Macfarlane, Robert and Morris, Jackie, *The Lost Words* (London: Hamish Hamilton, 2017)

Madson, John, *Where the Sky Began: Land of the Tallgrass Prairie* (Iowa City: University of Iowa Press, 1995 [1982])

Markandya, Anil et al., 'Counting the cost of vulture decline: an appraisal of the human health and other benefits of vultures', *Ecological Economics* vol. 67, no. 2 (September 2008), doi.org/10.1016/j.ecolecon.2008.04.020

Martin, Andy, 'The philosophy of trees: From the Sheffield tree massacre to the Australian rain forest', *The Independent*, 20 October 2017

Mayer, Frank H. and Roth, Charles B., *The Buffalo Harvest* (Denver: Sage Books, 1958)

McCarthy, Michael, 'Charles Rothschild: The banker who changed the world for good', *The Independent*, 12 May 2012

————, *The Moth Snowstorm: Nature and Joy* (London: John Murray, 2015)

Mikanowski, Jacob, 'A different dimension of loss: inside the great insect die-off', *The Guardian*, 14 December 2017

Millet, Lydia, 'Good grief: style and story in the age of extinction', *LENS Magazine*, 30 October 2016

Monbiot, George, 'Biodiversity offsetting will unleash a new spirit of destruction on the land', *The Guardian*, 7 December 2012

————, 'Forget the "environment": we need new words to convey life's wonders', *The Guardian*, 9 August 2017

Morris, Steven, '"A Berlin wall for wildlife": battle looms over Gwent Levels motorway plan', *The Guardian*, 18 October 2013

Nace, Paul, 'We're now at a million plastic bottles per minute – 91 percent of which are not recycled', *Forbes*, July 2017

National Trust, 'Places that make us: Research report', 2017

————, 'Wicken Fen Vision', www.nationaltrust.org.uk/wicken-fen-nature-reserve/documents/wicken-fen-vision-strategy-document.pdf

Nijhuis, Michelle, 'What roads have wrought', *New Yorker*, 20 March 2015

O'Connor, Betty, *Rights of Common: The Fight Against the Theft of Sydenham Common and One Tree Hill* (London: past tense, 2009)

OECD, 'Health at a glance: 2017 report', November 2017

Orwell, George, 'Some Thoughts on the Common Toad', *Tribune*, April 1946

'Pollution: think of the children' (Editorial), *The Lancet: Child and Adolescent Health* vol. 1, no. 4 (December 2017), p. 249

Preston, Richard, *The Wild Trees* (New York: Random House, 2007)

Price, John, *Not Just Any Land: A Personal and Literary Journey into the American Grasslands* (Lincoln: University of Nebraska Press, 2004)

Price, John T. et al., *The Tallgrass Prairie Reader* (Iowa City: University of Iowa Press, 2014)

Pyle, Robert Michael, *The Thunder Tree: Lessons from an Urban Wildland* (Corvallis: Oregon State University Press, 2011 [1993])

Rackham, Oliver, *The History of the Countryside: The Classic History of Britain's Landscape, Flora and Fauna* (London: Phoenix, 2000 [1986])

———, *Woodlands* (London: Collins, 2006)

Ramzy, Austin, 'A remote Pacific island awash in tons of trash', *New York Times*, 16 May 2017

Reece, Erik, 'Moving mountains', in Barry Lopez (ed.), *The Future of Nature: Writing on a Human Ecology* (Minneapolis: Milkweed Editions, 2007)

Reichman, O. J., *Konza Prairie: A Tallgrass Natural History* (Lawrence: University Press of Kansas, 1987)

Rose, Chris, 'Don't let our nightingales go quietly', *The Ecologist*, May 2015

Rotherham, Ian D., *Ancient Woodland: History, Industry and Crafts* (Oxford: Shire Books, 2013)

———, *Shadow Woods: A Search for Lost Landscapes* (Sheffield: Wildtrack Publishing, 2017)

Rothschild, Miriam and Marren, Peter, *Rothschild's Reserves: Time and Fragile Nature* (Colchester: Harley Books, 1997)

RSPB/State of Nature Partnership, *State of Nature 2013*, ww2.rspb.org.uk/Images/stateofnature_tcm9-345839.pdf

Sample, Ian, 'Plastics reach remote pristine environments, scientists say', *The Guardian*, 17 February 2019

Sánchez-Bayo, Francisco and Wyckhuys, Kris A. G., 'Worldwide decline of the entomofauna: a review of its drivers', *Biological Conservation* vol. 232 (April 2019), pp. 8–27, doi:org/10.1016/j.biocon.2019.01.020

Schlossberg, Tatiana, 'The immense, eternal footprint humanity leaves on earth: plastics', *New York Times*, 19 July 2017

Sedgwick, Isabel, *Wicken Fen* (n.p.: National Trust, 2016)

Slobodchikoff, Con, 'The language of prairie dogs', in Michael Tobias (ed.), *Kinship with the Animals* (Hillsboro, OR: Beyond Words, 1998), pp. 65–76

Smits, David D., 'The frontier army and the destruction of the buffalo: 1865–1883', *Western Historical Quarterly* vol. 25, no. 23 (1994), pp. 312–38

Solnit, Rebecca, *Hope in the Dark: Untold Histories, Wild Possibilities* (Edinburgh: Canongate, 2016 [2005])

Spalding, Mark, 'It's not too late to save coral reefs', *Global Solutions*, March 2018

——, 'Mangrove forests as incredible carbon stores', *Cool Green Science*, October 2013

Survival International, 'Dongria Kondh', www.survivalinternational.org/tribes/dongria

Suzukovich, Eli, 'Kiskinwahamâtowin (learning together): outdoor classrooms and prairie restoration at the American Indian Center of Chicago', in Gavin Van Horn and Dave Aftandilian (eds.), *City Creatures: Animal Encounters in the Chicago Wilderness* (Chicago: University of Chicago Press, 2017), pp. 106–13

Thomas, Edward, *The South Country* (Wimborne: Little Toller, 2009 [1909])

Toumbourou, Tessa, 'Mining paradise', *Inside Indonesia*, May 2014

Trajçe, Aleksandër, 'The gentleman, the vagabonds and the stranger: cultural representations of large carnivores in Albania and their implications for conservation', PhD thesis, University of Roehampton, London, 2016

Tschinkel, Walter R., 'Nest relocation and excavation in the Florida harvester ant, *Pogonomyrmex badius*', *PLOS One* (published online: 19 November 2014), doi.org/10.1371/journal.pone.0112981

Unger, David J., 'Saving America's broken prairie', *Undark: Truth, Beauty, Science*, April 2017

Welsh Government, 'M4 Corridor Around Newport: Strategic Environmental Assessment', 9 July 2013

——, 'The Well-being of Future Generations (Wales) Act 2015', https://gov.wales/topics/people-and-communities/people/future-generations-act/?lang=en

Whitty, Julia, *Deep Blue Home: An Intimate Ecology of Our Wild Ocean* (New York: Houghton Mifflin Harcourt, 2010)

Wilson, Edward O., *The Future of Life* (London: Abacus, 2003)

Woodworth, Paddy, *Our Once and Future Planet: Restoring the World in the Climate Change Century* (Chicago: University of Chicago Press, 2013)

Woolfson, Esther, *Field Notes From a Hidden City: An Urban Nature Diary* (London: Granta, 2013)

Wright, Mike, 'Farm Terrace Allotment holders vow to take fight "all the way" on BBC 1 The One Show', *Watford Observer*, 22 August 2014

———, 'Farm Terrace Allotments: Preserving site would "close the door" on future hospital development', *Watford Observer*, 24 July 2014

WEBSITES OF INTEREST

American Indian Center of Chicago: www.aicchicago.org
Balkan Lynx Recovery Project: http://ppnea.org/balkan-lynx
BirdWING: www.birdwing.eu
Buglife: www.buglife.org.uk
Children's Wood: www.thechildrenswood.co.uk
Farm Terrace Allotments: http://savefarmterrace.wixsite.com/savefarmterrace
Friends of Hopwas Wood: http://friendsofhopwaswood.co.uk
Friends of Midewin National Tallgrass Prairie: https://sites.google.com/site/
    midewinalliance/welcome
Friends of the North Kent Marshes: www.northkentmarshes.org.uk
Gaylord and Dorothy Donnelley Foundation: http://gddf.org
Great Crane Project: www.thegreatcraneproject.org.uk
Gwent Wildlife Trust: www.gwentwildlife.org
Hornbill Nest Adoption Project: http://ncf-india.org/projects/hornbill-nest-
    adoption-program
Konza Environmental Education Program: http://keep.konza.k-state.edu/
    index.html
Macedonian Ecological Society: http://mes.org.mk
Nature Conservation Foundation India: http://ncf-india.org
North Kelvin Meadow: https://northkelvinmeadow.com
Pakke Jungle Camp: www.pakkejunglecamp.org.in
People Need Nature: http://peopleneednature.org.uk
Plantlife: www.plantlife.org.uk/uk
Return of the Neophron: http://lifeneophron.eu
RiverWatch: https://riverwatch.eu
Rothschild Reserves: www.wildlifetrusts.org/about-us/rothschilds-list
Royal Society for the Protection of Birds: www.rspb.org.uk

Websites of Interest

Save the Blue Heart of Europe: www.balkanrivers.net
Save the Redwoods League: www.savetheredwoods.org
Sempervirens Fund: https://sempervirens.org
Suara Pulau Foundation: www.suarapulau.org/pages/en/welcome.php
Wildlife Trusts: www.wildlifetrusts.org
Wildlife Trust of India: www.wti.org.in
Woodland Trust: www.woodlandtrust.org.uk

INDEX